Constructing European Union Trade Policy

A Global Idea of Europe

Gabriel Siles-Brügge
Lecturer in Politics, School of Social Sciences, University of Manchester, UK

First published 2014 by
PALGRAVE MACMILLAN

Palgrave Macmillan in the UK is an imprint of Macmillan Publishers Limited,
registered in England, company number 785998, of Houndmills, Basingstoke,
Hampshire RG21 6XS.

Palgrave Macmillan in the US is a division of St Martin's Press LLC,
175 Fifth Avenue, New York, NY 10010.

Palgrave Macmillan is the global academic imprint of the above companies
and has companies and representatives throughout the world.

Palgrave® and Macmillan® are registered trademarks in the United States,
the United Kingdom, Europe and other countries

ISBN: 978–1–137–33165–6

This book is printed on paper suitable for recycling and made from fully
managed and sustained forest sources. Logging, pulping and manufacturing
processes are expected to conform to the environmental regulations of the
country of origin.

A catalogue record for this book is available from the British Library.

A catalog record for this book is available from the Library of Congress.

100721500Q

International Political Economy Series

Series Editor: **Timothy M. Shaw**, Visiting Professor, University of Massachusetts Boston, USA and Emeritus Professor, University of London, UK

The global political economy is in flux as a series of cumulative crises impacts its organization and governance. The IPE series has tracked its development in both analysis and structure over the last three decades. It has always had a concentration on the global South. Now the South increasingly challenges the North as the centre of development, also reflected in a growing number of submissions and publications on indebted Eurozone economies in Southern Europe.

An indispensable resource for scholars and researchers, the series examines a variety of capitalisms and connections by focusing on emerging economies, companies and sectors, debates and policies. It informs diverse policy communities as the established trans-Atlantic North declines and 'the rest', especially the BRICS, rise.

Titles include:

Gabriel Siles-Brügge
CONSTRUCTING EUROPEAN UNION TRADE POLICY
A Global Idea of Europe

Jewellord Singh and France Bourgouin (*editors*)
RESOURCE GOVERNANCE AND DEVELOPMENTAL STATES
IN THE GLOBAL SOUTH
Critical International Political Economy Perspectives

Tan Tai Yong and Md Mizanur Rahman (*editors*)
DIASPORA ENGAGEMENT AND DEVELOPMENT IN SOUTH ASIA

Leila Simona Talani, Alexander Clarkson and Ramon Pachedo Pardo (*editors*)
DIRTY CITIES
Towards a Political Economy of the Underground in Global Cities

Matthew Louis Bishop
THE POLITICAL ECONOMY OF CARIBBEAN DEVELOPMENT

Xiaoming Huang (*editor*)
MODERN ECONOMIC DEVELOPMENT IN JAPAN AND CHINA
Developmentalism, Capitalism and the World Economic System

Bonnie K. Campbell (*editor*)
MODES OF GOVERNANCE AND REVENUE FLOWS IN AFRICAN MINING

Gopinath Pillai (*editor*)
THE POLITICAL ECONOMY OF SOUTH ASIAN DIASPORA
Patterns of Socio-Economic Influence

Rachel K. Brickner (*editor*)
MIGRATION, GLOBALIZATION AND THE STATE

Juanita Elias and Samanthi Gunawardana (*editors*)
THE GLOBAL POLITICAL ECONOMY OF THE HOUSEHOLD IN ASIA

Tony Heron
PATHWAYS FROM PREFERENTIAL TRADE
The Politics of Trade Adjustment in Africa, the Caribbean and Pacific

David J. Hornsby
RISK REGULATION, SCIENCE AND INTERESTS IN TRANSATLANTIC
TRADE CONFLICTS

Yang Jiang
CHINA'S POLICYMAKING FOR REGIONAL ECONOMIC COOPERATION

Martin Geiger, Antoine Pécoud (*editors*)
DISCIPLINING THE TRANSNATIONAL MOBILITY OF PEOPLE

(continued in page ii)

Michael Breen
THE POLITICS OF IMF LENDING

Laura Carsten Mahrenbach
THE TRADE POLICY OF EMERGING POWERS
Strategic Choices of Brazil and India

Vassilis K. Fouskas and Constantine Dimoulas
GREECE, FINANCIALIZATION AND THE EU
The Political Economy of Debt and Destruction

Hany Besada and Shannon Kindornay (*editors*)
MULTILATERAL DEVELOPMENT COOPERATION IN A CHANGING
GLOBAL ORDER

Caroline Kuzemko
THE ENERGY-SECURITY CLIMATE NEXUS

Hans Löfgren and Owain David Williams (*editors*)
THE NEW POLITICAL ECONOMY OF PHARMACEUTICALS
Production, Innovation and TRIPS in the Global South

Timothy Cadman (*editor*)
CLIMATE CHANGE AND GLOBAL POLICY REGIMES
Towards Institutional Legitimacy

Ian Hudson, Mark Hudson and Mara Fridell
FAIR TRADE, SUSTAINABILITY AND SOCIAL CHANGE

Andrés Rivarola Puntigliano and José Briceño-Ruiz (*editors*)
RESILIENCE OF REGIONALISM IN LATIN AMERICA AND THE CARIBBEAN
Development and Autonomy

Godfrey Baldacchino (*editor*)
THE POLITICAL ECONOMY OF DIVIDED ISLANDS
Unified Geographies, Multiple Polities

Mark Findlay
CONTEMPORARY CHALLENGES IN REGULATING GLOBAL CRISES

Helen Hawthorne
LEAST DEVELOPED COUNTRIES AND THE WTO
Special Treatment in Trade

Nir Kshetri
CYBERCRIME AND CYBERSECURITY IN THE GLOBAL SOUTH

Kristian Stokke and Olle Törnquist (*editors*)
DEMOCRATIZATION IN THE GLOBAL SOUTH
The Importance of Transformative Politics

Jeffrey D. Wilson
GOVERNING GLOBAL PRODUCTION
Resource Networks in the Asia-Pacific Steel Industry

International Political Economy Series
Series Standing Order ISBN 978–0–333–71708–0 hardcover
Series Standing Order ISBN 978–0–333–71110–1 paperback

You can receive future titles in this series as they are published by placing a standing order. Please contact your bookseller or, in case of difficulty, write to us at the address below with your name and address, the title of the series and one of the ISBNs quoted above.

Customer Services Department, Macmillan Distribution Ltd, Houndmills, Basingstoke, Hampshire RG21 6XS, England

For Larissa

Contents

List of Tables and Figures

Tables

Figures

ix

List of Abbreviations

ACEA	Association des Constructeurs Européens d'Automobiles (European Automobile Manufacturers' Association)
ACP	African, Caribbean, Pacific (group of states)
ASEAN	Association of Southeast Asian Nations
BIT	bilateral investment treaty
CAP	Common Agricultural Policy
CARICOM	Caribbean Community
CARIFORUM	Caribbean Forum
CCP	Common Commercial Policy
CRNM	Caribbean Regional Negotiating Machinery
DG	Directorate-General (of the European Commission)
EAC	East African Community
EBA	Everything But Arms
ECB	European Central Bank
ECJ	European Court of Justice
ECLAC	Economic Commission for Latin America and the Caribbean (United Nations)
EDF	European Development Fund
EEA	European Economic Area
EFTA	European Free Trade Association
EMU	Economic and Monetary Union
EP	European Parliament
EPA	Economic Partnership Agreement
ERT	European Roundtable of Industrialists
ESA	Eastern and Southern Africa
ESF	European Services Forum
EU	European Union
FDI	foreign direct investment
FTA	free trade agreement
GATS	General Agreement on Trade in Services
GATT	General Agreement on Tariffs and Trade
GPA	Government Procurement Agreement
GSP	Generalised System of Preferences
HLWG	US–EU High-Level Working Group on Jobs and Growth
IEPA	Interim Economic Partnership Agreement

IMF	International Monetary Fund
INTA	Committee on International Trade (European Parliament)
IPE	International Political Economy
IPR	intellectual property right
IR	International Relations
KORUS	Korea–US (Free Trade Agreement)
LDC	least-developed country
MEP	Member of the European Parliament
MERCOSUR	Mercado Común del Cono Sur (Southern Common Market)
MFN	most-favoured-nation
NAFTA	North American Free Trade Agreement
NGO	non-governmental organisation
NTB	non-tariff barrier
ODI	Overseas Development Institute
OECD	Organisation for Economic Cooperation and Development
PA	principal–agent (analysis)
PTA	preferential trade agreement
QMV	qualified majority voting
SADC	Southern African Development Community
SEA	Single European Act
SMP	Single Market Programme
TRIPS	Agreement on Trade Related Aspects of Intellectual Property Rights
TTIP	Transatlantic Trade and Investment Partnership
UK	United Kingdom
UNICE	Union des Industries de la Communauté Européenne (Union of Industrial and Employers' Confederations of Europe)
US	United States
USTR	United States Trade Representative
WTO	World Trade Organisation

Acknowledgements

This book is the result of a number of years spent researching EU trade policy at the Universities of Sheffield, Oxford Brookes and Manchester. In the process, I have incurred a significant debt of gratitude with colleagues, friends and family who have provided important academic and moral support along the way.

First and foremost, I would like to thank Tony Heron. He has not only painstakingly read through various iterations of this book and offered invaluable guidance on how to improve it – covering everything from key conceptual issues to readability – but has also developed into a stellar academic mentor and friend. I can only hope this work lives up to his expectations to in some way repay him for all the support he has given me over the years. This book has also benefited tremendously from the very insightful comments of Colin Hay, Ben Rosamond, Simon Bulmer and two anonymous reviewers. They have all offered excellent advice which has helped me to refine the book's constructivist argument.

Several people have also helped me iron out conceptual and empirical issues by commenting on various parts of this book as they have appeared presented at several conferences and workshops. A special mention is owed to (in no particular order) Jan Orbie, Bart Kerremans, Alasdair Young, Fabienne Bossuyt, Ben Richardson, Ben Jacoby, María García, Aukje van Loon, Ferdi De Ville, Stephen Woolcock, Manfred Elsig, Andreas Dür, Mark Langan, Ben Clift, Len Seabrooke (who also came up the sub-title for the book), Peg Murray-Evans and Matt Bishop. I have similarly gained a lot from the many discussions I have had with colleagues at the Universities of Oxford Brookes and Manchester. Finally, at the University of Sheffield, an especially big thank you is owed to Sarah Cooke, without whose tireless efforts I would have often been lost. Any errors, of course, remain my own.

Thanks are due to the UK Economic and Social Research Council for generously funding the research this book is based on. Similarly, I would like to thank the publishers Taylor & Francis and Wiley and the *Journal of Contemporary European Research* for allowing me to draw on material in this book, in a substantially revised and expanded form, that was previously published as: 'Resisting Protectionism after the Crisis: Strategic Economic Discourse and the EU–Korea Free Trade Agreement' in *New Political Economy*, 16 (5), pp. 627–53 (from which I also reproduce

Figures 2.1 and 2.2 and Table 3.1); 'Competitive Liberalization and the "Global Europe" Services and Investment Agenda: Locating the Commercial Drivers of the EU–ACP Economic Partnership Agreements' in the *Journal of Common Market Studies*, 50 (2), pp. 250–66 (which I co-authored with Tony Heron) and 'The Power of Economic Ideas: A Constructivist Political Economy of EU Trade Policy' in the *Journal of Contemporary European Research*, 9 (4), pp. 597–617. I also draw on a couple of short passages previously published in 'Explaining the Resilience of Free Trade: The Smoot-Hawley Myth and the Crisis' in the *Review of International Political Economy*.

At Palgrave Macmillan, Christina Brian and Amanda McGrath have provided excellent editorial support, while I am extremely grateful to series editor Tim Shaw for the all the encouragement and advice I received from the moment we first discussed the book. Similarly, I would like to thank all those who agreed to share their time and insights with me for my research and should stress that their personal opinions in no way reflect the positions of the organisations they may have been working for.

I also have to thank those friends in Sheffield who put up with my slightly abrasive sense of humour and managed to make the most dreary of days passable. I am especially grateful to Chris, João, Defne, Jojo, Florian, Laura, Ellie, Nick, Jemma, and Tom. While he is unfortunately no longer around, I also have very fond memories of Mark Duncan and the many laughs we shared while living together and working in the Department of Politics.

I cannot forget to express my very deep gratefulness to my family, especially my parents José and Martina and my brother Oscar. I owe my parents so much that cannot adequately be put into words, from the love and affection they have always shown to the values and drive they have instilled in me. They have always put my education (and that of my brother) before anything else at great personal sacrifice and I hope to be able to repay them at some point in the future. My brother and I may not have always seen eye-to-eye, but in the past few years I have really come to appreciate what a loyal and caring friend he is. I wish him all the best in his future academic pursuits as it looks as though I am unlikely to remain the only academic in the family for long.

Lastly, and most importantly, my heartfelt gratitude goes out to my better half Larissa. It is no exaggeration to say that without her love, patience (especially when I may have 'zoned out' while writing the book) and support I do not know where I might have ended up at the end of all these years. This book is dedicated to her.

1
Introduction

The European economy stands or falls on our ability to keep
markets open, to open new markets, and to develop new areas
where Europe's inventors, investors, entrepreneurs can trade.
We should pursue this objective *by every means we can*.

Peter Mandelson (2005c: 4, emphasis added),
European Commissioner for Trade (2004–08)

**Trade has never been more important for the European
Union's economy.** In today's difficult economic circumstances,
it has become an important means of achieving much needed
growth and creating jobs without drawing on public finances.

European Commission (2013: 1, emphasis in the original)

Anyone following the ongoing problems of the Doha Round of trade
talks might be forgiven for thinking that trade politics has become a
sideshow in the international political economy. Even as the multilateral
negotiations have gone through multiple deadlocks, the world has experienced a flurry of preferential trade agreements (PTAs) of various shapes
and sizes. The World Trade Organisation (WTO) currently lists over 200
such agreements as being in force (WTO 2013). This broader trend
towards seeking discriminatory trade deals has also meant that the
agenda of 'behind-the-border' liberalisation – agreement on issues such
as the regulation of trade in services, government procurement and intellectual property rights – has grown in prominence; 'deep' liberalisation is
easier to negotiate between preferred partners. For advocates of free
trade, long frustrated with the slow pace of multilateral negotiations,
this is seen as a positive development. Writing on one of the most significant of these agreements to be proposed – a free trade agreement (FTA)

1

between the European Union (EU)[1] and the United States (US) – *The Economist* (2013) was to proclaim that 'it could anchor a transatlantic economic model favouring openness, free markets, free peoples and the rule of law over the closed, managed visions of state capitalism'. For the EU, the world's single largest trader (see Eurostat 2013: 94), the trade deal with the US substantiates the message of the epigraphs above: the pursuit of free trade is explicitly linked to European economic performance. Given the economic crisis currently rocking the continent, which is not only causing considerable economic hardship but has also constrained the public purse, trade opening is seen as a cheap means of generating much sought-after 'growth and jobs'. This is not new. Ever since its 2006 'Global Europe' communication – which led the EU to abandon an informal and self-imposed moratorium on new FTAs it had adopted in order to underscore its commitment to the Doha Round – the EU has seen the pursuit of PTAs as the means for delivering the sorts of market access gains that it allegedly needs to engender economic prosperity.

This book is about the drivers of the 2006 'Global Europe' communication and the sorts of agreements it has spawned – most notably with South Korea, which represents not only the first completed FTA to come out of 'Global Europe' but is also widely seen as the EU's most ambitious commercial agreement so far. 'Global Europe' is seen as a key moment in EU trade policymaking, leading the EU to actively embrace preferential market opening as the most significant instrument in its offensive trade arsenal. In the communication, the Commission – or more specifically its Directorate-General (DG) for Trade[2] – argued that while multilateral trade liberalisation remained the EU's 'priority', other, bilateral avenues had to be urgently sought (European Commission 2006g). In the context of a (then already) stagnating Doha Round this read like a wholesale espousal of bilateralism and went beyond the more *ad hoc* bilateralism of previous years, which had seen the EU sign agreements with Mexico, Chile and South Africa while still prioritising the multilateral trade route (what became known explicitly as the 'multilateralism-first' policy under Trade Commissioner Pascal Lamy; see Lamy 2002: 1401). Crucially, 'Global Europe' saw the EU target the emerging economies of East Asia.[3] These could provide significant market opportunities for its (competitive) upmarket exporters which the multilateral trading system was failing to deliver – especially as such countries were unwilling to discuss the sorts of regulatory issues that the EU had shown a keen interest in pursuing during the Round – and which the EU's commercial rivals (especially the US) were already pursuing through their own FTA agendas.

In this book I also consider the broader impact of 'Global Europe' on the European and international political economies. As 'Global Europe's' sub-title – 'Competing in the World' – made clear, it explicitly linked Europe's economic well-being to its ability to *compete* in the global economy. In doing so, policymakers were invoking the ideas embodied by the Lisbon Agenda of competitiveness. This overarching strategy document, announced in 2000, aimed to transform the EU into 'the most competitive and dynamic knowledge-based economy in the world, capable of sustainable economic growth with more and better jobs' by 2010 (European Council 2000). Much in the same way, 'Global Europe' promised to deliver 'growth and jobs' through 'activism in creating open markets and fair conditions for trade abroad' (European Commission 2006g: 6). This is important for three reasons. Firstly, the EU has sought not only to serve the interests of upmarket exporters, but has increasingly done so *at the expense* of other, hitherto protected sectors. The second, related point is that trade policy plays an increasingly important role in the discourse of economic policymaking within the EU, given the explicit linkages between 'internal' and 'external' competitiveness first stressed by 'Global Europe'. This is reinforced by the increasingly regulatory nature of the liberalisation sought by the EU. Thirdly, this mantra of competitiveness has ever more permeated the EU's trade relations with developing countries, especially with the African, Caribbean and Pacific (ACP) group of states. Not only has a renewed interest in the Economic Partnership Agreements (EPAs) being negotiated with the ACP dovetailed with the arrival of 'Global Europe', but increasingly, the Commission has pushed for these agreements to feature regulatory liberalisation that goes beyond WTO disciplines. This is justified on the basis that it enhances the economic prospects of developing states. The specific provisions, however, bear a striking resemblance to the texts of the EU's 'Global Europe' FTAs despite policymakers insisting that the EPAs lie at the heart of its international *development* (rather than commercial) strategy.

The EU continues to be wedded to an aggressive strategy of preferential market opening since the start of the Financial and Eurozone Crises. But, despite the continued impact of Global Europe, to my mind the true significance of EU trade policy has long been masked by its treatment – or more precisely, the relative lack thereof – in the International Political Economy (IPE) literature. Compared to the plethora of works written by political economists on trade policymaking in the US, the study of EU trade policy has been largely neglected (although this is beginning to change, see Poletti and De Bièvre 2013). Instead, the study of the EU's commercial relations and trade policymaking processes has generally been confined to the narrower field of EU Studies. Here, rather than consider the wider implications of EU trade governance within the international political economy, the focus has largely been on the institutional determinants of policymaking, the implicit argument being that this is justified by the EU's *sui generis* trade governance structure; the shift from 'multilateralism-first' to 'Global Europe' and the increasingly entwined 'developmental' and 'commercial' trade agendas of the EU, however, occurred *in the absence of any institutional change* to the EU's trade governance structures. Similarly, an almost exclusive focus on the *material* drivers of (EU) trade policy has obscured some of the deeper drivers of policymaking; the distributive politics of the liberalisation implied by 'Global Europe' cannot be explained by the allegedly unique institutional insulation of EU trade policy nor be simply 'read off' the material interests of societal actors (as in endogenous trade policy accounts). While I am not saying that rationalist approaches have nothing to offer the student of trade politics – I explicitly draw on such literature for important insights into the behaviour of interest groups – in this book I also consider the role of language and ideas. More concretely, such an approach helps to explain three inter-related puzzles raised by conventional understandings of EU trade policy: why was there a shift to bilateralism as implied by 'Global Europe'; why did this entail significant economic restructuring and why did it bring about the increased entwinement of the EU's 'developmental' and 'commercial' trade agendas?

Parsons' *A Certain Idea of Europe* (2003) contends that a set of specific ideas held by French elites – and their subsequent institutionalisation – explain the shape of European integration. Not entirely unlike him, my argument focuses on the role that a set of particular ideas about the EU's place within the world have had on the conduct of its trading relations. Promoted by trade policymakers in the European Commission, the notion that the EU had to adapt to the competitiveness challenges of the global economy and service the interests of exporters – what could be called 'a *global* idea of Europe', as in the subtitle of this book – is one which has had a considerable impact as part of the neoliberal drift of EU trade policy. In this sense, I join a group of 'critical IPE' scholars writing about the neoliberal shift (away from 'embedded liberalism') in EU policy in more specific policy domains, such as competition policy and corporate governance (Buch-Hansen and Wigger 2011; Horn 2011). In contrast to such largely neo-Gramscian perspectives – which have been criticised as not sufficiently attuned to the role of specific agents and ideas, especially as they are situated within a broader literature on the increasing marketisation implied by the 'relaunch of European integration' in the 1980s (see Gill 1998; van Apeldoorn 2002; Cafruny and Ryner 2003) – I am explicitly seeking to craft a constructivist IPE perspective on EU trade policy. Specifically, I focus on the role that particular agents (DG Trade, the Trade Commissioners and the constituency of exporters) and ideas play in constructing and reproducing neoliberalism in this specific policy field. Moreover, constructivists have not only studied the broader shift from 'embedded liberalism' to neoliberalism (for example, Blyth 2002) – which is not so much the focus of this book – but have also developed arguments on the strategic agency of supranational actors in the context of European integration that bear some resonance to my own (for instance, Rosamond 2002; Jabko 2006). These scholars show that ideas about competitiveness and the market have been deployed by the Commission as a compelling set of arguments to constrain other actors (see Hay and Rosamond 2002), such as those who might be opposed to trade liberalisation and the economic restructuring it implies. To rephrase Wendt's (1999) much-cited line, *trade is what (these) actors (choose to) make of it.* Moreover, I find that such ideas continue to hold sway in the current economic context – although their future is perhaps less certain – adding to discussions about the 'resilience' of neoliberalism since the start of the Financial and Eurozone Crises (see Crouch 2011; Schmidt and Thatcher 2013).

In order to situate my argument within current debates on EU trade policy, the next section provides an overview of such perspectives and their tendency to focus on the institutional determinants of trade policy. This section also briefly discusses the institutions of EU trade policy. I then offer an overview of the book's empirical focus and constructivist argument. The penultimate section serves as an outline to the remainder of the book and the chapter concludes with a short note about the primary sources used.

The (overstated) role of institutions in EU trade policy

The EU Studies literature on trade policy has largely adopted a rational choice institutionalist approach that sees institutions in a narrow sense as 'the humanly devised constraints that shape human interaction' (North 1990: 3; see also Hall and Taylor 1996).[4] This has meant a focus on the formal institutional machinery of EU trade policy, which is established in the various EU Treaties (see Figure 1.1; Woolcock 2012: 51–61). Most of it falls under the so-called Common Commercial Policy (CCP), originally set up by the Treaty of Rome in 1957. In the original CCP, the Member States had delegated negotiating authority for trade agreements

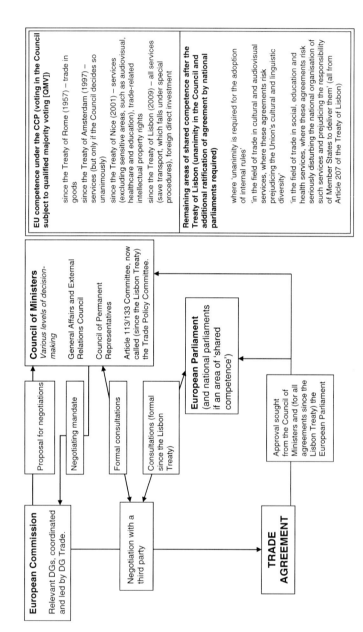

Figure 1.1   An overview of the formal EU trade policy process and the evolution of competences

Sources: Adapted from Woolcock (2010b: 390), Figure 16.1; the figure also draws on relevant EU Treaties.

with third parties in goods to the European Commission. That being said, approval from the Council of Ministers was still required to initiate and conclude any trade deals, while Member States also monitored the Commission via a specialised Council working group. Since the Treaty of Lisbon (which came into force in December 2009) this is known as the Trade Policy Committee, but was formerly known as the Article 133 and (before Amsterdam) the Article 113 Committee, after the article in the Treaties establishing the CCP. The Treaties of Amsterdam, Nice and Lisbon have since increased the number of trade issue areas that – as 'EU competence' – fall under the purview of the CCP, such that now only very few areas are subject to 'shared competence' between the EU and the Member States (where different policymaking procedures arise, see Figure 1.1). Since the Treaty of Lisbon, the European Parliament (EP) also has the prerogative of having to assent to all trade agreements (as well as being formally consulted during trade negotiations, where previously its involvement was at the Commission's discretion). Most of the existing research on EU trade policy written so far has, however, worked within the older institutional set-up privileging the Commission and Council.

Key to much of this research is the so-called 'collusive delegation' argument (Meunier and Nicolaïdis 1999; Meunier 2005; Woolcock 2005). Its basic proposition is that the delegation of trade policymaking authority from national governments to the supranational Commission in the Treaty of Rome was intended to 'insulate the process from protectionist pressures and, as a result, promote trade liberalisation' (Meunier 2005: 8). Taking this as a starting point, most scholars have focused on two aspects of EU trade policy: the nature of interest mediation within a 'multi-level' polity and the effects of inter-institutional conflict resulting from the delegation of trade policymaking authority. In the first school of thought – borrowing from the work on 'multi-level games' of Moravcsik (1998) and Putnam (1988) – EU trade policy has been conceptualised in terms of three distinct arenas of decision making: the domestic level (inside Member States), the supranational EU level (the Council) and the international level of negotiation with third parties (see Collinson 1999; for applications, see Young 2002; Meunier 2005). The focus here has generally been on the institutional parameters shaping the aggregation of diverse national interests into a single European position – such as the nature of voting rules in the Council (Young 2006: 12). For its part, research that has explored the delegation of trade policymaking authority in the EU has mostly adopted a methodology known as principal–agent analysis (PA) (see Pollack 2003; for applications to trade policy, see Meunier 2007; Elsig 2007). The PA approach is essentially concerned with the delegation of a task (in this case trade policy authority) from a principal (the Council of Ministers) to an agent (the Commission) and the various control mechanisms that the former can employ to ensure that the latter acts according to the mandate that has been set. Similarly, scholars have also studied conflict between different DGs with responsibility for different aspects of trade policy (for example, Larsén 2007). This builds on research that has shown that DGs' preferences often correspond to their area of functional responsibility (Peters 1992: 115–16; Egeberg 2002: 8) in what could be characterised as bureau-maximising logic.

Going back to the 'collusive delegation' argument that underpins much of this scholarship, the issue appears to be the implicit stress that is placed – albeit to varying degrees by different authors – on the EU's uniqueness as a trade policy actor. This is perceived to be a product of its *sui generis* institutional structure. Theoretically, this 'European exceptionalism' in trade can be traced to the broader disciplinary evolution of EU Studies, which has primarily been concerned with explaining the prospects for European integration (Ryner 2012: 654–5). Even moving away from the 'first debate' between neofunctionalism and intergovernmentalism to the so-called 'governance turn' (Kohler-Koch and Rittberger 2006) – where the tools of political science (such as PA) have been brought in to 'mainstream' EU Studies (see Rosamond 2007: 235–6) – the focus has still been on the institutional evolution of the Union. Indeed, it is not too difficult to see that those invoking 'multi-level games' to explain EU trade policy outcomes have implicitly sought to explain the institutional development of European integration by focusing on the design of the EU's policymaking institutions. In much the same way, the PA debate over the role of principals and agents – which stresses inter-institutional conflict between the Commission and the Council – seems to be a debate over which institution holds greater sway in the EU; as Meunier and Nicolaïdis (1999: 479) note 'the debate over trade authority has been above all a reflection and a test of a larger ideological battle over European integration', where the preferences of the Commission and Member States are seen to derive from their *functions* as, respectively, liberal agents of European integration and guardians of the national interest (see also Meunier 2005).

An institutionalist history of EU trade policy

Taking the 'collusive delegation' argument as a historical starting point, the underlying assumption of the EU Studies literature has been that institutional developments over the last twenty to thirty years have underscored the insulation of policymakers from special interests and produced a uniquely stable and liberal strategic orientation. The Single Market Programme (SMP), launched by the Single European Act (SEA) in the mid-1980s, is seen as the turning point for EU trade policy in the rational institutionalist literature in EU Studies. Hanson's (1998) account of the role of the SMP in EU trade policy has become extremely influential at this juncture. For one, he argues that the completion of the Single Market meant that Member States were no longer able to use national instruments to restrict trade. For another, the SEA's extension of qualified majority voting (QMV) into several areas of voting in the Council produced a 'liberal bias' in EU policymaking that made it difficult to introduce offsetting protectionist measures at the supranational level. This change in institutional set-up, so the conventional wisdom goes, had the unintended consequence of facilitating leadership in trade policy by the supranational (and more liberal) Commission vis-à-vis the intergovernmental (and more protectionist) Council of Ministers.

The ability of the EU to pursue an offensive agenda from the Uruguay Round onwards has also been strongly linked to the formal and informal transferral of supranational policymaking competence from Member States to the Commission (Woolcock and Hodges 1996; Billiet 2006; Young 2011: 720–2). Although there were a number of competence wrangles from the end of the Round through to the negotiation of the Treaties of Amsterdam, Nice and what became Lisbon, these did not entirely impede the Commission from exercising trade policymaking authority in new issue areas not previously delegated by the CCP (Woolcock and Hodges 1996; Young 2002). Moreover, the Commission would eventually formally acquire many of these powers (see Figure 1.1), cementing the narrative of the supranational insulation of policymakers from societal pressures. More recently, other authors have also pointed to the fact that there has been a trend towards the informal (and sometimes unintended) concentration of powers in the hands of the Commission.[5]

Whatever their theoretical merits, such explanations are consistent at a superficial level with the stability and liberal orientation demonstrated by EU trade policy during the 1990s and early 2000s. Given this emphasis, however, how did this literature explain the eventual shift towards bilateralism when it occurred in October 2006 with 'Global Europe'? Taking the PA metaphor as a starting point, the EU's trade strategy has been portrayed as a product of the Commission's continued efforts at exercising leadership – to varying degrees – in the face of the stagnation of the multilateral trade strategy and the emergence of competition in Asia. To Elsig (2007), it is suggestive of the Commission's power to reset the trade policy agenda according to its ideological preferences. For her part, Meunier (2007: 905) sees 'Global Europe' as evidence of nothing more than DG Trade's 'entrepreneurial ability to repackage Member State preferences into a consensual doctrine'.

The limitations of institutionalist explanations

The rational institutionalist view within EU Studies has some difficulty in explaining the important shift to 'Global Europe' in the *absence of significant institutional change* to the EU's trade policymaking machinery in the intervening period. Both the Treaties of Amsterdam (1997) and Nice (2001) predated the new strategy by several years. By the same token, the Treaty of Lisbon came into force only in December 2009. This means that neither multi-level game nor PA approaches, the two forms of rational institutionalist explanations commonly found in the EU Studies literature on trade policy, can provide an explanation of the shift. In the case of the former, there has been no change to the mechanisms for preference aggregation in the Council, which is its source of explanation of trade policy outcomes. Similarly, even if the bureau-maximising logic at the heart of the PA metaphor can explain why DG Trade may have had an institutional incentive to change course when the multilateral trade strategy did not yield results – in that this may have (for instance) prompted the Council to 'rein in' its delegated agent to address perceived failings in trade strategy – it is insufficient to explain the shift to 'Global Europe'. This is because it is dependent on a particular institutional setting to provide the parameters for conflict between an agent and a principal. Given that the institutions of trade policymaking were the same from 2004 to 2006 it is impossible to attribute the shift to the Commission's relative autonomy (or lack thereof) as in Elsig (2007) and Meunier (2007). In both of these accounts, the underlying (and underexplored) explanation of the shift really lies in a change of the Commission's ideological preferences and/or the systemic environment. As leading proponents of PA themselves concede, the approach is unable 'to make general claims about what agents do with the autonomy they possess' (Lake and McCubbins 2006: 344). Given the lack of an institutional catalyst, how does one explain the Commission's quite significant shift in policy? A similar puzzle also besets the study of EU–ACP relations, where insofar as an entwinement between the EU's 'developmental' and 'commercial' trade policy is identified, this is attributed – in an argument drawing on 'bureaucratic politics' explanations of EU trade policy – to a shift of responsibility for conducting trade negotiations from DG Development to DG Trade in 1999 (see, for example, Ravenhill 2004: 130–1).

This however, does not fit the timing of the EPA agenda, which only really picked up steam under Mandelson's tenure from 2004 onwards and, as for the PA approach, provides little insight into the actual content of the negotiations.

While acknowledging the increasing importance of the supranational Commission (and more specifically DG Trade) within EU trade policy-making, highlighted by the historical narrative in EU Studies, I argue in this book that that the underlying view of trade policy as 'exceptionally' depoliticised is problematic. By this I mean, quite simply, that rational institutionalist accounts overlook a number of important determinants of political economic outcomes. The first issue is that such accounts are often based on the *assumption* that functional integration has served to insulate policymakers, with little empirical evidence invoked to support the argument that interest groups have played a negligible role in European trade policymaking (Dür 2008: 29). A second, related problem is the tendency of rational institutionalist accounts to overlook the wider international systemic context within which trade diplomacy is rooted (Billiet 2006; for an exception, see Sbragia 2010). In both of these senses, 'Global Europe' is a case in point; by joining the fray of preferential market opening of recent years the EU's practices increasingly resemble those of its main commercial rivals. While it must be said that there exists an incipient literature which points to the role of interest groups and (albeit less frequently) systemic pressures within EU trade governance, much of it still uses a rational institutionalist framework, deploying either a 'policy networks' approach stressing 'resource dependencies' between different actors (Shaffer 2003), or a multi-level governance approach (Collinson 1999) or PA (De Bièvre and Eckhardt 2011). This runs the risk of reproducing the problems enumerated above; apart from the obvious adoption of the PA approach, 'resource dependence' and multi-level governance are, after all, very close incarnations of, respectively, functional rationality and multi-level games.

That is, however, only part of the problem faced by institutionalist explanations of EU trade policy. One of the key contentions in this book is that such rationalist approaches overlook the role of ideas in shaping agents' behaviour in policymaking; one cannot capture the specific distributive consequences of 'Global Europe' by focusing only on materially given interests (more on this in the next section). Although a non-rational choice, historical institutionalist account of EU trade policy could be constructed to accommodate the role of ideas (as in Parsons 2003), the fact remains that it would still rely on an 'institutional logic of explanation' emphasising the effects of path dependence and unintended consequences (Parsons 2007: 67–8). 'Global Europe', however, represents a deliberate change of strategy that is not necessarily driven by processes of institutionalisation. For example, although the EU enlargement of May 2004 may have affected the balance of Member State interests in the Council and their relative power vis-à-vis the Commission (see Elsig 2010), it was not accompanied by any shift in policy while Lamy was still Commissioner. More generally, the Commission's ascendancy within EU trade comitology long preceded 'Global Europe'. While it may partly explain the focus taken in this book on the role of the Commission (and more specifically DG Trade) it does not account for the content of the Commission's policy proposals. Similarly, although neoliberal ideas have shaped EU trade policy since at least the 1990s, their effects are better understood if we focus on the role of agents in propagating them; after all, they have led Commissioners to pursue somewhat different policies and have featured in quite purposive (rather than unintended) policy strategies. Trade has been what policymakers made of it at a given moment in time, rather than what they inherited from their predecessors. In this vein, I concur with Bell's (2012: 667–8) assessment that one should not 'conflate' ideas with institutions, as the latter 'have properties that help structure thought and behaviour at one remove from the immediacy of thought or action by agents at any given point in time'. In other words, an 'ideational' 'logic of explanation' can be distinguished from 'institutional explanation' (for this terminology and argument, see Parsons 2007). Having established the limitations of institutionalism for studying the case at hand, I provide an overview of the argument I make for a constructivist IPE of EU trade policy.

The argument: Trade is what you make of it

My first objective in this book is to situate the study of EU external trade within the IPE literature on trade policy, arguing, in essence, that the EU is not as 'exceptional' a trade actor as it is often made out to be within EU Studies. In this vein, I am joining a number of other accounts of EU trade policy which have similarly borrowed arguments from this broader literature (see, for instance, Dür 2007; Sbragia 2010). More specifically, I turn to a set of works on North–South preferential liberalisation to argue that European service suppliers played an important role in pressuring EU decision-makers to compete for preferential access to emerging markets; the argument is that such sectors had a particular interest in discriminatory market opening as it would allow them to make 'first entry' and subsequently benefit from an oligopolistic market position

(Manger 2009). I argue that DG Trade policymakers drafting 'Global Europe' were sensitive to the vociferous demands of these services lobbyists, which were increasingly concerned about rivals (especially the US) in East and South Asia. This was reflected in the EU's subsequent bilateral services and investment agenda – which has remained in place with the 2010 'Trade, Growth and World Affairs' communication – and in the EU–Korea agreement, where service suppliers fought hard to not only ensure parity with the Korea–US FTA but to also exceed the US's discriminatory gains. Similarly, these commercial drivers account, in part, for the similarity between the EPAs and 'commercial' FTAs in the sense that European services lobbyists also pressured policymakers to ensure that the EPAs contained meaningful services and investment liberalisation provisions.

While offering important insights, rationalist IPE approaches are not a sufficient explanation of *why* DG Trade chose to pursue such a preferential strategy and *how* it was successful in doing so. Firstly, interest groups – content to seek liberalisation gains through the Doha Round until this began to stagnate – mobilised later than expected in response to the competitive threat posed by rivals, with DG Trade not heeding their arguments until even later. Secondly, and more importantly, the emphasis on collective action problems in the IPE literature on trade policy – that protectionists are more likely to mobilise and shape policy than the 'winners' from liberalisation due to the concentration of the costs and diffuse nature of the benefits – sits uneasily with the fact that the EU has been able to push through its aggressive trade policy premised on trading away protection for market access. This is particularly puzzling in light of the mobilisation of protectionists in opposition to the EU's 'Global Europe' agenda, especially the EU–Korea FTA which proved an important threat to the automobile industry at a time of economic crisis. The fact that import-competing sectors had access to policymakers at all levels in the EU also precludes an explanation premised on institutional insulation, as in much of the literature on EU trade policy. In a similar vein, while rationalist IPE explanations centred on commercial interests provide some insight into why the EU's 'developmental' and 'commercial' agendas became entwined, they offer insufficient clues as to *why* DG Trade apparently chose to heed the arguments of services lobbyists when negotiating agreements with the ACP that policymakers *stressed* were 'developmental' in intention.

In order to study this increasingly neoliberal bent in EU trade policy, my second theoretical contribution in this book is to develop a novel constructivist framework which emphasises that social and political reality is *constructed by agents* through ideas rather than being *fixed* by particular material (or what could be called 'structural') constraints. This builds on a growing tradition of constructivist IPE scholars who have argued that ideas are crucial determinants of political economic outcomes in the face of uncertainty in the social world (Blyth 2002; Abdelal *et al.* 2010a), and also adds to the emerging group of authors seeking to bring ideas and language into the generally quite rationalist study of global trade politics (see, for example, Wilkinson 2009; Trommer 2013). While providing a compelling explanation of why ideas matter, the constructivist IPE literature, however, has been open to the charge of some critical scholars that it fails to account for the success of *certain* ideas over others (Bieler and Morton 2008); uncertainty is too parsimonious an analytical device to provide an answer to this essential question. As a result, my framework also draws on a literature focused on discourses of external economic constraint, such as the 'hyperglobalisation' myth prevalent in policymaking circles. This literature has broadly argued that ideas matter in IPE because political actors treat them *as though they were material straightjackets* (Hay and Rosamond 2002; Schmidt 2002b, 2008). This is particularly relevant in trade governance, where neoclassical trade theory has been particularly influential (Deraniyagala and Fine 2001), leading policymakers to believe that free trade is desirable because it allows for the reorganisation of production along the more efficient basis of international comparative advantage. Such ideas have not only shaped the neoliberal beliefs internalised by political actors – the so-called 'reflexive' dimension to discourse – but have also been at the heart of discursive strategies to construct ideational imperatives to legitimate otherwise controversial neoliberal economic programmes – the 'strategic' dimension to discourse, also known as rhetoric (for this distinction, see Rosamond 2000; Hay and Rosamond 2002).

More specifically, my argument is that the beliefs of policymakers in DG Trade led them to pursue certain policies, which they sought to legitimise using a different set of ideas (rhetoric). Ideas have shaped both what policymakers have *thought* in private and *said* in public. On one hand they have internalised a neoliberal discourse on the desirable, but ultimately contingent nature of trade liberalisation – explaining, in large part, *why* DG Trade pursued the policies it did and heeded certain interest groups over others. However, a far more necessitarian discourse was used in public pronouncements in order to legitimate an agenda of market opening. This allows me to explain *how* DG Trade was successful in the pursuit of its neoliberal agenda by appealing to competitiveness constraints posed by globalisation, which had been the leitmotif of the widely endorsed Lisbon Agenda of macroeconomic reform (as well as of its successor, 'Europe 2020'). However, rather than simply assuming that these ideas have been invoked strategically, as in some of the literature on 'globalisation discourses', this assessment is based on developing a way of determining the strategic invocation of ideas. In this way, I begin to address one of the central dilemmas in this literature: establishing whether pronouncements are truly rhetorical (or instrumental) or are in fact simply the reflection of underlying beliefs (Hay and Rosamond 2002: 165). I develop a novel analytical strategy premised on contrasting the private (or 'coordinative') discourse of policymakers with their public (or 'communicative') declarations, using insights from Schmidt's (2002b) discursive institutionalism. This allows me to conclude that policymakers *strategically* used such ideas as instruments of power. I also briefly consider the failure of a similar discourse of external constraint to legitimate the EPAs, given that only one regional grouping has so far signed up to an agreement with the EU.

Finally, my constructivist IPE approach also allows me to explain why the arguments of certain, export-oriented interest groups were heeded by policymakers at particular junctures (while defensive sectors, whose arguments were judged to be unconvincing, were marginalised). I do so by recasting these groups' attempts at influence in terms of strategic discourse, premised on appeals to the external *threat* of commercial rivals. I am thus able to accommodate the insights of rationalist IPE concerning the role of interest groups and systemic pressures in EU trade policy under a common, constructivist ontological roof, allowing for a greater contingency of outcome (including the later than expected mobilisation of interest groups, which only came after the Doha Round began to run into trouble). Moreover, focusing on the reflexive dimension to discourse also allows me to account for the fact that policymakers chose to heed the arguments of exporters even in the case of supposedly 'developmental' trade agreements with the ACP. It is not too difficult to see how policymakers in DG Trade 'bought' the argument of the services lobby and other groups that regulatory liberalisation was 'good' for development.

Outline of the book

Having provided an overview of my argument I now put forward a road-map for the remainder of the book. The first step is to explicitly state the three analytically distinct, yet inter-related research questions and puzzles around which this work is organised:

1 What prompted the European Commission's DG Trade to adopt a preferential trade strategy ('Global Europe') in October 2006 and why did this come about at the time that it did?
2 Why was this strategy premised on trading away protection for market access and how was DG Trade able to push this through, particularly at a time of economic crisis and against the opposition of powerful sectoral interests?
3 Why have the EU's 'commercial' and 'developmental' trade agendas become increasingly entwined in the wake of 'Global Europe'?

In Chapter 2 I begin the process of addressing these questions by providing a theoretical framework to inform the remainder of the book. I find that although existing literature in IPE that focuses on the determinants of North–South preferential trade liberalisation provides some answers to my research questions, particularly in terms of the emphasis placed on discriminatory services and investment liberalisation, it is still missing a crucial appreciation of the role of ideas in trade policymaking. I therefore make the case for a constructivist approach to IPE and develop my own specific framework for analysing EU trade policy. This focuses on: i) actors' internalisation of particular neoliberal ideas derived from neoclassical trade theory and ii) the power of discourses of external economic constraint, particularly when deployed instrumentally by those same actors to legitimate potentially controversial policy decisions. I propose an improved analytical technique for determining the *strategic* nature of such appeals to external constraints. Finally, I proceed to broaden the study of such rhetorics by considering how one can conceptualise their use by both policymakers *and* interest groups in the determination of trade policy outcomes. In sum, my aim in this chapter is to arrive at a constructivist IPE of EU trade policy that considers not only *material* dynamics but also the important (yet often neglected) role of ideas in trade policymaking. In doing so, I do not seek to dismiss interest group–based accounts of trade policy but rather try to accommodate them within my constructivist approach.

In Chapter 3 I develop the empirical argument that sits at the heart of this book, charting the rise of the 'Global Europe' strategy from my constructivist perspective. I begin by situating 'Global Europe' in a historical context, charting the shift from 'embedded liberalism' to neoliberalism in EU trade policy which coincided with a more proactive multilateral orientation. I then turn to the role of interest groups in shaping the EU's subsequent turn to bilateralism. The focus here is on the European services lobby, which constructed an external, competitive *threat* in order to pressure policymakers into shifting their strategy as the Doha Round looked increasingly stalled. Services and investment liberalisation hence also became particularly significant domain in the new 'Global Europe' strategy. A specific template was designed by DG Trade (the so-called 'Minimum Platform') for negotiations in this area that was aimed at matching competitors' preferential liberalisation gains. I then consider the discursive drivers of these developments. I focus on the neoliberal beliefs of policymakers, which led them to seek to boost EU competitiveness by reorganising its political economy along the lines of international comparative advantage. More specifically, it drove officials in DG Trade to not only seek to trade away the EU's remaining 'pockets of protection' for market access – as argued in the key 2005 'Trade and Competitiveness Issues Paper' (European Commission 2005a) – but also to consciously and deliberately construct an ideational imperative for liberalisation. This linked the 'Global Europe' strategy to the wider Lisbon Agenda and its emphasis on globalisation as a non-negotiable, external constraint.

In Chapter 4 I follow on from this to consider how the 'Global Europe' agenda has played out in practice, focusing on the first agreement concluded as part of this strategy, the EU–Korea FTA, which has been widely held up as the EU's most significant and ambitious trade agreement to date. I consider the distributive politics of the agreement and find that these embodied precisely the sentiments expressed in the 2005 'Issues Paper'; protection in the automobile industry was being leveraged in exchange for a substantial liberalisation of services and investment in South Korea. Thus, after briefly discussing the influence of services lobbyists during the negotiations, I proceed to consider *how* the Commission was able to pursue these trade-offs following the 2008 Financial Crisis. This galvanised opposition to the FTA, particularly from the powerful European automobile sector and its allies among Member States and in the EP. In this respect, the ideational imperative created by 'Global Europe', which characterised trade liberalisation as a necessary outcome in order to serve the Lisbon Agenda of competitiveness, served it well. Import-competing sectors were forced to fight an uphill (and ultimately fruitless) struggle against the EU–Korea agreement.

In Chapter 5 I focus on the increasing entwinement between the EU's 'developmental' and 'commercial' trade agendas in the wake of 'Global Europe' by turning to the EPA negotiations on WTO-plus issues between the EU and the ACP group. This chapter thus sheds light on how – despite the professions of policymakers to the contrary – the reach and scope of 'Global Europe' extends beyond purely commercial trade agreements. This is indicative of a broader convergence around neoliberal ideas in trade policymaking. I begin by situating EU–ACP trade relations in historical perspective to show how it was only under Mandelson that the EPA agenda became part and parcel of the EU's wider bilateral trade agenda, as exemplified by a renewed emphasis on not only completing the EPAs but also including ambitious WTO-plus liberalisation provisions in these agreements. I then turn to consider how these provisions bear a striking similarity to those featured in the EU's commercial FTAs, focusing specifically on the services and investment provisions of the only EPA completed to date with the Caribbean region. Subsequently I explore the drivers of convergence between both agendas, finding that services lobbyists played a role in pressuring policymakers who themselves had an independent interest in pursuing such an agenda. This was based on their prior conviction that regulatory liberalisation was beneficial for development. Finally, I turn in this chapter to consider a further element of similarity between the EPAs and 'Global Europe', namely the strategic deployment of a discourse of no alternative to economic liberalisation. Its failure to overcome opposition to the EPAs is an interesting counterpoint to the success of 'Global Europe's' discursive agenda in a 'commercial' context and suggests that problems may lie ahead for DG Trade's discursive strategy.

In Chapter 6, the book's final substantive chapter, I focus on the evolution of the 'Global Europe' agenda since the economic crisis. I present evidence to suggest that 'Global Europe's' successor, the 'Trade, Growth and World Affairs' strategy of November 2010, is driven by a similar concern with securing market access overseas for the EU's upmarket producers. A new emphasis on 'reciprocity' in trading relations, while potentially reading like a turn towards mercantilist-inspired protectionism, is in fact about improving leverage in negotiations with emerging country partners. This has led to two specific initiatives: a reform of the Generalised System of Preferences (GSP) scheme designed to exclude emerging economies the EU is negotiating FTAs with from receiving unilateral preferences, and an instrument to open foreign government procurement markets through selective and targeted closures of the EU market. Finally, and most importantly, I find that the key driver of these developments has been continuity in the beliefs of policymakers, who still subscribe to a positive-sum view of trade liberalisation. Moreover, officials continue to legitimate this agenda by locating trade policy within the macroeconomic consensus of the day, 'Europe 2020' – which serves as a successor to the Lisbon Agenda – and its emphasis on globalisation as an external constraint. While this neoliberal rhetoric remains successful, it faces several potential challenges: the economic crisis, the emergence of high-end competitors for EU producers in emerging economies and the increasing contestation of the discourse of no alternative in the field of 'developmental' trade relations.

Finally, I bring this book to a conclusion in Chapter 7. I begin by discussing how I have contributed to scholarly understanding of 'Global Europe' and EU trade politics. I then turn to my three main theoretical insights and how these might inform a future research agenda. These contributions are: bringing the study of the EU into IPE, considering the role of ideas within trade policy (a field usually dominated by rationalist scholars) and, in the process, offering several distinct insights to constructivist scholarship.

Sources

Before turning to the theoretical discussion in Chapter 2, I conclude this chapter by briefly discussing the nature of the primary sources relied on in drafting this book. These have been of two types: interviews with the main participants in the EU trade decision-making process and policy documents. I conducted a total of 83 face-to-face interviews as well as three telephone interviews with relevant European Commission officials (predominantly, but not exclusively in DG Trade);[6] other EU officials (including in the Council Secretariat), Member State officials; interest group representatives; WTO officials; non-governmental organisation (NGO) representatives and officials of other organisations (such as the ACP Secretariat). These took place over a series of fieldtrips to Brussels (two one-month trips over September/October 2009 and April/May 2010, a few days in December 2009 and 'follow up' interview sessions in May 2011 and January 2013), Geneva (three weeks in March 2010) and London (a few days in October and December 2009). The interviews were conducted in a loosely semi-structured format. Anonymity was offered to and, in practically all cases, taken up by participants, so the majority of references to interviews have been anonymised using a fairly general formulation acceptable to participants (for example, rather than mentioning a specific DG, interviews are simply referenced as being with 'European Commission officials'). Moreover, I have drawn more extensively on Commission rather than Member State officials, for two reasons. On the practical side, it was more difficult to gain access to Member State representatives. There is, however, also a conceptual rationale; as I have noted above, the literature on EU trade policy has increasingly noted the concentration of power in the hands of Commission officials and the waning influence of Member States.

I also draw on qualitative textual analysis of relevant policymaking documents issued by the European Commission, other EU bodies, interest groups and other relevant actors as well as (their) public statements and speeches. As MacDonald (2001: 205) writes, a document (or more broadly a text) can be analysed at two levels of meaning: 'the surface or literal meaning' or 'the deeper meaning arrived at by some form of interpretative or structural analysis'. This highlights the two objectives that textual analysis served in this book. At the 'surface' level, it contributed to an understanding of developments in EU trade policy, contributing also, in part, to 'methodological triangulation' (see Denzin 2006) with interview data. Primary texts were, however, also analysed in a 'deeper' sense in order to understand the discursive dimension to EU trade politics. More specifically, textual analysis (especially of Commission documents) was used to determine both policymakers' beliefs and to identify the more strategic use of ideas. To avoid overburdening the text at this stage, I have chosen to explain this decision in the Appendix to this book, which justifies the process for coding and selecting certain texts for analysis. This method is explicitly informed by my constructivist IPE framework, to which I now turn.

2
Trade Is What You Make of It: The Social Construction of EU Commercial Policy

In the previous chapter I showed how much of the literature on EU trade policy has tended to work with an implicit acceptance that the EU is somehow an 'exceptional' entity as a result of its institutional structure, with the latter seen as the main factor explaining EU trade policy. This body of work, I argued, struggled to explain the timing and content of the EU's preferential trade strategy, which increasingly resembled that of its principal commercial rivals. In this chapter, my aim will be to arrive at a theoretical framework that draws on a broader literature in IPE in order to explain these developments. This framework is developed in two steps. I begin by considering a rationalist IPE literature which has emphasised the important 'domestic–societal' and 'systemic' drivers of preferential trade liberalisation. I argue that recent strands of this literature (in particular Manger 2009), seeking to combine insights from both 'levels of analysis', represent an improvement on rational institutionalism in that they draw attention to important features of the current wave of North–South preferential liberalisation of which the EU is a participant. Following on from this, my second purpose in this chapter is to show that, although the mainstream IPE literature begins to answer some of the questions raised in this volume regarding the EU's preferential trade strategy, it still does not appreciate the important role of ideas in trade policymaking.

I therefore seek to develop a constructivist IPE framework which, rather than dismissing the mainstream literature, incorporates the important insights of interest-group-based explanations of trade policy. Although existing constructivist IPE approaches have made a good case for studying ideas as causes, they have not always had an answer to the question of why certain ideas matter, opening themselves up to

21

criticism by neo-Marxist scholars (Bieler and Morton 2008). This is because, following Blyth (2002), they have often relied quite heavily on the notion of agential uncertainty to establish the importance of ideas, such as Woll's (2008) influential constructivist study of interest group behaviour in the area of trade in services. In contrast, I make the case for a constructivist approach that – while premised on the insights of Blyth's constructivism into the importance of ideas as ordering narratives in the context of an uncertain social world – focuses on the role of discourses of external constraint and stresses their importance as instruments of power (drawing on, amongst others, Hay and Rosamond 2002; Schmidt 2002b, 2008). In doing so, I propose an improved theoretical method for determining the strategic invocation of such discourses, addressing one of the central dilemmas in this literature (see Hay and Rosamond 2002: 165). I then proceed to broaden the study of such rhetoric by considering how one can conceptualise its use by both policymakers *and* interest groups in the determination of trade policy outcomes – drawing on rationalist IPE accounts of preferential trade liberalisation. In sum then, I aspire in this chapter to make the case for an IPE of EU trade policy. In addition to so-called 'material' factors, this takes on-board the crucial role played by ideas in shaping political economic outcomes, in particular those of the dominant neoliberal paradigm in trade policymaking. In other words, I see trade as being what actors make of it.

The remainder of the chapter is divided into four sections. In the first, I consider the insights of mainstream IPE literature into the drivers of preferential liberalisation among developed countries. In the next, I make the case for constructivism in IPE. I show how – despite the difficulties some constructivist accounts have in showing *why* certain ideas trump others – the prevalence of neoliberal thinking in trade policymaking circles suggests that one important reason that certain ideas matter (in an uncertain social world) is that they are treated *as though they were material constraints*. This allows me, in the third section, to build on constructivist IPE by drawing on insights from a literature that has emphasised the discursive construction of external constraints. This section sets out my specific framework which – while drawing on some of the insights of rationalist IPE – emphasises the constructed nature of social reality and, more specifically, augments the study of strategically invoked economic discourses to study the EU's (neoliberal) trade governance. The final section concludes by summarising the arguments presented in this chapter.

The rationalist IPE literature on preferential trade

The first body of work that I draw on is an emerging literature in IPE on North–South preferential liberalisation. By focusing on the drivers of this trend from a developed country perspective it has emphasised the role of domestic lobbyists and their sensitivity to systemic competition for market access. Before turning to this specific group of authors, however, I need to provide a brief overview of the broader literature on preferential liberalisation (which has often been referred to as 'regionalism')[1] which has largely emerged within a mainstream, rationalist framework.[2] This has tended to organise work around two levels of analysis – the 'systemic' and the 'domestic–societal'.

In the 'systemic' literature on preferential liberalisation, many explanations have been influenced by neoliberal institutionalist notions of state preferences (see Keohane 1984) – namely, a concern with 'absolute' rather than 'relative gains', as in neorealist writing (for this distinction, see Grieco 1988). A strain of this literature has emphasised the concern of states with welfare gains or losses from the formation of PTAs. The starting point is the idea taken from Viner (1950) that a PTA 'diverts' as well as 'creates' trade. A state may thus be motivated to cooperate with other states to join or form a PTA on defensive grounds in order to protect its export interests, or it can be prompted to proactively form or join such an economic grouping to benefit from 'trade creation' effects (for example, Pomfret 1988; Yarbrough and Yarbrough 1992). The commonality of such approaches is that they stress the 'contagion effect' of PTAs (Mansfield 1998), in other words, the *strategic interaction* between different trade agreements. Moreover – and in contrast to other authors in a systemic IPE tradition who emphasise the mediating role of international institutions in shaping the proliferation of FTAs (for instance, Mansfield and Reinhardt 2008) – this literature sees PTAs as developing independently of the multilateral trading system.

For their part, domestic studies of trade have tended to work within an 'endogenous' trade policy framework literature, mostly based on the US experience, wherein trade policy is seen as determined by the outcome of interest group competition (for a review, see Hiscox 2002).[3] The formal framework developed by Grossman and Helpman (1994) has been particularly influential. It offers a pluralist view of state–society relations where certain lobbyists are heeded on the basis of their ability to mobilise the necessary resources (financial contributions) to influence elected officials. Drawing on this approach to study the phenomenon of regionalism (and why it may be preferred to multilateral liberalisation) are those who emphasise the role of economies of scale and imperfect competition (for a review, see Mansfield and Milner 1999). As prime exponents of this literature, Casella (1996) and Milner (1997) hypothesise that in an industry marked by increasing returns to scale – which traditional economic theory dictates will tend towards imperfect competition – a firm's scale of production in relation to minimum efficient scale (the scale of output minimising unit costs) is endogenous to market size. This may lead such firms to support regionalism because it allows them to increase their market size and move down their cost curves enough to increase their profits and offset the decline in price resulting from trade liberalisation (the implication being that the decline in price resulting from multilateral liberalisation may be too great to offset the reduction in costs). Building on these insights, Chase (2005) introduces a novel element into his framework: the notion that PTAs also help to safeguard production-sharing arrangements across different countries (as differences in national factor endowments may allow production to be carried out more efficiently abroad). In this way, the literature on 'imperfect competition' serves to empirically refocus the debate on regionalism to study the emerging trend of North–South PTAs (from the perspective of developed countries).

Combining 'systemic' and 'domestic' explanations of regionalism

Although I have considered them separately so far for heuristic purposes, it would be wrong to overstate divisions between 'systemic' and 'domestic–societal' schools of thought. Even though they may have their own distinct logics of explanation, several works within IPE have invoked both to explain preferential liberalisation. The most prominent of these has been Baldwin's (1993) 'domino theory of regionalism'. Baldwin argues that the fear of trade diversion from a PTA will prompt interest groups to lobby their governments to seek to join this agreement to offset any potential loss of competitiveness. These 'pressures for inclusion' (Lawrence 1996) set a chain of 'dominoes' in motion, as more and more states are lobbied by their exporters to join existing preferential trading arrangements. This links the insights of 'systemic' accounts of regionalism stressing strategic interaction effects to domestic–pluralist explanations of trade policy. The implicit argument is that one cannot explain the phenomenon of regionalism exclusively by appealing to endogenous factors (for a very similar argument, see Dür 2010).

Although Baldwin's work may have been suitable to study the 'open regionalism' of the early 1990s – as perhaps best embodied by Asia

Pacific Economic Cooperation (see, for example, Bergsten 1997) – it contributes less to one's understanding of the more fragmented system of bilateral agreements that has developed in recent years. In this vein, a more interesting 'combined' literature on the drivers of preferential liberalisation has sought to link the notion of strategic interaction to the literature stressing the importance of imperfect competition and increasing returns to scale. In particular this scholarship has stressed the importance of FDI in manufacturing and services as drivers of a competitive North–South regionalism. Thus, although owing an intellectual debt to the 'imperfect competition' school of regionalism – particularly in framing the debate in terms of North–South PTAs and emphasising the role of market structures – Manger (2005, 2009) rejects Chase's (2005) main insight that the existence of production-sharing arrangements necessarily leads to preferential liberalisation. Manger instead argues that preferential liberalisation is often preferred by domestic firms over multilateral liberalisation because its discriminatory nature can help generate economic rents, by restricting 'access to this benefit of location, [assuming] host countries impose a sufficiently high tariff on imports from nonmembers' (Manger 2005: 810). Facing such 'proactively' strategic agreements, firms in a third country may lobby their respective governments to seek PTAs that offset the advantages gained by their competitors.

Manger also makes a unique contribution to the field by considering the role that services liberalisation plays in driving regionalism, particularly for those firms that are established or are seeking a commercial presence in a host country through investment ('mode 3' suppliers in General Agreement on Trade in Services [GATS] parlance). He contends that in emerging economies, such services markets – which include telecommunications, professional services, retail banking and other financial services and utilities – are often marked by large economies of scale, requiring significant 'sunk' investments (see Manger 2008: 2459–60). These market structures give 'first-movers' an advantage over potential competitors, allowing them to establish a dominant market position and deter further entry. As a result, services firms may lobby their governments for preferential access to such markets for two reasons. Firstly, incumbent service operators with significant sunk investment may favour preferential liberalisation of investment because it – even if applied non-discriminatorily, which the lifting of foreign equity restrictions often is – allows them to take advantage of their 'first-mover' advantage to improve on their dominant position. Secondly and more importantly, where regulation is very important for a given sector, preferential liberalisation itself creates 'first-mover' advantages for potential entrants.

This is because the elimination of regulatory restrictions previously blocking or hampering the operation of foreign service suppliers is usually carried out on a discriminatory basis. The exclusion of outsiders from an FTA ensures that firms benefitting from its provisions may be able to establish a dominant position through 'first-entry'. In extreme cases of limited-licensing – often found in telecommunications – and standard-setting, latecomers may be, respectively, completely prevented from entry or severely disadvantaged by the adoption of different regulations to that of their home market (Manger 2009: 44–8).

A 'combined' IPE perspective on North–South regionalism

There is a clear link between the insights of 'domestic–societal' accounts stressing the role of interest groups to the wider systemic pressures that lead states to pursue preferential trade policies, particularly the strategic interaction effects of PTA 'contagion'. What is also clear, moreover, is that one cannot explain the phenomenon of regionalism by appealing exclusively to either 'systemic' or 'domestic–societal' explanations, as they only paint part of the picture. Without an external, systemic competitive *threat* there would be no imperative for firms to act, but likewise, without domestic political forces there would likely be no (direct) source of pressure on policymakers. This suggests that the 'combined' literature on regionalism has the greatest explanatory potential. With this in mind, in Table 2.1 I summarise some of the main features of the 'domestic–systemic' literature on regionalism (and the 'imperfect competition' school on which it builds). It becomes clear that that the consensus here is that regionalism is a phenomenon that is largely independent of multilateral dysfunction because it offers firms the possibility of seeking goals that are distinct from those of multilateral trade negotiations, namely, *discriminatory* and *partial* liberalisation. This, in turn, has meant that such scholars have relied (where relevant) on insights that are compatible with the systemic literature on strategic interaction effects – as opposed to the systemic IPE works looking at the mediating effect of multilateral institutions (see above) – as these objectives are difficult to reconcile with multilateral liberalisation.

In order to understand the preferences of firms for *partial* and *discriminatory* liberalisation I have to first consider the role played in such accounts by Olson's (1965) 'logic of collective action', which stresses the asymmetric nature of interest group mobilisation; pressure groups will only mobilise *after* the emergence of a common economic interest. This has traditionally been understood to mean that the 'losers' from a particular economic policy are more likely to mobilise than the 'winners', due to the concentrated and more immediate nature of the losses

Table 2.1 Preferential liberalisation, firm interests and systemic pressures

Sectors Concerned	Nature of Firm Interest in Preferential Liberalisation	Nature of Liberalisation Sought by Firms
Services (especially mode 3 suppliers)	Regulatory liberalisation in the services sector (Manger 2008, 2009)	(Mainly) discriminatory
	Liberalising investment for incumbent service operators (Manger 2009)	Both discriminatory and non-discriminatory
All (a focus on manufacturing is implicit, given the emphasis on trade creation and trade diversion effects)	Restoring exporter competitiveness (Baldwin 1993; see also the 'protection-for-exporters' argument in Dür 2010)	Discriminatory
	Increasing market size (Casella 1996; Milner 1997)	Partial
Manufacturing engaged in production sharing	Safeguarding production sharing arrangements (Chase 2005)	Partial
	Generating economic rents for production sharing arrangements (Manger 2005, 2009)	Discriminatory

Source: Author's interpretation.

incurred and the greater diffusion of, and uncertainty regarding, the benefits. A consistent narrative within the endogenous trade literature has been that this explained why protectionist interests often had the upper hand in trade policymaking when this was in the hands of politically malleable legislators, such as the US Congress (see Baldwin 1985; Destler 2005), while exporters were generally at a disadvantage (Dür 2010: 20–5). Although some scholars have provided insights into the conditions under which exporters may mobilise and exert pressure, the fact remains that such approaches have still accepted the importance of collective action dynamics and thus postulated very specific conditions under which exporters can be seen to exert influence (for instance, 'reciprocity' and trade policy insulation) (Bailey *et al.* 1997; Gilligan 1997).

This understanding of interest group mobilisation has also permeated the literature concerning preferential liberalisation.

In terms of firms' preference for partial liberalisation, the main insights are offered by the literature stressing economies of scale in production (Milner 1997; Casella 1996; Chase 2005). This preference for more limited market opening as opposed to (more comprehensive) multilateral liberalisation is seen to derive from the ability of firms to fully internalise the benefits of increased returns to scale from partial liberalisation without suffering from an offsetting decline in price through increased competition. Speaking more broadly, most theorists considering the role of interest groups in trade policy (whether from an 'endogenous' or 'domestic–systemic' perspective) have agreed that bilateral trade agreements are not prompted by a dysfunctional multilateral trade round, but rather allow for 'liberalisation without political pain' (Ravenhill 2003: 299). In other words, they are likely to appeal to exporting industries while minimising the threat to import-competing firms – by, for example, excluding sensitive sectors – and are thus politically more palatable than more comprehensive (multilateral) liberalisation (Dür 2010). In this vein, Manger (2012) argues that North–South preferential liberalisation is driven by vertical trade specialisation (trade in similar products differentiated on the basis of quality, more on which below) rather than complete specialisation, as this entails lower adjustment costs. More generally, in the face of both exporters and protectionists mobilising, existing approaches have tended to suggest that governments will continue to respond to import competitors (for instance, Dür 2010: 34; Manger 2012: 629–33). Turning to the specific aims of this chapter, firms' desire for *partial* liberalisation provides a useful insight into the causes of the current fragmented system of preferential liberalisation and, more generally, highlights the importance of distributive politics in shaping states' market opening strategies.

The stress placed by authors on the discriminatory liberalisation logic to regionalism is also underpinned by an Olsonian understanding of collective action dynamics (Olson 1965). In the case of the 'domino theory of regionalism', it was fear of a *loss* of market share from discriminatory liberalisation, rather than a concern with securing additional market access, that was the driving force behind interest group activism. In the Manger framework there is also an emphasis on such defensive considerations for incumbent firms engaged in production sharing which are seeking to offset rivals' gains to protect their economic rents. However, it is not only the 'losers' which seem to mobilise effectively to push for discriminatory market opening. Manger's framework to explain North–South regionalism is based on the notion that firms have a distinct interest in discriminatory, as opposed to non-discriminatory (or multilateral), liberalisation for offensive reasons. Such liberalisation can generate economic rents for firms engaged in production sharing, while in the case of services, discriminatory regulatory liberalisation gives suppliers a 'first-mover' advantage in terms of penetrating new markets. Neither of these advantages would be derived from market opening in the most-favoured nation (MFN) mould of multilateral trade talks, where competitors cannot be excluded from taking advantage of liberalisation gains. In fact, for Manger the extremely competitive nature of preferential liberalisation for services – and to a lesser extent for production-sharing manufacturers – provides a powerful Olsonian 'common economic interest' that rallies interest groups and leads them to seek PTAs. As a result, it is not too difficult to see why, where PTAs serve as vehicles for discriminatory liberalisation, systemic pressures (in the form of strategic interaction effects) are particularly relevant. What is more noteworthy is the fact that this is particularly relevant in the case of regulatory liberalisation, as implied (but not explicitly stated) by Manger. This is because of the consequences of standard-setting or (even more extreme) limited-licensing for latecomers. As a result, this literature – which emphasises the unique opportunities that 'behind-the-border' liberalisation affords economic actors to exploit market structures in emerging economies – is particularly useful at explaining the North–South focus, regulatory content and competitive edge to much of the current regionalism. In subsequent chapters I will show how all of these factors were relevant in the case of 'Global Europe' (although, as will become apparent in Chapter 3, the stagnation of the Doha Round did also matter in shaping interest group preferences, albeit not in the rationalist manner of some systemic IPE accounts).

So far then, the literature highlighting the *discriminatory* and *partial* nature of regionalism points to important features of the current system of preferential market opening from a developed country perspective. More generally, accounts linking 'domestic–societal' to 'systemic' accounts of regionalism overcome the problems associated with focusing on simply one 'level of analysis' as has often been the case in mainstream IPE (see Katzenstein *et al.* 1998); as I have highlighted above, neither is a sufficient explanation of preferential liberalisation. Strange's (1994: 218) widely cited assessment of the discipline is particularly apposite at this juncture:

> [t]he whole point of studying international political economy rather than international relations is to extend more widely the conventional limits of the study of politics and the conventional concepts of who engages in politics and of how and by whom power is exercised to influence outcomes.

As becomes apparent from the passage cited above, Strange was wedded to a notion of IPE as a discipline concerned with studying power within a social whole (see also Strange 1970). Applying this meta-theoretical insight to the specific phenomenon of preferential liberalisation, it is clear how 'domestic–systemic' accounts provide a compelling and parsi-monious account of how trade policymaking operates: facing an *external threat*, in the form of (potential) commercial gains by rivals, interest groups engage in the domestic policy process by pressuring their policy-makers, who respond by pursuing a regionalist trade agenda. However, Strange was not just making a point over the need to transcend bound-aries between different levels of analysis. Among other things, the 'criti-cal' IPE school with which she became associated – and which is explored in a little more detail in the next section – sought to 'extend more widely the conventional limits of the study of politics' (Strange 1994: 218) by considering the socially constructed nature of the politi-cal world and the resulting power of ideas (and those who deploy them). The mainstream, or so-called 'rationalist', accounts of trade policy reviewed so far have, unfortunately, mainly focused on the material determinants of policy and have thus disregarded a key determinant of political economic outcomes. In the next section I will thus show that, from a theoretical perspective, one needs to take the role of ideas more seriously if one is to understand the behaviour of the EU and the key actors in its trade policymaking. It is important at this stage to empha-sise that I am not saying that conventional accounts of trade policy cannot explain the EU's trade strategy or its policy outcomes. On the contrary, I suggest that they point to important features of the EU's approach, as will become apparent in subsequent chapters. My analysis simply highlights that ideas and language play an important role in shaping trade policy outcomes in *mediating* so-called 'material factors': trade is what actors make of it.

The social construction of neoliberal rationality

Using the term constructivism inevitably evokes a tradition in International Relations (IR) theory mostly associated with the writings of Wendt (1999) (and, to a lesser extent, Ruggie 1982). Wendt's work sought to engage with structural realist (or neorealist) accounts of international order by underscoring the intersubjective nature of international relations and the anarchy problématique; rather than being given materially 'state identities and interests are in important part constructed by [...] social structures' (Wendt 1994: 385) so that 'anarchy is what states make of it'. In this vein, scholars have recently sought to reconceptualise the international trade regime in terms of an 'intersubjective communication among participants' (Wolfe 2005: 340). However – and while acknowledging Wendt's important contribution to the field – in this book I follow others in seeking to move beyond IR constructivism's structural determinism, neorealist-inspired state-centrism (on these issues, see Adler 1997: 330–7; Hay 2002: 199–200) and 'rump materialism', or the idea that 'brute material facts' can still affect international relations in a number of ways (Wendt 1999: 109–11; for a critique, see Smith 2000: 154). Instead, I seek to recast constructivism as an ontologically consistent framework – based on the premise that ideas *do matter all the way down* – and one which emphasises the role of agency. Rather than being constituted at the level of state interaction, it is agents themselves which construct social reality. Quoting Hacking (1999: 6, 12), directly, Hay's argument is that X is socially constructed when:

- X need not have existed, or need not be as it is. X, or X as it is present, is not determined by the nature of things; it is not inevitable. [...]
- In the present state of affairs, X is taken for granted; X appears to be inevitable.

> Hay (2002: 201, original numbering altered to bullet points)

This leaves me with a rather intuitive ontological position on which to base the constructivism in this volume: the belief that social and political reality is *constructed* by agents through ideas rather than being *fixed* by particular material (or what could be called 'structural') constraints, as in rationalist accounts. This is not to say that material factors do not exist or matter, but rather that, in a social context, what is decisive is *how* they are interpreted by relevant actors. A deep and wide river cutting off one's path will always be a river – save in the case of intervention by *force majeure* – no matter how much one believes it not to be there. However, its effects on human behaviour will not (necessarily) be as circumscribed, as we can choose whether to circumnavigate or attempt to cross it. In practice, of course, most ('sane') people would choose to do (what is probably considered to be) the 'rational' thing and take a detour, but this does not detract from the underlying ontological argument that it is the *interpretation* of material facts that is the underlying variable to understanding human behaviour rather than the facts themselves. As Blyth (2002: 10) notably put it, 'structures do not come with an instruction sheet'. One could always foresee a context in which it was 'appropriate' to show some bravado (maybe in the company of boisterous friends) and attempt to swim across. Thus, although there may be material constraints to action, what is ultimately the determining factor is how an actor responds to these. This is what, according to Adler (1997), could be called the 'middle ground' between rationalism – where ideas are best adjunct to material forces – and 'interpretivist' approaches (such as post-structuralism or the Frankfurt School) – where the emphasis is almost entirely on language and meaning in constituting reality. Making the case for such a constructivism, Adler (1997: 324) argues that 'collective understandings, such as norms, endow physical objects with purpose and therefore help constitute reality'.

A similar ontological position has informed a growing and self-consciously constructivist literature in IPE, which has emphasised the role of ideas in the international political economy, focusing in particular on the construction of actor interests. This has taken its cue from the work of economic sociologists and Polanyi (1944) to highlight the socially embedded nature of economic activity. Its primary exponent has been Blyth (2002) and the emphasis he places on 'Knightian uncertainty'.[4] Borrowing from the work of Beckert (1996) – who in turn draws on the work of the economist Knight (1921) – Blyth (2002: 30–4) underscores how, in moments of crisis, actors are faced with unique situations in which they are unable to determine their interests. Crucially, he differentiates this type of uncertainty (which he labels as 'Knightian') from the notion of 'uncertainty as complexity' found in the work of certain rationalist scholars (such as North 1990). Here actors know their interests but are uncertain as to how to realise them and therefore face a situation of 'risk' rather than uncertainty. In contrast, actors' 'interests in […] an environment [of uncertainty] cannot be given by either assumption or structural location and can be defined only in terms of the ideas that agents themselves have about the causes of uncertainty' (Blyth 2002: 32). Moreover, such ideas are not independent of the functioning of the economy (as say theories of the workings of the solar system are) given that they have a direct bearing on the nature of causal relations between actors by shaping their perceptions of each others' interests (Blyth 2002: 33). Combining an emphasis on the 'uniqueness' of moments of Knightian uncertainty with an insight into the endogeneity of ideas, Blyth's key argument is that actors' behaviour is not a product of their material interests, but rather of their *perception* of these interests; these ideas are what render interests 'actionable' in moments of crisis (Blyth 2002: 39). A similar claim as to the importance of ideas in political explanation has been made more recently, and forcefully, in Blyth (2010) where it is argued that situations of uncertainty are pervasive in the social world rather than just characterising moments of crisis. The corollary of this line of reasoning is that one must move beyond seeing the study of ideas as just an important aspect of social organisation (as in Blyth 2002) and towards seeing them as 'fundamental' to our understanding thereof.

Turning to issues of epistemology, an important feature of this constructivist IPE literature is the emphasis many of these works place on attributing a specific *causal* role to ideas.[5] In this, it stands in contrast to Wendt's claim that the ideational often does not have an analytically separable effect on outcomes and that its effects are thus 'constitutive'. In contrast, Parsons (2007: 105–13) argues that Wendt works within a very narrow conception of Humean causality. Parsons' view, instead, is that Hume's 'constant conjunction' – in particular, the notion that 'for *A* to be a cause of *B*, *A* must exist independently of *B* [and] *A* must occur before *B* in time' (Parsons 2007: 105) – can still hold when dealing with ideational explanation that Wendt refers to as constitutive. The key is that the analyst must be prepared to ask 'careful, specific questions about causes and effects' (Parsons 2007: 112) as '[c]lassical causal logic does not ask we imagine an effect without its causes [but rather that] we ascertain the cause and effect without using the same information for both' (Parsons 2007: 109). This shared epistemological position distinguishes such constructivist IPE scholars not only from Cox's (1981, 1987) historicism – which, as I will note below, sits uneasily with causality-based explanations – but also (albeit for different reasons) from 'neo-positivist' works (to borrow a term from Jackson 2010) which incorporate ideas into their analysis. Blyth (2002) has shown that in such accounts, ideas are simply used as devices to correct for the failings of existing rationalist research programs (see, for example, Goldstein and Keohane 1993; or, in the trade sphere, Drake and Nicolaïdis 1992) rather than invoke specific ideational logics of explanation. The key difference between such works and a constructivist perspective is an appeal to a different logic of explanation, one ideational and contingent, the other material and static (for more on the nature of 'logics of explanation', see Parsons 2007).

Both of these metatheoretical insights have spawned considerable research into different aspects of the international political economy, including the paradigmatic shift from 'embedded liberalism' to neo-liberalism (a good selection can be found in Abdelal *et al.* 2010a; see also Best and Widmaier 2006; Best 2008). Even in the field of trade policy – traditionally a bastion of rationalist writing – there have been some authors working in the tradition of constructivist IPE (for instance, Bukovansky 2010). Especially influential has been Woll (2008), who developed a model for firm preference formation premised on the idea of uncertainty and applied it to explain the mobilisation in favour of liberalisation in the GATS of previous monopolies in telecommunications and air services in the EU and US.

However, while accepting the basic ontological and epistemological premises of this constructivist literature – namely, that agents construct social reality through ideas and that such ideas can be studied as causal phenomena – in this book I rely on more than just the analytical device of uncertainty. Indeed, while this constructivist IPE literature has been very convincing at making the case for both of these metatheoretical premises, an excessive reliance on this specific, and parsimonious analytical device is very clear in Blyth (2002). Despite seeming to privilege ideas at the expense of the material, he succumbs to a 'residual materialist' pitfall (Hay 2004b: 208–10). Specifically, Hay critiques Blyth's (2002) framework for not resolving the issue of where actors' ideas emerge from during times of Knightian uncertainty and, most importantly, why certain actors' ideas trump those of others. The problem is, in Hay's opinion, that Blyth's overly parsimonious emphasis on uncertainty in moments of crisis must rely on material explanations (such as access to particular non-ideational 'resources') to account for the success of a particular actor's 'crisis-narrations' in reshaping political economic institutions.

Arguably, part of this issue – which is ultimately tied to the view that it is crises that create a moment of Knightian uncertainty – is resolved in subsequent work where Blyth (2010; see also 2006) argues for a more general theory of the importance of ideas. More specifically, he maintains that the social world does not conform to the expectations of a positivist social science – 'equilibrium, linearity, exogeneity and normality' – and that instead 'we live in a world that is actually disequilibrial and dynamic, where causes are endogenous and nonlinear, and where outcomes of interest are *not* normally distributed' (Blyth 2010: 87, emphasis in the original). The argument is, however, premised on a similar distinction between risk and uncertainty as found in his earlier work, although uncertainty is now more clearly shown to characterise *all* social interactions, rather than just moments of crisis (see Seabrooke 2010: 84–6). As a result, and although the ontological primacy of ideas is established, it is not entirely clear from this framework why certain ideas matter rather (or more) than others. In other words, living in an uncertain world may explain why studying ideas is necessary, as such ideas are necessary for agents to navigate social reality (Blyth 2010: 96) but it does not clarify how we are to account for the success (or not) of particular ideational constructions in shaping social interactions. A similar emphasis on uncertainty in many of the constructivist accounts discussed above means that ideas are often simply invoked as a *'deus ex machina'* in view of the failure of rationalist accounts to provide an explanation of particular political phenomena (Hay 2004b: 210). It should be stressed at this stage that this holds even for constructivists who do not rely on uncertainty to establish the importance of ideas (for example, Weaver 2008; Chwieroth 2010). Such authors have tended to engage in an exercise of methodological bracketing, where the importance of ideas is established by eliminating alternative (material/institutional) explanations. Parsons (2003: 10–15; see also 2007: Ch. 4) refers to this as the 'how much problem' in ideational analysis, in other words, the issue of specifying the degree to which ideas determine political outcomes. Although a justifiable first step in terms of building a constructivist theoretical framework, it does not get one further in terms of determining the importance of some ideas over others. In sum, much of the existing constructivist IPE literature – while providing an adequate explanation of why ideas *qua* ideas matter – have not sufficiently addressed the question of why *certain* ideas matter and shape political outcomes, beyond considering their importance as ordering narratives given an uncertain social world and/or necessary variables to explain social outcomes. This has resulted in criticism from, among others, historical materialists who claim that such a framework is 'unable to explain *why* a particular set of ideas became part of the structure and not another, rival set of ideas' (Bieler and Morton 2008: 104, emphasis in the original).

Unfortunately, many of those who have begun to address such questions have tended to operate within an ontologically inconsistent framework, where actors may behave according to an ideational logic even though their interests have been given materially.[6] My aim in the remainder of this section is therefore to respond to the critics of constructivism in IPE by showing *why* certain ideas may matter in an ontologically constructivist fashion. This explanation is centred on the purchase and nature of neoliberal ideas in academic and policymaking circles, not unlike the constructivist research agenda into the rise of said policymaking paradigm in the international political economy. Much like this literature, I do so with reference to the specific content and nature of these ideas rather than to external material factors. But to avoid the pitfalls of relying exclusively on uncertainty as an 'enabling' device for ideational explanation, I turn to a literature that has focused on the discursive construction and internalisation of external constraints. Indeed, the belief that human beings are rational utility-maximisers – seen by many to be at the heart of neoliberalism (see, for example, Best and Widmaier 2006) – provides a powerful imperative for behaviour when internalised by political actors (Hay 2004a: 59–60).

Why do ideas matter? A 'critical' perspective on neoliberal rationality

I contend that one powerful reason why certain ideas matter in the international political economy is that they are treated by actors *as though they were material straightjackets*. More specific to the case at hand, and as others have pointed out, it is neoliberal tenets that are being treated as increasingly 'normalised', that is, as reflections of a reality in which the rational *homo œconomicus* is the main determinant of social outcomes, rather than as a 'normative' framework, advocating policies seen as desirable (Hay 2004c; see also Best and Widmaier 2006). Such findings echo Polanyi's (1944: 45) view that markets are ultimately socially embedded and historically situated rather than spontaneous and natural as nineteenth century liberals and twentieth/twenty-first century neoliberals have claimed. In this vein, the key point I wish to stress at this juncture is that the rational-actor assumptions neoclassical economic models are premised on are ultimately constructed and contingent, rather than given and fixed. As Maier (1988: 4–6), puts it, such (critical) political economy 'interrogates economic doctrines to disclose their sociological and political premises [...] regard[ing] economic ideas and behaviour not as frameworks for analysis, but as beliefs and actions that must themselves be explained'.

Thus, I argue that an answer to the question of why ideas matter *causally* in the international political economy can be found by accommodating rationalist insights within an ontologically consistent constructivism (for a very similar argument, see Saurugger 2013). Although much maligned by constructivist scholars, the notion of rationality employed by rational choice scholars can still serve as a useful 'as if' heuristic to understand the hypothetical consequences of purely rational-egoistic behaviour on which neoclassical economic models are premised (Hay 2004a: 59–60). Going one step further, one could argue that in certain contexts, actors have internalised particular 'rationalities' so that their behaviour does correspond to that of rationalist models. Actors may at one point act as though there were particular material constraints to their behaviour, but this constructed and internalised rationality – in contrast to its counterpart in a rational choice model – is always subject to change; actors' perceptions of material constraints are not fixed (although in practice they may be quite stable). Actors may also be driven by behaviour not grounded in beliefs about the fixed nature of social reality (as in the sociological institutionalist literature in IR and EU Studies, for instance, Reus-Smit 1997; Checkel 2005). Schmidt (2008: 306–7) follows others in making a similar distinction between such 'cognitive' and 'normative' ideas. Referring to Hay's (2002: 64) argument that epistemology is always dependent on ontology, one can see that although epistemologically I am talking about two distinct analytical logics of explanation they are both still logically dependent on a view of social reality as a constructed and inherently contingent phenomenon. This helps one to see that rather than seeing these two logics as necessarily oppositional, they can be figuratively accommodated under the same 'ontological roof'. Thus, the insights of rationalist approaches can be reconciled with a form of ideational logic of explanation that makes such rationalism contingent on the ideas internalised by actors.[7]

It should become clear that I am not only drawing from the constructivist (and by proxy from economic sociology) but also from the (earlier) 'critical' approach of Cox (1981). He proposes a historicist approach that stresses the context-bound nature of theory. Knowing the historical circumstances surrounding the origin of a theory is imperative to come to understand for *whom* and for *what* – to paraphrase his oft-cited adage that 'theory is always for someone and for some purpose' (Cox 1981: 128) – it has been conceived. His starting point is, in other words, to uncover the interests and power relations that underpin theories of political behaviour. Cox refers to this as 'critical theory', which he contrasts with 'problem-solving' theory, approaches that take the *status quo* as an ahistorically defined (that is, as a timeless) given and simply seek to 'tinker' with the existing order. In the case of the rationalist trade policy literature considered in this chapter, such biases are not too difficult to observe as it has been, in the main, premised on an (automatic) acceptance of the neoclassical economic tenet of the desirability of trade openness. Systemic theories of IPE drawing their inspiration from Keohane (1984), for example, have been concerned themselves with the ability of the multilateral trading system (and the global 'public good' of free trade) to survive hegemonic collapse, while a primary concern of the endogenous trade policy literature has been to explain 'sup-optimal' trade policy outcomes such as protectionism in terms of 'collective action' logics.

I – and constructivist IPE scholars more broadly – are therefore indebted to Cox (and the neo-Gramscian school of IPE, more generally), as it exposes such theoretical shortcomings in mainstream/rationalist approaches to the study of IPE and alerts us to the power of economic ideas. That being said, I do not wish to go down the neo-Gramscian route, for a number of reasons. For one, and from an epistemological perspective, Cox's 'interpretive, hermeneutic, historicist mode of knowledge' (Cox 1996: 29) is difficult to reconcile with the sort of causal IPE approach that I seek to develop. Secondly, it is driven by a narrow problématique of its own, centred on explaining the persistence of inequitable relations of production between social classes. As a result, and most importantly, although the explicit aim of such approaches is to deconstruct the hegemony of neoliberal ideas, the structural dominance of such ideas is taken largely as a given, tied as it is in such accounts to the interests of the capitalist class. In other words, not only is such a framework underpinned by a materialist conception of social relations but ideas are also treated as an *exogenously* determined factor (tied to social class), much as in the 'augmented' rationalist approaches considered above (for instance, Goldstein and Keohane 1993). This means that due consideration is not given to the role of particular agents in generating and propagating certain ideas. This is most evident in the 'new constitutionalist' approach of Gill (1998) which focuses on the legal 'locking in' of the neoliberal paradigm via such mechanisms as European integration (particularly monetary union). This has been criticised precisely for being overly deterministic and not paying sufficient attention to the role (and possibilities) of agency in ideational construction (Parker 2008). Neo-Marxian perspectives have also been found to be overly holistic; in other words, they are insufficiently fine-tuned to the several specific forms that liberalism has taken – especially within the history of European integration (Rosamond 2013: 11).[8] In the current context of the Eurozone Crisis, for example, German ordoliberalism (and its emphasis on the need for *Ordnungspolitik*, or a rule-based political economy with a strong state at its heart) is often conflated with neoliberalism (which dichotomises markets and the state) (Berghahn and Young 2013; contrast with van Apeldoorn and Overbeek 2012: 2–3).

As a result, and before developing my theoretical argument any further, I take a pause to consider what specific form neoliberalism has taken in trade policy. Indeed, even if we leave the specific problems of the neo-Gramscian literature behind, the expression 'neoliberalism' has been said to be so ubiquitous in contemporary political analysis as to lack analytical purchase. That being said, many scholars would probably agree that 'some term is needed to describe the macro-economic paradigm that has predominated [for much of the past three decades]' (Watkins 2010: 7). This has led some, such as geographer Peck (2010: 33), to seek to 'bring[] neoliberalism to ground' by studying in detail the evolution of the term. Although my aim is a slightly different one, in that I focus on the role of neoliberalism in a more specific context rather than offer a comprehensive history of the term, in the next sub-section I seek to give neoliberalism a more concrete meaning for the purposes of this book by considering its specific implications for the arena of trade policymaking – and to distinguish it from other forms of economic thought.

The intellectual basis of neoliberalism in trade: Neoclassical trade theory

The embodiment of neoliberalism found in trade policymaking circles is based on modern neoclassical trade theory. This gained significant traction amongst trade economists from the 1970s onwards, accompanying the broader shift within the discipline from the previous Keynesian paradigm to a bold restatement of classical economic ideas (Best and Widmaier 2006: 618–26; for a critical review of the neoclassical literature on trade, see Deraniyagala and Fine 2001). The starting point for many such trade economists is the work of the nineteenth-century 'classical' political economist Ricardo (2002 [1817]). Contrary to the prevailing mercantilist doctrine (see below), he argued that countries could benefit from specialising in the production of certain goods, even if they were technologically less advanced, provided they had a *comparative advantage*, that is, the opportunity cost in terms of lost productive capacity of producing the good was lower than for other countries. Given free trade, specialisation based on differences in comparative labour productivity (premised on technological differences between countries) would enable countries to allocate production more efficiently and increase general welfare. This model premised on the gains from *inter-industry* trade was subsequently modified by two Swedish economists, Heckscher and Ohlin, in the early twentieth century (a collection of their writings can be found in Heckscher and Ohlin 1991). Their model allowed for inter-industry gains from free trade without the need for technological differences between countries, recasting comparative advantage in terms of differential factor endowments. Countries that were rich in labour and poor in capital, for instance, would specialise in the production of labour-intensive goods and import goods that were capital-intensive, with the resulting free exchange of goods allowing for a more efficient

allocation of resources. In the more recent neoclassical economic literature on trade, these two frameworks have often been amalgamated to
form the Heckscher-Ohlin-Ricardo model (for example, Fisher 2011),
with the argument that 'the greater the difference [in terms of comparative advantage between countries], the greater the gain' from free trade
(Ethier 2009: 70).

In addition, and beginning in the 1970s and 1980s, economists began
postulating that important gains may also arise for countries with similar factor endowments trading freely with one another. They were
responding to the puzzle raised by the Heckscher-Ohlin approach as to
why most trade in the world takes place between developed economies
with similar factor endowments. The argument was that countries will
specialise only in the production of a subset of goods of a particular type
due to economies of scale in production resulting from imperfect competition. Increased returns to scale, moreover, could be facilitated by the
increased market size resulting from *intra-industry* trade (see the seminal
pieces by Grubel and Lloyd 1975; Krugman 1981; note also the clear link
here to the arguments of the IPE literature that sees market structure and
increasing returns to scale as determinants of regionalism). This form of
horizontal intra-industry trade reflects specialisation in the production of
similar goods differentiated by their variety as opposed to their factor or
technology dependence. However, such models did not account for so-
called *vertical* intra-industry trade, where similar products are differentiated by quality. As a result, models were also devised by economists
which relied on the Heckscher-Ohlin-Ricardo framework, using differences in technology and relative factor endowments to explain why certain economies export high-end goods while others operate at the lower
end of the production chain (although these differences in technology/
factor endowments cannot be so great as to lead to complete specialisation, as under the inter-sectoral trade models; see Flam and Helpman
1987; Egger *et al.* 2007). As a result, in modern, neoclassical trade theory
the gains from specialisation possible under free trade (when compared
to autarky) accrue from both inter-industry (specialisation in a small
number of sectors) *and* intra-industry trade (specialisation in a greater
number of sectors) patterns. The former is seen to apply more readily to
North–South trade and the latter to characterise trade between more
developed economies. The argument is also that intra-industry specialisation patterns will imply less 'painful' adjustment costs, allowing for
the maintenance of a greater variety of production sectors.

The key summative point to take from this sub-section is that neoclassical
economists, which clearly represent economic orthodoxy (Fine 2001),

believe that exposing the domestic economy to the forces of international markets culminates in a more efficient allocation of resources through specialisation (be it inter-industry or intra-industry); possible processes of economic adjustment resulting from import competition are thus positive and are to be welcomed as they lead to increases in general economic welfare in the form of greater consumer choice, lower production costs and so forth. In the longer run, moreover, specialisation may also produce so-called 'dynamic gains from trade' in the form of increased accumulation of and improvements to the productivity of factors of production (see, for example, Baldwin 1992; Bernard and Jensen 2004). As a result, at the heart of neoclassical trade theory lies an understanding of competitiveness as deriving from either comparative advantage in inter- and vertical intra-industry trade or economies of scale in horizontal intra-industry trade, which countries should foster by opening up their markets. This translates into the neoliberal beliefs so common among trade policymakers that they have to put the prescriptions of neoclassical economics into practice (in this book I distinguish between neoclassical economic theory and neoliberalism, the latter being an embodiment of the former as a political project among policymakers). Moreover, neoclassical economic theorists have argued – together with sympathetic political scientists – that while free trade (even when pursued unilaterally) may be the economically preferable outcome, it is politically contingent. 'Protectionist' interests can still seize the policymaking process given collective action dynamics (I have discussed this 'Olsonian' literature above; see also the seminal work by Grossman and Helpman 1994). There is therefore a deep distrust of the role of policymakers, which are said to be prone to capture by special interests. Even Krugman (1994), having made the theoretical case for government intervention in a series of works on 'strategic trade policy' (Krugman 1986), subsequently dismisses such a role for government on similar grounds.

As a result, neoclassical economics stands in marked contrast to both mercantilism and Keynesian economics, which in different ways have advocated political intervention to mediate the effects of unfettered markets. The tradition of mercantilism may have had its heyday in the seventeenth and eighteenth centuries, stressing the importance of maximising net exports – achieved, at the time, by accumulating bullion – as a means of exercising state power (Viner 1948). Such ideas, however, remain prominent in public discourse (as shall become apparent in subsequent chapters; see also Fairbrother 2010: 332). Moreover, the 'economic nationalist' writings of List (1904 [1841]) in the first half of the nineteenth century – which stressed the importance of national economic development and advocated the use of protection in order to achieve this goal, most notably via the 'infant industry' argument – can also be broadly seen as falling within the mercantilist tradition of economic thought (Hettne 1993: 214). More recently, these Listian ideas have found resonance amongst 'dependency theorists' and heterodox 'institutionalist' economists such as Chang (2002). For his part, Keynes (1931) would write that free trade policies should be contingent on achieving broader socioeconomic fairness, such as promoting employment. This view came to shape the 'embedded liberal' compromise of the postwar period, which saw interventionist, Keynesian welfare states operating within a broadly liberal international trading system (see Chapter 3). Keynes' reflections would (in part) be formalised by the work of later 'Kaldorian' (post-Keynesian) economists, who have emphasised the need for interventionist trade policies to guard against shortages of international demand and have emphasised the strategic importance of the manufacturing sector (for a contemporary application, see Kitson and Michie 1995).

The discursive construction of external economic constraints

Having provided an overview of the specific embodiment of neoliberalism found in trade policy, I can now return to my broader theoretical argument. In the previous section I argued that the notion that ideas are treated as though they were material constraints offers an explanation of why ideas *qua* ideas matter; in our case, the ascendancy of neoliberal economic thinking and its emphasis on the 'naturalness' of the rational *homo œconomicus* means that certain logics of behaviour are treated as particularly compelling. Linking this to the insights of the 'critical IPE' literature one could say that just as 'problem-solving' theory is deliberately deployed to mask the ultimately contingent nature of theorising, the same can be said of economic ideas about the nature of social reality. It thus becomes important to not only understand the impact – in an uncertain social world – that this 'material' rationality has when internalised but also how it can serve as a platform to advance actors' interests. What matters, in other words, is not only how agents interpret economic parameters and to what extent these act as constructed constraints on their behaviour, but also how such ideational constructions are used to serve particular ends.

This suggests that it may be fruitful to consider a literature that has concerned itself with the discursive construction of globalisation as such an economic constraint. These authors may not have, strictly speaking, 'hitched their wagon' to the specific constructivist IPE literature considered previously – and especially its emphasis on uncertainty. Schmidt and Hay, two key authors in this field, respectively refer to their frameworks as 'discursive' and 'constructivist' 'institutionalism'. That being said, their approach to the study of ideas has very much drawn on similar ontological and epistemological foundations (an emphasis on the social construction of reality through agents and an emphasis on causality in explanation) – the three approaches are often considered as joint expressions of a broader constructivist turn in the study of politics (see, for instance, Bell 2011) – and has been similarly preoccupied with studying the effects of the neoliberal economic policy paradigm. What they have provided more of – than the self-professed constructivist IPE literature so far, by avoiding an excessive reliance on the analytical device of uncertainty – is a way of understanding why certain ideas may matter without sacrificing ontological consistency.

In this book I therefore seek to build on the fundamental premises furnished by the constructivist IPE literature by drawing on the insights of Hay, Schmidt and others. Blyth's (2010) more recent and sophisticated argument regarding the pervasiveness of uncertainty not only helps to establish the ontological importance of ideas, but is also perfectly compatible with the notion that in an uncertain social world, agents cling to 'as if' material constructions (see, for instance, Blyth 2002: 33–4, 2010: 96; contrast this with the position adopted in Gofas and Hay 2010: 24–6, 48). Given that actors face an uncertain social world – in the sense described by Blyth (2010) – it makes sense to argue that 'as if' material ideas will be particularly influential as a means for those actors to navigate that world. There is also something to be gained by adopting the epistemological rigour of this constructivist IPE literature (in particular that of Parsons 2007), especially its notion that ideational causation can still be understood in (broader) Humean terms. This is because of the premium that Parsons consequently places on clearly specifying causes and effects. In this sense, I am differentiating my position slightly from that of Gofas and Hay (2010) who reject Humean causation in favour of a 'critical realist' understanding – 'all of those things that bring about, produce, direct or contribute to states of affairs or changes in the world' (Kurki 2006: 202, cited in Gofas and Hay 2010: 39–40) – which is a more 'loose' conception of the term. However, one should not overstate the differences between both approaches. Even if they seek to move beyond Humean causality, Gofas and Hay (2010: 15) are ultimately interested in underscoring 'the causal significance of constitutive processes', which is not too different to Parsons' (2007) position that the constitutive is ultimately causal. There is thus an underlying common commitment to causality in ideational explanation.

Returning to the literature on discursive constraints itself, this takes as its point of departure the debate between advocates of the 'hyperglobalisation thesis' – which argue that increasing global economic integration has robbed national governments of policy autonomy, as increased competition in the international market place has rendered state intervention in the economy ineffective (for example, Ohmae 1995) – and its skeptics (including, for instance, Hirst and Thompson 1999). Rather than accepting the parameters of this rationalist argument – that is to say, entering into a debate over whether globalisation is an empirically verifiable *material* process that restricts the choices facing political actors – such writers adopt the constructivist view that it is the ideas that agents hold (and invoke) about 'globalisation' that are key (see, among others, Rosamond 2000; Hay and Rosamond 2002; Watson and Hay 2003; Hay and Smith 2010). In a seminal article, Hay and Rosamond (2002: 148, emphasis in the original) quite effectively condense the central argument of this approach, noting that 'policymakers acting on the basis of assumptions consistent with the hyperglobalisation thesis may well serve, in so doing, to bring about outcomes consistent with that thesis, *irrespective of its veracity* and, indeed, *irrespective of its perceived veracity*'. They draw on the example of international tax competition to emphasise their line of reasoning: irrespective of whether high corporate taxes induce capital flight, as the hyperglobalisation thesis implies, the outcome will be the same if governments work under the assumption that it does (namely, corporate tax cuts). The perceived material rationality of the hyperglobalisation thesis becomes meaningful in shaping outcomes only because it is internalised by actors, in other words, because it is treated by them as though it were a *real*, material constraint rather than just a (contestable) economic framework.

The key to understanding this process is a study of what this literature terms 'globalisation discourse', tapping into a Foucauldian understanding of knowledge. Here discourse is defined as 'a broad[] matrix of social practices that gives meaning to the way that people understand themselves and their behaviour. [...] More precisely, a discourse makes "real" that which *it* prescribes as meaningful' (George 1994: 29–30, emphasis in the original). Analysing discourse thus becomes the study of the process of social construction, focusing on the nexus between power and knowledge. Globalisation is not simply seen as a (material) conditioning structure but rather as a zone of (political) contestation (Amin and Thrift 1994), where control of knowledge about this *so-called* economic process becomes an exercise of authority in the international political economy. Such a framework problematises economistic understandings of IPE in the sense implied by Maier (1988) above. It also stresses the fact that power is being exercised when such discourses are invoked, borrowing from the critical approach of Cox (1981).

Despite appealing to postmodernist understandings of discourse, this literature can hardly be classified as such. The aim is to redefine discourse in more general terms so that it 'encompasses not only the substantive content of ideas', which have so far been the focus of postmodernist accounts, 'but also the interactive processes by which ideas are conveyed. Discourse [in this literature] is not just ideas or "texts" (what is said) but also context (where, when, how and why it was said)' (Schmidt 2008: 305). Hay and Rosamond still draw a distinction between 'globalisation as discourse' (the structural dimension) and 'globalisation as rhetoric' (the agential dimension). But as causal constructivists, their focus is on this newer dimension to discourse, that is, its construction through human agency. As a result, they define discourse as 'a repertoire of discursive resources […] at the disposal of political actors' and rhetoric as 'the strategic and persuasive deployment of such discourses, often in combination, as means to legitimate specific courses of action, policy initiatives, etc.' (Hay and Rosamond 2002: 152). Moreover, they stress that 'an analysis which confines itself exclusively to discourses of globalisation is overly structural, giving insufficient attention to the active and frequently creative role of agents in the formulation of ideas which may become sedimented as discourse' (Hay and Rosamond 2002: 151).

In this, they seem to be combining two previous strands of work on economic discourses of globalisation. To see this I turn to Rosamond (2000), who notes a distinction between so-called 'strategic' and 'reflexive' pathways to the study of economic discourse. In the former, actors consciously use particular discourses to construct reality in order to serve their interests; in such a case a strategically invoked discourse is separable from actors' interests or *exogenous*. Work focusing on the 'reflexive' dimension to discourse, for its part, 'invites us to think about how the spread of intersubjective understandings alters both cognitive *and* material reality […] [T]he social construction of market imperatives contributes to the realisation of those market imperatives and to the altered "globalising" behaviour of various actors' (Rosamond 2000: 11, emphasis in the original). In Hay and Rosamond (2002), although the emphasis of explanation may be on charting the frequently strategic deployment of globalisation discourses to serve the interests of particular actors (principally European policymaking elites), there is also an appreciation of how 'ideational structures become institutionalised and normalised' (Hay and Rosamond 2002: 147). In other words, they are also interested in the internalisation of ideas by actors. Moreover, Hay and Rosamond reject the premise that actors can have interests that are separable from discourse, as a superficial reading of the 'strategic' pathway would suggest. As a result, the explanatory emphasis is not on the interests that actors may have independently of discourse (as the latter is constitutive of the former) but rather on whether particular actors choose to invoke such beliefs to serve interests that are partly constituted by these (or other) beliefs. For instance, a policymaker may (or may not) choose to *strategically* appeal to a particular economic discourse to justify a course of action, but this is a product of interests that are in part derived from having internalised a particular discourse, whether of 'external constraint' or not.

Using the term strategic may at first seem like a concession to rationalism, with its emphasis on instrumentality in actor behaviour, and, more broadly, to a 'neo-positivist' treatment of ideas (Jackson 2010) as in Goldstein and Keohane (1993) where interests are seen as analytically separable from ideas. But although using the term *strategic* implies *deliberate* ends-orientated action, as in rationalist accounts, in this case actor interests are socially constructed rather than externally (and materially) given. In other words, the world which such actors inhabit is itself a social construction and not immutable; we should not see it so much as a steel cage (of 'brute', material 'facts') but rather as a balloon which can be pricked (or deconstructed) by a needle (or alternative discourse). Indeed, Blyth's (2010) argument in defence of constructivism is that the contingency of the social world means that we cannot study it using the tools of a positivist social science; actors' interests will always be socially constructed given uncertainty about the way in which the (social) world works. Ultimately, such a view is more ontologically consistent than a view of discourse (or ideas) as 'exogenous' to actor interests (see also Rosamond 2013).

Hay and Rosamond (2002: 152–7) begin by setting out a typology of discursive constructions of globalisation that exist amongst political actors, which is organised along two axes. For one, such discourses can be associated with either a positive or a negative view of the outcomes of globalisation. Additionally the nature of the outcome can also be seen to be dependent on political choices – as in Hay and Smith (2005) who engage in a more sophisticated exercise of discursive mapping. Along the second axis, the process of globalisation itself can be portrayed or interpreted as either politically contingent or inevitable. It is this latter typology which forms the brunt of the literature's analytical argument, that policymakers *strategically* invoke a view of globalisation as inexorable (in other words, they make use of 'globalisation rhetoric') in order to legitimate potentially painful and/or contentious neoliberal socioeconomic reforms aimed at further marketisation of the political economy; in sum, they are 'rendering the contingent necessary' (Watson and Hay 2003). The power of such rhetorics thus resides in that they present a (politically) contingent phenomenon as immutable (economic) fact. Moreover, it also underscores the often coercive nature of rhetoric – as distinct from discourse, the broader set of ideas in circulation – that some have claimed has often been absent from political analysis. The argument is that regardless of whether a particular set of ideas has been internalised by one's opponents, rhetoric 'can prove critical to success in political contests' as it might leave them 'without access to the rhetorical materials needed to craft a socially sustainable rebuttal' (Krebs and Jackson 2007: 36).

Augmenting the study of economic discourse

Determining intentionality in the invocation of globalisation as an external economic constraint by policymakers is thus of paramount importance if one is to locate the sources of discursive power in constructing the neoliberal project. Existing studies, however, have largely premised their work on theoretical assumptions and have not done much to determine this fact theoretically or empirically. This is due to a supposedly 'intractable' and 'inherent' methodological dilemma in the study of discourse (Hay and Rosamond 2002: 165). The problem is that it is impossible to determine from policymakers' pronouncements themselves whether these are a reflection of their true beliefs or not, which makes it difficult to ascertain whether the invocation of external economic constraints is done disingenuously (as part of a discursive strategy). This is because there are two possible explanations for an invocation of an economic constraint in the case of a decision maker who believes that constraint to be *real* (Actor A in Figure 2.1). For one, they may be *choosing* to invoke such ideas strategically to serve particular ends; in other words, they would be making a rhetorical use of such ideas. They may, however, just be 'reflexively' (to use the term as in Rosamond 2000) repeating a discourse they have already internalised, leaving one with no *a priori* method for differentiating between both cases. Only where the researcher knows that a policymaker does not believe a constraint to be *real* (Actor B in Figure 2.1) can one say with any certainty that they

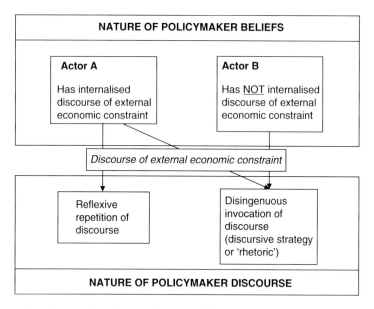

Figure 2.1   The methodological dilemma of discourse analysis
Source: Siles-Brügge (2011: 632), Figure 1; reproduced with permission and slight changes.

are invoking such an economic discourse strategically, but this is not something that can be determined from the actor's invocation of a constraint *per se*.

One of my contributions in this book is to provide an analytical strategy to overcome this methodological dilemma. Hay and Smith (2010; see also Hay and Rosamond 2002: 158–9) – who engage in a more in-depth empirical mapping exercise of discourses of globalisation in the Anglosphere – hint at this when they suggest that the disparity between discourses they find in different settings suggests a strategic appeal to such ideas. Their data

> reveal[] an interestingly stark contrast between public discourses and private understandings [...] In so doing it lends some further credence to the view that, in public contexts, elected politicians may invoke globalisation discourse strategically – and as a source of non-negotiable external imperatives – in insulating otherwise contentious policy choices from critique [...] Private understandings of globalisation, our data show, are far less necessitarian in character.
>
> (Hay and Smith 2010: 926)

Hay and Smith's argument rests on an important distinction between 'coordinative' (private) and 'communicative' (public) discourses. The former refers to the process of policy construction – more specifically, 'the common language and framework through which key policy groups come to agreement in the construction of a policy program' (Schmidt 2002a: 171) – while the latter is about a process of engagement with the public in order to legitimate such policies (for more detail, see Schmidt 2002b: 230–9). Here I build on these insights to develop a more general empirical strategy to determine whether or not a policymaker is deploying a discourse strategically.

Referring back to Figure 2.1, Hay and Smith's empirical findings suggest a case where policymakers do not hold globalisation to be a genuine *constraint* (Actor B), as highlighted by the invocation of contrasting discourses of 'globalisation as constraint' and 'globalisation as contingent' in different discursive settings. The basis of the argument is that discourses evoked within a communicative setting are likely to be part of a discursive strategy (or rhetoric) when an actor has not internalised them (that is, in the case of Actor B) because of the nature of the setting; what need does a policymaker, who does not believe in a particular constraint, have to refer to such a constraint other than to legitimate a particular course of action?[9] The discourses originating in a coordinative setting, in turn, are more likely to correspond to the actual views of policymakers (again, as a result of their setting). As such, any discrepancy between discourses present in communicative and coordinative settings is strong evidence to suggest a strategic appeal to particular economic ideas. In sum then, one can be quite confident in identifying a policymaker's appeal to a particular external economic constraint as rhetorical if this discourse is *not* invoked consistently across different discursive settings (see Figure 2.2). There is, however, a clear limitation to such a framework in that it only serves to identify an actor who has not internalised a particular discourse but is using it strategically (Actor B from Figure 2.1). The researcher is still left with an 'intractable' methodological problem that does not allow one to identify policymakers who may have internalised such beliefs but are still invoking them disingenuously (Actor A from Figure 2.1); the scope of any uncertainty, however, is considerably reduced.

This novel analytical strategy, which is based on the study of texts (for more on the methodological issues this raises, see the Appendix), is the first step towards my wider aim in this book of improving understanding of strategically invoked economic discourses. As noted above, it is fundamental that one is able to identify the strategic nature of economic

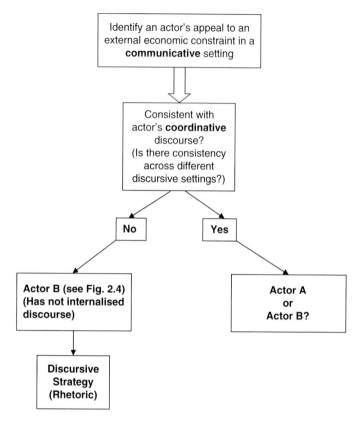

Figure 2.2   Identifying an actor's discursive strategy
Source: Siles-Brügge (2011: 633), Figure 2; reproduced with permission.

rhetoric in order to begin locating the sources of discursive power. A second step in this direction is to more broadly recast the study of how economic constraints have been constructed as a rhetorical device. This is an important step in situating these insights within a broader constructivist IPE, as I have argued above. The literature on discourses of external constraint has focused on the invocation of globalisation as an economic imperative by policymakers in a European national context and this, as I will show, was also relevant in the case of EU trade policy. Indeed, the European focus of this literature makes it particularly easy to transpose to the (supranational) EU context (as is also suggested by Rosamond 2000). The hyperglobalisation thesis, however, is only one of the products of the neoclassical economic thinking that holds so much sway among policymaking elites; even if this is a key aspect of the neoliberal project there are clearly other discourses of economic constraint that have mattered in economic governance. Although Hay and Rosamond (2002) also refer to European integration as a discursively constructed constraint and Rosamond (2002) explores the 'construction of "Europe" as an economic space' by focusing on the discourse of 'competitiveness', only the former has been picked up significantly in subsequent work. What is more, the literature on legitimating economic discourses has tended to focus on the Member State rather than the EU context, despite the important role played by neoliberal ideas in the construction of the EU political economy (on this latter point, see van Apeldoorn 2002). The literature on globalisation discourse I have referred to above has been focused on the Anglosphere while European integration discourse has been seen as a crucial determinant of, among others, French policy outcomes (Schmidt 2002a).

In this book I therefore seek to broaden understanding of how strategically invoked discourses operate in practice by focusing on the arena of EU trade policymaking and the ideas that have been invoked in order to legitimate particular trade policy decisions. In addition to expanding the study of economic discourse to a key arena of the neoliberal project, and thus locating myself within a more expansive constructivist IPE, this enables me to consider in more detail the operation of discursive strategies. This is because I will be focusing on the behaviour of a well-defined actor (the Commission's DG Trade) legitimating specific policy decision (liberal trade outcomes) rather than the more diffuse generalisations usually found in the literature on strategically invoked discourses (and the literature referring to neoliberalism more generally), where the focus has been, by and large, on indeterminate policymaking elites legitimating broadly defined neoliberal agendas (this explains the turn to a more Humean conception of causality, as in Parsons 2007). Indeed, the Commission has been shown in a related constructivist literature within the field of EU Studies to have a history of strategically crafting an image of the market to further the cause of integration (Rosamond 2002; Jabko 2006). My aim, however, rather than focusing on the drivers of integration, is to problematise and deconstruct the economistic understandings that have characterised the study of trade politics, so far the purview of rationalist scholars who have treated interests as purely materially given.

I also seek to broaden the research agenda of this particular strand of constructivism by focusing on the use of economic rhetoric by interest groups. The use of such ideas as instruments of pressure on policymakers is a dimension that remains relatively unexplored by the literature. It is, however, very relevant in light of the previously reviewed literature on economic regionalism; it is clear that 'domestic–systemic' explanations in IPE derive much of their explanatory power from the importance accorded to external and material competitive threats (what in the IPE literature are referred to as 'systemic' factors) and their invocation by particular interest groups. Following this sub-section's theoretical discussion (and the above finding that one can reconcile material and ideational logics of explanation under a common constructivist ontological 'roof'), I can quite easily reconceptualise the supposedly 'economic' arguments made by such groups as discourses of external economic constraint invoked to serve their perceived interests. The appeal here is to the specific systemic pressures facing exporters. In this way, I can simply 'graft' a constructivist ontology onto existing rationalist models of trade policymaking – in this case specifically those addressing the drivers of regionalism (although obviously the possible applications of this schema could go beyond this particular literature). Although the interests of such groups are thus not strictly material – in the sense that it is the *interpretation* of material circumstances that leads them to perceive their interests in a particular way – their interests can be taken to be 'as if' rational because they are created with a clear purpose in mind, to serve the (perceived) economic interests of their constituency. Bearing this in mind, it is not too difficult to see how all pronouncements by interest groups must be seen as strategic (that is, as economic rhetoric, to use the terminology of the globalisation discourse literature); it is implied by their relationship to policymakers. Even if one may be uncertain as to the true beliefs of economic interest groups (that is, whether they are Actor A or B from Figure 2.1), the goal of their pronouncements will always be to influence policymakers.

The novelty of such a constructivist perspective to interest group pronouncements lies in two key differences to a purely 'rationalist' approach. For one, explaining the influence of such groups with policymakers is not just a matter for 'material' variables. The focus of explanation in subsequent chapters will also be on how and why interest groups' (strategic) *arguments* are themselves effective, rather than just taking the rationalist view that such arguments matter because of the Olsonian dynamics of collective action in the trade policymaking sphere. In other words, I will be refocusing attention to the use of language as an instrument of power. The second difference to the mainstream IPE models of interest group behaviour is that 'as if' rationality is always contingent, rather than fixed. The interests of pressure groups are always subject to

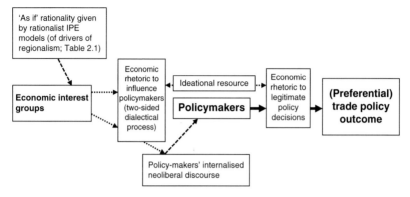

Figure 2.3 A constructivist IPE of EU trade policy
Source: Author's elaboration.

a changeable perception of material factors and are themselves also dependent on ideational constructions (see Figure 2.3) – allowing the eventual deadlock in the Doha Round (which the rationalist 'combined' IPE models reviewed above may have downplayed) to be a factor in shaping their preferences (see Chapter 3). Moreover – and despite the parallels to Woll's (2008) constructivist approach to the study of interest groups in trade policy, including a reliance on the concept of uncertainty to establish the importance of ideas – it goes beyond such a framework by focusing on the internalisation of rational/material logics to establish *why* certain ideas matter rather than others.

The picture is also slightly more complex when it comes to determining the interests of decision makers and their deployment of particular discourses, which is why I devised the analytical strategy discussed above. In a nutshell, I am relying on a study of coordinative discourse to arrive at policymakers' true beliefs (read interests) and contrasting this with their communicative discourse to establish strategic agency. The question remains, however, as to why interest groups' (strategic) discourses hold any truck with policymakers and why such policymakers may privilege one particular group of business interests (exporters) over another (for example those interested in the maintenance of protection). To address this issue, I am aware of the 'duality' of economic discourse alluded to above – the fact that it serves not only as a strategic instrument for policymakers (and interest groups) but also becomes internalised by actors. The so-called 'reflexive pathway' of discourse analysis (Rosamond 2000) suggests that I also focus on how 'the spread of the discourse itself alters the *a priori* ideas and perceptions which people have of the empirical phenomena which they encounter; in so doing, it engenders strategies and tactics which in turn may restructure the game itself' (Cerny 1995: 620). It is thus clear how the ideas held by policymakers can be shaped by the arguments deployed by interest groups; the fact that DG Trade held particular neoliberal ideas made it particularly susceptible to the discursive constructions of pro-liberalisation groups (such as exporters) calling for preferential market-opening, especially if we consider that with the stagnation of the Doha Round this was perceived as one of the only avenues to obtain new market access (see Chapter 3). Likewise, it made it relatively impervious to protectionist arguments, given the shared emphasis on market opening and developing (exporter) competitiveness. The logical corollary, and second aspect of this 'reflexive' dimension to discourse alluded to by Cerny above, is that these new ideas, when internalised by policymakers, also 'engender[] [new] strategies and tactics'. In this vein, I argue that interest groups' discourse of 'competitive threat' is itself a useful *ideational resource* for policymakers. They can draw upon this in constructing their rhetoric of external constraint in defence of their preferential liberalisation policies, which are a product, in large part, of (discursive) interest group activism. The dialectical (or reflexive) process of discourse construction has therefore come full circle, shaping the nature of interests but also the ideational strategies used to advance them.

Theoretically this marks an improvement on previous models where the interests of policymakers and interest groups are considered fixed, in terms of either functional rationality (rational choice institutionalism) or economic interest (mainstream IPE). Even where the role of neoliberal ideas held by policymakers in the Commission (and DG Trade, more specifically) is acknowledged (largely) in the neo-Gramscian literature as the driver of free trade policies (see, for example, Hurt 2003; Bieler 2013) they have been invoked as a, to use Hay's (2004b: 210) term from before, *deus ex machina*. This approach's treatment of ideas bears some resemblance to the way that rationalist accounts privilege externally given interests, with insufficient attention being paid to the issue of *why* ideas as such may matter. In contrast, the approach taken here is to not to simply read off externally given interests (or ideas) but to focus on the 'dialectics' of discursive change, in other words, on the process of constructing social reality and in particular, on the role played by economic rhetoric in this process. This is reflected in Figure 2.3, where I provide an overview of my theoretical argument. Crucially I see trade policy as what actors *make of it* in two senses: it is not only shaped by actors' views on it, but also by the way in which it is portrayed by those actors.

Conclusion

In this chapter I began by considering how mainstream IPE accounts of regionalism marked an improvement on the EU Studies approach. These have emphasised that trade policy is determined either as a result of systemic pressures, following domestic political competition between various economic interest groups, or as a result of a combination of both series of factors. This latter, 'combined' IPE literature (and, in particular, Manger 2009) is, in my eyes, particularly useful at highlighting important features of the current wave of regionalism, such as its North–South focus, its competitive and discriminatory logic and the emphasis on regulatory liberalisation. However, it still neglects the important role played by ideas in constructing social reality. Going beyond (but still building) on much of the extant constructivist IPE literature's focus on uncertainty in explaining the importance of social construction (especially that inspired by Blyth 2002), I have argued that certain ideas matter (in an ultimately uncertain social world) because they are treated *as though they were material constraints*. This is particularly noteworthy if one considers the purchase of neoliberal economic discourses in policy-making (and academic) circles, in this case specifically those derived from neoclassical trade theory. As a result, in the final section of this chapter – drawing on the work of, amongst others, Hay and Rosamond (2002) and Schmidt (2002b, 2008) – I have developed a constructivist approach that emphasised both actors' strategic use of discourses of economic constraint and their internalisation of particular neoliberal discourses as important determinants of policy. This, however, did not seek to detract from the insights of rationalist IPE when it came to explaining the preferences of interest groups and their influence with policymakers, which I have accommodated within my ontologically consistent constructivism.

As I noted in the introduction, in this chapter my aim has been to construct a theoretical framework that moves beyond the widespread rational institutionalist view that EU trade policy is uniquely depoliticised. In this book I am thus taking the first step on a long road to bringing the study of EU trade policy – for long the preserve of scholars stressing its 'exceptionalism' – into the discipline of IPE. In subsequent empirical chapters I will illustrate how, rather than being the product of a uniquely depoliticised policymaking machinery, the EU's trade strategy has been shaped over the years by a lively politics of interest – not unlike that found in other major trading nations like the US, which have been the subject of a voluminous literature in IPE. I have also made theoretical inroads in Chapter 2 by introducing the role of ideas to the study of (EU) trade politics, where rationalist scholars with narrower understandings of the political have traditionally dominated. Along the way, I have augmented existing constructivist approaches and sought to marry them with relevant insights from the rationalist mainstream. In Chapter 3 I will chart the rise of 'Global Europe'. This will not only help underscore my theoretical arguments – pointing in particular to the importance of considering the rise of a neoliberal paradigm and (exporter) interest group politics in EU trade policy – but will also illustrate the wider historical significance of this strategy.

3
Charting the Rise of 'Global Europe'

'Global Europe' was the defining document in EU trade policy from 2006 until late 2010, when it was superseded by the 2010 'Trade, Growth and World Affairs' strategy (see Chapter 6). After the long strategic lull that followed the failure of the EU's ambitious Doha agenda at Cancún – and given the increasing perception after the 2005 Hong Kong Ministerial that the Doha Round was moribund – it announced an end to the moratorium on FTAs and a more activist trade policy premised on securing market access for exporters through FTAs. Although clearly bearing the imprint of Trade Commissioner Peter Mandelson under whose watch it originated, 'Global Europe' shaped EU trade policy beyond his tenure. It did so most visibly in terms of the trade agreements it spawned but also, and very importantly, by forming a key part of an emerging neoliberal trade order with clear antecedents in the SMP. In both senses, it became a key strategic reference point for officials working in DG Trade and also played a major role in shaping its successor, the post-Lisbon Agenda 'Europe 2020' trade strategy. One cannot, therefore, understand the drivers of the EU's recent (preferential) trade agenda without first charting the rise of 'Global Europe'.

The existing EU Studies literature on 'Global Europe' has largely deployed a PA approach and portrayed the strategy as an effort by the Commission to continue exercising leadership in trade policy in the face of a multilateral impasse. However, it is difficult for explanations stressing the importance of institutional pressures to account for the shift in strategy, in the *absence of significant institutional change* to the EU's (formal and informal) trade policymaking machinery in the intervening period (see Chapter 1). In this chapter, in contrast, I deploy a constructivist IPE approach to highlight the role that neoliberal ideas and interest group activism have played in shaping 'Global Europe'. While the neo-Gramscian literature on European integration has been useful at pointing to the role of neoliberalism in the governance of EU economic relations, it has generally overlooked the role that more distinct agents and ideas have played in constructing the European political economy. That is not to say that one needs to abandon the label 'neoliberalism' entirely to refer to economic policymaking in Europe, as it bears considerable resonance in the area of trade policy, but rather that one needs to adopt a more fine-grained approach to its study. After all, over the course of the past twenty years, the EU has pursued quite different trade policies (an emphasis on multilateralism followed by a turn to preferentialism) while still sharing a broadly neoliberal concern with promoting exporter competitiveness.

After setting the historical scene in the first section, providing an overview of the broad shift from 'embedded liberalism' to neoliberalism in EU trade policy, I turn in the second section to the role that exporters have since played in shaping EU trade policy. More specifically, they have strategically deployed a discourse of external competitive threat at particular junctures, driving the Commission's DG Trade to change its previous 'multilateralism-first' stance and embrace preferential trade liberalisation efforts in 'Global Europe'. Services lobbyists were particularly vociferous in their demands for preferential market opening and therefore also enjoyed particular influence with policymakers. In the third section, I show how this influence was ultimately not only reflected in the EU's turn to preferentialism but also in the specific bilateral services and investment agenda developed by policymakers, which has been *the* key component of the EU's preferential liberalisation agenda. In the fourth, I show how the 'Global Europe' communication also played an important discursive role. It came to embody DG Trade's rhetoric of external economic constraint; this 'global idea of Europe' served to legitimate the Commission's neoliberal trade agenda – which was premised on seeking market openness in exchange for trading away 'pockets' of protection. This discourse may have had its origins in the SMP of the 1980s, but it was given a key impetus by Commissioner Mandelson. This also explains the close relationship to exporters of Mandelson's DG, with which it not only shared ideational affinity, but upon which it also came to draw as an ideational resource. I conclude in the final section of this chapter by summarising why ideas and interest groups have mattered in shaping 'Global Europe'.

From 'embedded liberalism' to neoliberalism in EU trade policy: A defensive participant in global trade turned proactive multilateralist

The EU has not always played a proactive role in the governance of global trade, even though it did have a common trade policy from its inception. Given the aim of establishing a customs union, Member States of the EU agreed in its founding document, the 1957 Treaty of Rome, to establish the CCP to govern their trade relations with third parties. Moreover, the CCP had a decidedly liberal bent, with its stated objective in Article 110 being 'to contribute [...] to the harmonious development of world trade, the progressive abolition of restrictions on international trade and the lowering of customs barriers'. The Treaty of Rome, however, is often depicted as a compromise between those interests that favoured the establishment of the customs union (for the benefit of industrial producers) and the accompanying CCP and those seeking domestic support for European agricultural producers via what became Common Agricultural Policy (CAP) (see, for example, Hayes 1993: Chs. 6, 7; Moravcsik 1998: Ch. 2). Regardless of whether one accepts this historical interpretation of European integration, the fact remains that the combination of CAP and CCP put the EU on the defensive in the global trading system during the 1960s and 1970s. While broadly supportive of liberalisation efforts in the area of industrial tariffs during both the Kennedy (1964–67) and Tokyo Rounds (1973–79), conducted under the auspices of the General Agreement on Tariffs and Trade (GATT), the EU resisted considerable US pressure to liberalise its agricultural markets (Preeg 1970; Winham 1986).

The GATT system was part of the broader 'embedded liberal' economic system agreed to at the end of the Second World War (Ruggie 1982: 393–8). This involved a compromise between liberal economic doctrine and a concern with accommodating national Keynesian economic management and the nascent welfare state. As Ruggie (1982: 393) put it, the goal was 'to devise a framework which would safeguard and even aid the quest for domestic stability without, at the same time, triggering the mutually destructive external consequences that had plagued the interwar period'. While a system of fixed exchange rates was agreed to at the Bretton Woods conference, in the trade sphere the end result of subsequent negotiations was a broadly liberal system whose cornerstone was the principle of non-discrimination that became enshrined in the GATT. The General Agreement of 1947, however, also included a number of 'safeguards, exemptions, exceptions, and restrictions [...] to protect a variety of domestic social policies' (Ruggie 1982: 396). This included a major exception to free trade principles in agriculture, where 'the original GATT articles [...] were in large measure written to be consistent with US farm-support legislation existing in 1947' (Winham 1986: 152). Within a global trading system that was so *'permissive'* of domestic intervention in the economy (Howse 2002: 116), the EU was able to couple a liberal trade policy (the CCP) to a system of agricultural support (the CAP), which was at least partly driven by a 'need to integrate farmers into emerging welfare states and democratic politics' (Rieger 2005: 170).

The 'golden age' of post-war growth and prosperity would eventually give way to oil crises, stagflation and the collapse of the Bretton Woods system of fixed exchange rates in the 1970s. As argued by Strange (1979), the economic crisis of this period was symptomatic of fundamental changes in the international economic system, including increased competition from newly industrialised countries and changed demand patterns for manufactured goods. This resulted in the so-called problem of 'surplus capacity' in industrial production, 'a situation in which demand is insufficient to absorb production at prices high enough both to maintain employment and to maintain profitability for all the enterprises engaged' (Strange 1979: 304). The longevity of the economic crisis seemed to support this view of long-term industrial decline, which in Europe was particularly acutely felt in the textile, steel and ship-building sectors (on this, see Tsoukalis and da Silva Ferreira 1980; Kahler 1985). This meant there was considerable pressure within the EU to protect manufacturing industries. As elsewhere in the developed world, policy-makers implemented a wide array of non-tariff barriers (NTBs) to trade, including most notably quantitative restrictions. Although such measures had existed and been implemented in the past, over the course of the 1970s and early 1980s they mushroomed, as scholars began to speak of a 'new protectionism' (see, for example, Balassa 1978). Within the EU this was also accompanied by (largely) national and *ad hoc* industrial policy aimed at addressing the problem of surplus capacity (Tsoukalis and da Silva Ferreira 1980: 376). As Howse (2002: 101) notes, it became 'easy to view activist industrial policies as a beggar-thy-neighbour approach to declining industries [...]; that is, as protectionist cheating on the [embedded liberal] bargain'. The fact remains, however, that these measures could be seen as compatible with the embedded liberal paradigm as domestic policy responses to less favourable macroeconomic conditions. Indeed, this was the argument advanced by Ruggie himself. Not only were the measures fairly limited in scope, but they were also intended as a means to 'slow down structural change and minimize the social costs of domestic adjustment', rather than fundamentally challenge the principle of open markets (Ruggie 1982: 412). In this sense the 'new protectionism' would ultimately underscore the broader crisis of 'embedded liberalism' in trade. The remedies pursued to address the problems of surplus capacity – import relief and industrial policy – were perceived by policymakers as ineffective, failing to halt the decline of EU industry.

The new protectionism thus signalled the breakdown of the 'golden age' of high growth and near full employment of the 'embedded liberal' age – and its marriage of Keynesianism and classical economic liberalism – and would eventually lead to the emergence of a neoliberal paradigm of economic management in the late 1970s/early 1980s (on this broader ideational shift, see Blyth 2002; Best and Widmaier 2006). In this respect, the key turning point for the EU was the signing of the SEA by EU Member States in Luxembourg and The Hague in 1986 – and its subsequent entry into force in 1987. After a decade and a half of stagnation, the Community was said to be embarking on a new phase of development in the SMP and what became the Economic and Monetary Union (EMU), formalised in the 1992 Treaty of Maastricht. The SMP was of particular importance to the future conduct of trade policy. Premised on the principle of mutual recognition of standards introduced by the SEA and the liberalisation of capital flows – unthinkable during the Bretton Woods era of fixed exchange rates – it was to have obvious deregulatory effects (van Apeldoorn 2002: 131). As a number of authors have claimed, the aim here was to boost the 'competitiveness' of European industry through neoliberal restructuring, aimed at introducing greater market discipline into the social order (see, for instance, van Apeldoorn 2002: 158–89). Crucially, this was seen in the context of needing to improve the EU's waning export competitiveness in a global marketplace, following the perceived failure of the 'new protectionism' and industrial policy to halt the long-term structural decline of certain industries (see European Commission 1987; Cockfield 1988; Sandholtz and Zysman 1989: 108–10).

This is, of course, a very stylised reading of the history of the European political economy which might give the impression that neoliberalism became the only set of significant policy ideas from the 1980s onwards – something for which I have previously criticised neo-Gramscian approaches. This is, of course, not the case. Caporaso and Tarrow (2009) have illustrated that the collapse of the 'embedded liberal' compromise of the post-war period did not mean an end to battles between competing visions of the free market and the importance of social protection; the Single Market has implied a continued struggle between tendencies towards both neoliberalism and the greater 'social embedding' (in a Polanyian sense) of markets – as exemplified (in their study) by the jurisprudence of the European Court of Justice (ECJ) in social matters. Similarly, it makes sense to see EMU as not just a neoliberal but also a distinctively ordoliberal project – with a non-market institution (the European Central Bank [ECB]) seen to be playing a key role in the maintenance of a rules-based market order (Berghahn and Young 2013: 774–6).

These clarifications, however, do not detract from my more specific argument that EU trade policy came to be underpinned by the same neoliberal paradigm also shaping (although not entirely dominating) the SMP. Indeed, the influence of this set of economic ideas was also felt at the level of the global trading system, which was transformed following the completion of the Uruguay Round (1986–94). Where, under embedded liberalism, the GATT had been fairly 'permissive' of domestic intervention, the newly established WTO significantly moved beyond the realm of tariffs into the domain of liberalising domestic regulation (the so-called 'new issues'), establishing a new, legally binding dispute settlement mechanism to enforce global trading rules (Howse 2002; Chorev and Babb 2009). Crucially, the EU embraced this new trade multilateralism by the end of the Uruguay Round.

Although the EU's defensiveness on agriculture meant that there was initially a reluctance to engage in further multilateral trade talks in the early 1980s – with a considerable hiccup during the talks at Blair House in 1992 that saw EU Member States reprimand the Commission for exceeding its mandate – the EU would eventually make a series of unprecedented concessions on agriculture as part of the final Uruguay Round agreement (Devuyst 1995). For my purposes, the importance of these concessions lies less in the changes actually made to the CAP – which did not undermine the principle of agricultural protectionism as a separate trade regime within the EU – but rather in highlighting the fact that the EU's offensive trade agenda had grown more prominent in determining its strategic orientation in the multilateral context (Paemen and Bensch 1995; Daugbjerg and Swinbank 2009: Ch. 7). The EU also emerged from the Round as a keen advocate of pursuing the 'new issues' – including through the WTO trade-related intellectual property rights (TRIPS) agreement, which enshrined intellectual property rights protection at the multilateral level, and the GATS, which sought to extend the coverage of global trading rules to the liberalisation of services – while supporting the strengthening of dispute settlement (Paemen and

Bensch 1995; Woolcock and Hodges 1996). In sum, following the turn to neoliberalism EU trade policy became reoriented towards serving export interests in a multilateral setting. I consider the ideational implications of this shift in the fourth section of this chapter, after having discussed the role that interest groups (and specifically exporters) have played in shaping the EU's new proactive trade diplomacy in the next two sections.

Exporters and the discourse of external competitive threat

Despite the marked shift towards serving exporter shifts, pro-liberalisation European business interests had played a relatively negligible role in supranational trade policymaking during the Uruguay Round negotiations (Cowles 2001: 161; Lietaert 2009: 6; Woll 2009: 281), having been marginalised at the expense of protectionist agricultural interests in the preceding decades.[1] In contrast, one of the cornerstones of the Commission's 1996 'Market Access Strategy' – penned shortly after the conclusion of the Round and the establishment of the WTO – was a concerted effort on behalf of the Commission to involve outward-oriented business interests in policymaking.[2] The aim was to have them *'provide the Commission* with adequate information [...] to eliminate barriers [to trade]' (European Commission 1996a: 12, emphasis in the original). In this vein, the Commission established regular communication channels between itself and exporters, including the Market Access Database (an online service on collating information on market access conditions for EU exporters based on the trade barriers reported by business) and regular 'Market Access Symposia' (European Commission 2007c: 3). Contrary to the expectations of the 'collusive delegation' literature, which postulates that policymakers in the EU are insulated from societal pressures, exporters thus became increasingly involved in European trade policymaking following the turn to multilateralism. Rather than representing an awakening of the European business community to the potential opportunities of multilateral liberalisation, however, this was the product of Commission efforts to develop a more proactive constituency in favour of trade liberalisation. Crucially, it did so by stressing the economic benefits accruing from multilateral (as opposed to bilateral) market opening, also prefiguring the emphasis on 'regulatory' liberalisation that would subsequently distinguish the EU's approach to the Doha Round (European Commission 1996a: 5, 1999).

These new areas were to feature prominently in the EU's 'wish-list' for these multilateral trade talks, eventually launched in the Qatari capital of Doha in November 2001 (European Commission 1999). Whereas the US was always lukewarm to the inclusion of the so-called 'Singapore Issues' (government procurement, trade facilitation, trade and investment and trade and competition) in the Doha Round – eventually preferring to conduct negotiations on what were still WTO-plus provisions in the context of its bilateral trade strategy of 'competitive liberalisation' – the EU became the most avid advocate of pursuing these in the framework of WTO talks (Young 2007: 125–6). In addition, the EU committed itself to an informal 'moratorium' on new FTAs in 1999 in order to signal its commitment to the multilateral trade talks (Woolcock 2007: 2). The EU did not abandon this 'moratorium' – under what became explicitly known as the policy of 'multilateralism-first' with Pascal Lamy (see Lamy 2002: 1401) – after the debacle at the Cancún Ministerial in September 2003 even when other competitors (particularly East and South Asian nations and the US, the latter through its policy of 'competitive liberalisation') were stepping up their efforts in seeking bilateral trade deals (see Zoellick 2002; Ravenhill 2008). Moreover, even though the era of multilateralism of the 1990s and early 2000s witnessed the EU sign a total of three FTAs – with South Africa, Mexico and Chile – and attempt to launch negotiations on a fourth with the Southern Common Market (known by its Spanish acronym MERCOSUR), these were not part of a concerted and premeditated strategy of seeking preferential market opening. The few bilateral trade agreements that were signed were generally *ad hoc* – and, with the exception of South Africa, largely defensive – rather than the product of an offensive bilateral trade strategy (Doctor 2007; Dür 2007; Larsén 2007). As if to underscore this point, in a 1995 paper on FTAs, the Commission highlighted the need to 'respect scrupulously [any WTO] obligations' (European Commission 1995: 1).

The deliberate involvement of exporters in setting these priorities was evidence that DG Trade was concerned about the political contingency of liberal trade policies. This was certainly the sentiment put across in the 1996 'Market Access Strategy', which also expressed a fear that the EU's trade policymaking machinery might be exposed to protectionist pressures (European Commission 1996a: 2). The internalisation of such views is also reflected in the story of the cross-sectoral European services lobby[3] – which together with the Union of Industrial and Employers' Confederations of Europe (known by its French acronym, UNICE), the most important representative of broad business interests in Europe (Greenwood 2011: 76–8) – would become one of the most significant trade lobbyists in Brussels (see also Dür 2008: 33–4; for more on the services lobby, see Lietaert 2009).[4] Having noted how effectively US service industries had 'cooperated' with US negotiators during the Uruguay Round – in contrast to EU services negotiators, which had largely felt they lacked adequate 'support' from their industry – Trade Commissioner Leon Brittan actively encouraged the CEOs of major European services firms to reorganise themselves into a more cohesive and inclusive organisation in order to push for trade liberalisation. The European Services Forum (ESF) thus came into being in early 1999 to serve as a vehicle to aggregate the preferences of the European service interests and feed these into the EU position during the Doha Round services talks. The Commission's aim, as Brittan stated at the event launching the ESF was to 'build a strong, coherent and active European constituency in favour of international trade in services liberalisation in a multilateral context' (Brittan 1999: 1). The ESF thus owed its existence to the multilateral trade strategy – as embodied by the 1996 'Market Access Strategy' – and the concern among policymakers of resisting protectionist pressures. Much the same can be said of UNICE's increased role in trade policy-making; while Cowles (2001: 161) notes that prior to the mid-1990s 'it did not have any significant consultations with the Commission', interactions between the Commission and UNICE became more institutionalised in the latter half of the 1990s, with EU's position in the Doha Round reflecting the stated preferences of this umbrella organisation of EU business interests (Dür 2008: 33; Woll 2009: 281).

Business shifts its position[5]

In the first couple of years of the Doha Round, both the ESF and UNICE supported the Commission's 'multilateralism-first' strategy. At this stage, the few ongoing bilateral/regional trade agreements that the EU was pursuing were largely perceived as a side-show by the ESF and UNICE, both of whom noted that they were focused on securing gains at the multilateral level. Consequently, days before the Cancún summit, in a position paper co-authored with other international business groups, UNICE and the ESF stressed that 'while regionalism/bilateralism can be a useful means for liberalisation, multilateral liberalisation is our end goal' (ESF *et al.* 2003: 2).

The undoing of the EU's ambitious WTO agenda at the Cancún Ministerial in September 2003 – which resulted in the dropping of the Singapore Issues (save trade facilitation) from the Doha Round agenda and led to a prolonged deadlock in the Round – meant that expectations amongst European business leaders were considerably dampened. Although it would take another three years before the announcement of 'Global Europe', the Cancún Ministerial was the key turning point in the Round for the EU and the beginning of the end of its multilateral trade strategy (and associated discourse), as interest groups grew increasingly impatient with the lack of tangible new liberalisation gains. As noted above, prior to Cancún, European business groups were relatively unequivocal in their support for the EU's 'multilateralism-first' approach. Following the Cancún debacle (as early as November 2003), however, the ESF was quick to change its position; it now argued that

> the European services industry cannot ignore situations where its major competitors are gaining new markets via bilateral free trade agreements. The EU should therefore, as an additional policy tool, conclude the ongoing bilateral and bi-regional free trade agreements and *be ready to open new ones when appropriate.*
>
> ESF (2003b, emphasis added)

At this stage, European trade policy entered what could best be described as a lull. In his subsequent public interventions as Trade Commissioner, Pascal Lamy stressed the continuing commitment of the EU to multilateralism, even in the face of United States Trade Representative (USTR) Robert Zoellick's threat of intensifying US 'competitive liberalisation'. Lamy (2003, 2004) also underlined the need for a 'period of reflection' in EU trade policy. In the end, the EU stuck to its self-imposed moratorium by not initiating any new FTA negotiations between September 2003 and the end of Lamy's tenure as Commissioner in November 2004.

Things only started moving again after the arrival of Peter Mandelson. He began to re-orientate EU trade towards the competitiveness agenda of the Lisbon Strategy by participating from their creation in two informal Commissioners' groups dedicated to addressing the EU's competitiveness challenges. But although UNICE presented a paper in March 2005 that welcomed this move and called for the initiation of bilateral trade negotiations with emerging economies (UNICE 2005), the increasing restlessness of businesses at the lack of market access prospects was not yet reflected in Commission thinking by September 2005. This is when DG Trade presented its so-called 'Trade and Competitiveness Issues Paper' at the Fifth Market Access Symposium – a regular gathering of policymakers and industry representatives organised by the Commission. This was considered to be the precursor to the 'Global Europe' communication by policymakers as the Symposium itself was intended to feed into a communication on the 'External Aspects of Competitiveness' scheduled for release in autumn of 2006. The 'Issues Paper' reiterated the 1996 'Market Access Strategy's' emphasis on providing European exporters with 'adequate access to third markets' (European Commission 2005a: 3). But although it acknowledged the fears increasingly expressed by European business leaders – noting that EU producers did not have adequate access to the growing markets in East and South Asia and were losing market share to key competitors – there was widespread disappointment within the European business community at the time over the lack of decisive action in the document. The principal complaint voiced at the Market Access Symposium and during private consultations was that this was a largely 'academic' paper (European Commission 2005b). Indeed, its practical prescriptions – that opening third party markets 'should be primarily pursued through an ambitious strategy in the Doha Round [...] [and] complemented by bilateral or regional initiatives' (European Commission 2005a: 6) – were still rather modest, implying only a softening of the EU's multilateralist trade strategy. In the face of a troubled Round and the increasing turn to bilateralism of the EU's competitors, it seemed to offer little in the way of market access to address European industry's perceived lagging competitiveness in Asian emerging markets. Indeed, the 'Issues Paper' made no specific plans for new FTA negotiations.

European business' impatience with the lack of specific 'policy levers' in the 'Issues Paper' was symptomatic of its general state of anxiety. In the Far East, the key competitors that business claimed to be worried about – and which were explicitly mentioned in the 'Issues Paper' – were naturally not the emerging economies themselves – as Asian 'noodle-bowl' FTAs typically included only modest 'behind-the-border' liberalisation (Ravenhill 2008). Rather, the two countries singled out by the 'Issues Paper' had been the US and Japan. After four decades of multilateralist trade policy, the latter had signed its first FTA with Singapore in 2003 and a 'basic accord' with the Philippines in 2004, with negotiations underway with South Korea, Malaysia and Thailand by 2006 (Manger 2005). The US, in turn, had by 2006 signed an FTA with Singapore and was also negotiating with South Korea, Malaysia and Thailand as part of its policy of 'competitive liberalisation' (Schott 2004). Moreover, over the course of late 2005–06 it became increasingly apparent to observers (including actors within the EU) that the Doha Round of multilateral trade talks was stagnating. Although there was 'modest' movement towards resolving some issues at the Hong Kong Ministerial of December 2005, this was not enough to prevent the breakdown of multilateral trade negotiations in Geneva in July 2006 (Wilkinson and Lee 2007: 3–4, 7–12; for the EU perspective, see Young 2007).[6]

Tracing business input into 'Global Europe'[7]

The period between the release of the 'Issues Paper' (September 2005) and the announcement of 'Global Europe' (October 2006) provides strong evidence of the involvement of exporters in trade policymaking. During this so-called 'broad consultation exercise' (European Commission 2006c: 1), the Commission actively sought the input of business leaders. The Commission began drafting the strategy around March of that year, releasing a draft for comment to the Member States and UNICE in June and the final communication in October (European Commission 2006c). In order to trace interest group input into the 'Global Europe' strategy, I consider the evolution in Commission thinking following the reactions of business to its proposals. I focus on the texts of the three 'versions' of the 'Global Europe' communication produced by DG Trade and their responsiveness to three sets of business demands. The three Commission texts are the 'Issues Paper' (European Commission 2005a) – which served as an intellectual springboard for the strategic re-orientation of policy and formed the basis of most subsequent consultations with business and other stakeholders – a June 2006 draft communication (European Commission 2006d) and the final text of the 'Global Europe' communication (European Commission 2006g). Of all the business organisations involved in this consultation, the outcome mostly strongly reflected the input of the cross-sectoral UNICE and ESF. These also appeared to be the two interest groups in closest contact with officials (see Corporate Europe Observatory 2008).

The first set of demands concerned the EU's strategic orientation. DG Trade had only vaguely alluded to bilateral and regional trade agreements in the 'Issues Paper', with business reacting strongly to what was perceived as an insufficiently 'practical' paper. DG Trade was to later explicitly state in the 'Impact Assessment Report' that accompanied the 'Global Europe' strategy, that, in drafting 'Global Europe', it was heeding the calls of business for more concrete policies following the publication of the 'Issues Paper'. Above all, '[r]egarding market access, business representatives requested more action at bilateral level [...] [with] [a]ttention to be given to countries which have or are negotiating free trade agreements (FTAs) with EU competitors and where we are losing market share' (European Commission 2006h: 5). This is an almost *verbatim* repetition of the summary findings of a January 2006 meeting with business federations (European Commission 2006b: 1).

This points to a second set of demands from business – which were voiced particularly strongly by the services lobby – that could broadly be classed as requests for so-called 'economic criteria' in EU FTAs.

There were three such criteria that were routinely requested following the publication of the 'Issues Paper'. The first was what could be called the 'market potential' criterion, namely 'the size of the market and its growth prospects [which] are proxies for [EU] current and long-term commercial interests in a country, including investment opportunities' (European Commission 2006d: 12). The second, related criterion was the 'level of protection' faced by EU exporters in such markets. Finally, the third and most significant was the 'protection of EU export interests' criterion, which stated that markets should not only be targeted on the basis of existing levels of protection, but also that the EU should take competitors' FTAs into account. The ESF claimed to be particularly sensitive to such developments, pointing to the highly competitive nature of preferential (and discriminatory) liberalisation in services markets. European service providers privately noted how they were competing with a very assertive US bilateral WTO-plus strategy for 'first-entry' into Asia's highly regulated services markets (see also ESF 2007a: 2). However, it was not the only group that voiced concerns. It is not difficult to see in this third economic criterion a general reflection of business demands for a more assertive trade policy in the face of trade activism from competitors in East and South Asia, particularly if one notes the partners singled out by the Commission in both 'Global Europe' texts (which included India, Association of Southeast Asian Nations [ASEAN], South Korea). The economic criteria themselves were one of the elements most strongly welcomed by UNICE in its discussion of the 'Global Europe' draft, particularly as it was felt that in the past the EU's preferential trade policies had been driven by geopolitical interests that did little to serve the interests of industry (UNICE 2006).

Business (especially the ESF, but also UNICE) also repeatedly requested that services be explicitly addressed in the communication. Interestingly, although the 'Issues Paper' did stress that there were gains to be made from external services liberalisation, these were simply listed alongside other areas where the EU should make market access gains (tariffs, NTBs, other 'behind-the-border' barriers) (European Commission 2005a: 37). The only specific sub-heading dedicated to services focused on internal liberalisation in the context of the Single Market (European Commission 2005a: 24). In contrast, in the 'Global Europe' draft from June 2006, policymakers were to cite almost word for word a previous ESF statement on the issue stating that '[t]he services sector should be at the very heart of EU trade policy to maintain EU's [sic] comparative advantage' (European Commission 2006d: 7). Policymakers drafting the strategy themselves admitted that they were paying particular attention to include references to services and investment liberalisation in light of the ESF's previous complaints that the 'Issues Paper' had overlooked these areas of trade policymaking. Services and investment liberalisation would come to form an integral part of the EU's 'Global Europe' agenda through the so-called 'Minimum Platform on Investment', a template for services and investment liberalisation in future FTAs that was drafted with this new trade activism in mind.

In sum, then, the strong pressure from business groups, and in particular the services lobby, in the face of increasing competition from rival economies in East and South Asia seems to have played an important role in prompting the Commission to change tack in 2006 and abandon its multilateral strategic orientation. The Commission's initial (somewhat non-committal) position in the 'Issues Paper' gave way to specific proposals that mirrored the requests of interest group lobbyists. The final 'Global Europe' communication specifically proposed a new series of FTAs with ASEAN, South Korea and MERCOSUR; these agreements were based on the economic criteria requested by business and the liberalisation of services trade featured also prominently (European Commission 2006g: 11). Both the timing and content of the EU's strategic pronouncements on trade therefore fit the theory that interest groups and their responsiveness to systemic events are important factors in the determination of trade policy and challenge the dominant institutionalist narrative of the 'depoliticisation' of EU trade policy. The evidence has suggested that business was not hampered by a lack of 'sufficient interest convergence' (Elsig 2007: 940), as has been argued in that literature. The most influential business groups lobbying on the 'Global Europe' strategy – namely UNICE and the ESF – both embodied the strong and largely cohesive views held by their membership at the time. Similarly, there was little pressure for action from Member States in the Article 133 Committee (this view is shared by Elsig 2007: 938–9). Although they were growing impatient with the lack of progress in Doha, they were internally divided as to whether it would be wise for the EU to abandon the multilateral track.

The discursive dimension to business lobbying: From multilateralism to constructing an 'external threat'[8]

Although the content of the new strategy and the nature of the arguments invoked by interest groups seem to correspond to accounts in the rationalist IPE literature on North–South preferentialism (especially Manger 2009) they do not tell the full story. Why did exporters only mobilise sometime *after* a potential competitive threat had emerged in the form of US and Japanese preferential trade policies? What is crucial here is the discursive climate created by Commission officials in the 1996 'Market Access Strategy', where they emphasised the gains accruing from multilateral (rather than bilateral) trade opening (European Commission 1996a: 5). To be sure, the Commission's policy of engaging with exporters was premised on the oft-articulated goal of negotiating market access more effectively at the WTO. As a result, interest groups did not shift their position when initially faced with the US' 2002 'competitive liberalisation' policy and Japan's concurrent turn to preferentialism after decades of multilateralist trade policies (see Schott 2004; Manger 2005). This points to the important 'reflexive' dimension to discourse, namely the reading particular pressure groups had of their economic interests. In tune with the Commission's pronouncements in the 'Market Access Strategy', they saw these tied to the prospects for multilateral liberalisation. For those interest groups that were slower to change course, such as UNICE, the 'internalisation effect' of the discourse was particularly marked. Even in the case of the ESF, which shifted its discourse to push for bilateral FTAs soon after Cancún, the emphasis on multilateralism held sway for some time after the announcement of preferential trade policies by the EU's main competitors. In an instrumental sense, the ESF may have judged that its influence with policymakers was maximised if it appealed to this widely held (and/or invoked) belief. However, the belief itself also reflexively shaped the nature of the ESF as an actor. FTAs had not originally been foreseen in the ESF's mandate as the organisation was intended to exist for no longer than four years (the time the Round was expected to take to complete).

Frustration with the EU's pickings in the Round and its associated discourse of multilateralism – which originated in the 2003 Cancún summit debacle and became more pronounced with the stagnation of the Round over 2005–06 – was likely to be a driver of these groups' turn to preferentialism for a number of reasons.[9] For one, the ESF's entire *raison d'être* was tied to the Round; without substantial ongoing multilateral negotiations to liberalise services trade, its members were losing interest in the organisation. Indeed, membership of ESF has decreased considerably from 2003 to 2013 (contrast ESF 2003a, 2013). This also reflected the general feeling among services lobbyists and negotiators that the Doha Round – by focusing on trade-offs between industrial and agricultural market access – had side-lined the issue of services. But even in the case of UNICE, whose membership comprised more diverse interests than the ESF, member organisations were increasingly frustrated at the lack of tangible gains from multilateralism. These feelings were expressed by the business constituency more generally at the January 2006 meeting that the Commission held with European business group-ings. In the minutes, the Commission noted that '[r]egarding market access, the [business] federations are clearly disappointed so far and not optimistic for the future about the outcome of multilateral negotia-tions' (European Commission 2006b: 1). In order to keep their constitu-ency happy, therefore, both groups had to produce market access gains by *whatever* means possible. Fairbrother (2010: 320) notes a similar dynamic among business leaders in the US; there was general support for a neoliberal view stressing the benefits of free trade but this was not unconditional, as such groups 'primarily value[d] trade for its benefits to producers'.

Building on these insights, the aim here is to explore not only this 'reflexive' dimension to interest group discourse, but also its 'strategic' side. How and why was their *use of language* an effective means of influ-encing policymakers? The logical corollary to my constructivist ontol-ogy is that one has to recast the arguments made by business representatives in favour of a bilateral liberalisation track as contingent and, crucially, as economic rhetoric (or strategically invoked discourse) rather than the reflection of external, fixed interests, as in rationalist accounts.[10] Concretely, interest groups developed their own rhetoric on the necessity of pursuing preferential liberalisation in response to exter-nal competitive pressures. This is particularly noticeable for services, whose primary lobbyist, the ESF, went from supporting 'multilateralism-first' to calling for bilateral FTAs to respond to 'competitive threats' in the space of two months (see ESF 2003b, 2006, 2007a; ESF *et al.* 2003)!

The fact that most of the emphasis was on stressing the *importance* of these external competitive pressures (rather than say, noting the stagna-tion of the Doha Round and the need to pursue liberalisation elsewhere) is important in underscoring the ultimately constructed nature of this discourse. Such supposed systemic constraints had been present previ-ously but not invoked. Asian regionalism and the US' bilateral trade pol-icy of 'competitive liberalisation' both predated Cancún, while Japan had already signed an FTA with Singapore (acknowledged by the ESF to be an important services hub for the region) in January 2003. Similar argu-ments would eventually also feature in UNICE calls for 'economic crite-ria' in FTAs. In fact, there was a convergence amongst other interest groups around the ideas expressed by the ESF and UNICE on the need to respond to the competitiveness threat in Asia. Even the largely defen-sive automobile industry voiced fears of Japanese bilateralism in Asia

(European Commission 2006a: 35; see also European Commission 2005b, 2006b). This reflexive sedimentation of the 'external competitive threat' discourse is not surprising if one considers the fact that it underscored the potential *losses* from rivals' preferential trade policies: the Olsonian 'logic of collective action' became a constructed economic imperative, its real importance deriving from the fact that its message was treated *as though* it were a *material constraint.* That is why some of the (rationalist) academic arguments for preferential liberalisation have considerable analytical purchase (especially Manger 2009). They highlight, among other things, the importance of such pressures for (mode 3) service suppliers, accounting for the prominence of the ESF in these debates. However, such explanations fail to tell the full story of the contingent nature of interest group mobilisation, which was tied to internalising particular 'as if' rationalities (such as the discourse of multilateralism, which became increasingly discredited as the Round failed to make progress).

There was also an important strategic motivation for interest groups to refer mostly to such competitive threats – and not frustration with multilateralism – in their dealings with the Commission. Although these latter arguments were certainly present in the rhetoric of both the ESF and UNICE, centre stage was given to the 'external competitive pressure' discourse. Much as the appeal to globalisation as a non-negotiable constraint has been used in other settings to legitimate tough policy choices, the competitive threat rhetoric was a useful discursive tool to more forcefully push policymakers into reversing their previous policy stance and pursuing negotiations that had the potential promise of access to other markets. It was also testament to the important 'reflexive' effect of the discourse of multilateralism in EU trade policy. Scholars have often referred to the EU as a 'principled' trade power concerned with maintaining a rules-based, multilateral trading system – particularly under the leadership of Trade Commissioner Pascal Lamy (Meunier 2007; Abdelal and Meunier 2010). Regardless of whether one considers this a plausible explanation of Commission motives, it is clear that under Lamy's and his successor's tenure, interest groups continued to subscribe to the idea that multilateral trade liberalisation was preferable while (at least somewhat disingenuously) noting that external competitive pressures made it *necessary* for the EU to pursue bilateral trade negotiations, naturally only as a *complement* to multilateral efforts (ESF 2003b: 1; UNICE 2005: 3). In this vein, such rhetoric even permeated the statements of interest groups *after* negotiations collapsed in the Round in July 2006 (ESF 2007a: 1).

The EU's bilateral services and investment agenda[11]

The Singapore Issues had figured prominently on the EU's wish-list going into the Doha Round. The timing of most business groups' turn against 'multilateralism-first', coming soon after the Cancún Ministerial, also underscores the importance attached by business (especially exporters) to these issues (see ESF *et al.* 2003; UNICE 2005). Of these, services and investment liberalisation was to occupy a special place in EU trade policymaking in the 'Global Europe' era.

In July 2006, the Council of Ministers – on advice of the Commission – adopted the so-called 'Minimum Platform on Investment for EU FTAs'.[12] This was largely aimed at investment in services (mode 3), which represented the bulk of the EU total at 68 per cent of total outward foreign direct investment (FDI) stocks in 2005, compared to only 21 per cent in manufacturing (Eurostat 2008: 17). This template for 'a Title on "Establishment, trade in services and e-commerce"' in subsequent FTA mandates was formulated in anticipation of the 'Global Europe' strategy. A draft was circulated to the Members States in July 2006 and approved by the Council of Ministers in November 2006 (European Commission 2006e). Handling services and investment liberalisation under one chapter was a considerable innovation within EU trade policy which, up to a point, seemed to correspond to institutionalist arguments stressing principal–agent dynamics, functional integration and, more broadly, the concentration of power in the hands of the Commission. The 'Minimum Platform' expanded the Commission's existing negotiating competence for mode 3 service delivery under the Treaty of Nice to cover 'establishment' in all sectors. It did this by drawing a distinction between the post-establishment protection and promotion of investment on one side – which remained the exclusive purview of Member States through their various bilateral investment treaties (BITs) – and the pre-establishment liberalisation of investment on the other, which was to be negotiated by the Commission.[13]

In my view, however, the importance of the 'Minimum Platform' lay not so much in its expansion of trade negotiating competence, as would be argued by institutionalists, but rather in the emphasis that it placed on services and investment liberalisation in *future* FTAs. The central focus of any trade-related investment negotiation was always going to be services – where the Commission already had negotiating competence under the Treaty of Nice – given that investment in services comprised the lion's share of EU FDI. This is underscored by the fact that one unit in DG Trade was already tasked to handle both issues jointly by the time the 'Minimum Platform' proposal was submitted to the Member States for consideration in July 2006 (European Commission 2006e: 1). Moreover, the fact that the Commission had compromised to accept a GATS-style template (see Note 14 of this chapter) does not detract from the argument I make in this section that the 'Minimum Platform' captured the competitive essence of the preferential liberalisation sought by both the ESF and DG Trade. This is a point I will return to shortly.

To reiterate, then, what was particularly noteworthy about the 'Minimum Platform' was the emphasis placed on services and investment liberalisation within the context of the 'Global Europe' strategy. The fact that it was referred to as a '*Minimum* Platform' was not only a reference to its nature as an institutional compromise between the Council and Commission:[14] it also referred to the 'minimum' being sought from trade partners in future FTAs. In this respect, the emphasis placed by the 'Minimum Platform' on the need for a 'consistent' approach in services and investment – which is not something that has figured as prominently to date in FTA mandates in other areas such as government procurement and intellectual property rights (IPRs) – is significant, pointing to a common set of drivers for all agreements negotiated on the basis of its liberalisation provisions. This was in no small measure the feat of ESF lobbying and its strategic deployment of a discourse of external economic constraint. That being said, the intention was still – albeit on the basis of the 'Minimum Platform' – to adapt the FTA negotiating mandate to the particular circumstances of a trading partner, particularly with a view to match any market access gains acquired by a competitor through an FTA or otherwise. This desire for competitiveness-driven adaptability was also reflected in a novel 'review clause' for investment, which, in the words of its drafters, was included 'with a view to allow in the future a possible upgrading of establishment provisions' (European Commission 2006f: 2).

The most significant innovation, however, was the 'Minimum Platform's' MFN clause covering establishment provisions. Generally speaking, the purpose of such clauses in international services and investment agreements based on the GATS-style model is to ensure that new trade preferences granted by a party to others are extended automatically to the signatories of a particular agreement. MFN forms the basis of the GATS itself, with a general exemption in Article V for regional economic integration agreements and more specific exemptions listed under an Annex to the agreement. What is particularly telling in this case is not just the inclusion of the provision itself, but rather the nature of the MFN exemption in the 'Minimum Platform' for preferences granted under regional economic integration agreements. Whereas under GATS Article V, an MFN exemption exists for practically all such agreements (provided they have 'substantial sector coverage' and eliminate 'substantially all discrimination'), in the 'Minimum Platform' the wording is more restrictive. It provides an MFN exemption only for a 'regional economic integration agreement requiring the Parties thereto to approximate their legislation' (European Commission 2006e: 7). The explanatory memorandum attached to the 'Minimum Platform' spells out the EU's motivations quite unmistakably:

> By [wording the clause] so, the EU is in a position to obtain as many advantages as possible that could stem from other preferential agreements to which one of the EU's contracting parties would also be a party (*the EU should at least obtain the treatment granted by US FTAs*) without prejudicing some EU preferential policies (ex: in the framework of the EEA [European Economic Area] or of EU-accession processes).
>
> European Commission (2006f: 2, emphasis added)

Significantly, the MFN clause in the 'Minimum Platform' is phrased in such a manner as to apply retroactively: in other words, it would affect all preferential treatment granted by the partner in question even if it had been granted *prior* to the entry into force of the agreement with the EU.

This marked stress on seeking (at least) parity with EU competitors – with the US singled out as a particular target – is not altogether surprising, given the context of the 'Minimum Platform' proposals and their clear link to the 'Global Europe' strategy. It is rare to find such a provision for services and/or investment in the EU's previous bilateral trade agreements. Neither the EU–Chile FTA – widely heralded as a benchmark for future trade agreements by EU officials prior to 'Global Europe' – nor an important draft EU–MERCOSUR FTA text from 2004 contained such a clause (European Commission 2006f: 4).[15] Even where such an MFN clause had been included for establishment in services – such as in the EU's FTA with Mexico from 2000 – this followed the wording of the GATS, providing an exemption for any 'agreements concluded by one of the Parties with a third country which have been notified under Article V of GATS' (EC–Mexico Joint Council 2001: 3). Similarly, although the EU–Mexico FTA contained a review clause for services, ostensibly to 'upgrade' the agreement, the EU's bilateral agenda at the time was subordinated to its multilateral trade strategy. The review of services provisions, which according to the review clause had originally been scheduled to take place in 2004, was originally postponed because both parties were interested in pursuing services negotiations at the multilateral level (O'Boyle 2005). That is not to say that the services and investment provisions in either the EU–Chile and/or EU–Mexico FTA were insignificant. Particularly for telecommunications and financial services, there is evidence of strong interest group pressures seeking at least parity with US liberalisation efforts in the region (Manger 2009: Chs. 4, 6). That being said, these two FTAs have to be seen within the context of the EU's wider multilateral strategy. Business lobbying efforts represented a response to localised market pressures (as they were generally more concerned about Doha) rather than the wider systemic forces that the ESF and other corporate representatives appealed to in the run-up to 'Global Europe' (when they were also growing frustrated with multilateralism).

The inclusion of the review and MFN clauses as a 'minimum' requirement for future FTAs were thus significant policy innovations that reflected policymakers' susceptibility to the ESF's (and others') post-Cancún systemic/external competitive threat rhetoric. The ESF requested specifically that the EU's future FTAs 'should also include a clause guaranteeing that any preferential treatment granted to third countries in the future is automatically extended to the EU' (ESF 2007a: 2). In this respect, the 'Minimum Platform' embodied the essence of 'Global Europe' – regulatory liberalisation aimed at securing market access gains for outward-oriented sectors – and the success of the economic discourses advanced by these sectors. This was underscored by DG Trade's desire to secure liberalisation gains at *any* cost, which would prove to be politically sensitive.

DG Trade and the strategic use of discourse: 'A global idea of Europe'

Despite their delay in mobilising in response to so-called 'competitive threats', one could still account for the relative influence of exporters in the drafting of 'Global Europe' in a rationalist sense; the strategy represented a distinct opportunity for them while there was no explicit threat to import-competing businesses. The absence of protectionist interest groups from the debate is thus not too difficult to explain in terms of collective action dynamic – although this still begs the question as to why the Commission gave exporters privileged access to its policymaking machinery while drafting the strategy. The bigger issue and what is particularly puzzling at this juncture, however, is that in drafting 'Global Europe', DG Trade envisaged trading away existing 'pockets' of protection in order to serve its regulatory liberalisation agenda.[16] This is most explicit in the case of the EU–Korea FTA, where a substantial opening of the automobile sector was traded in exchange for (among other things) liberalisation in services and investment (see Chapter 4). Similarly, the existing domestic IPE literature cannot explain how DG Trade managed to push through the negotiation and ratification of the EU–Korea FTA and its agenda of aggressive liberalisation in the face of the opposition of major import-competing interests, particularly given the onset of the 2008 Financial Crisis which heightened societal pressures for trade protection within Europe. The aim in this section is to begin formulating an answer to these puzzles. I focus on the neoliberal beliefs held by policymakers in DG Trade, which were the drivers of a strategy – as embodied by the 'Global Europe' communication – that aimed to render the contingent process of trade liberalisation discursively *necessary*.

The beliefs of policymakers in DG Trade[17]

I begin by focusing on the specific beliefs internalised by policymakers within DG Trade. In order to determine these, I turn to the coordinative discourse present in Commission documents (for more on the selection and coding of these texts, see the Appendix). Specifically, I find that EU trade policymakers espoused a view that the marketisation, economic restructuring and integration of the EU into the world economy were desirable outcomes in themselves. Over the course of the 1990s – roughly coinciding with the broader shift towards neoliberalism underpinning the SMP (see the historical section above) – these ideas became encapsulated in the trade sphere in the notion that the competitiveness of the EU – understood in terms of an increasing emphasis on 'value-adding' and exporting upmarket goods and services where the EU had a comparative advantage (see European Commission 1996a, 2005a) – should be served through the elimination of restrictions to trade. Thus, in the 1996 'Market Access Strategy', DG Trade clearly espoused a neoliberal economic 'positive sum' view of free trade (European Commission 1996a: 2). Crucially, open trade policies were seen in the context of neoliberal economic restructuring; the 'Market Access Strategy' argued that although market opening could lead to political pressure from affected industries, the process of economic restructuring would bring new business opportunities to Europe based on the principles of 'comparative advantage and free trade' (European Commission 1996a: 2). It is not too difficult to see how this resonates with the neoclassical trade theory discussed in Chapter 2.

Moreover, the Commission argued that global trade was increasingly leading to intra-industry specialisation (European Commission 1996a: 3). The subtext was that Europe should concentrate on exporting high-end goods and services where it was judged to be 'competitive' (in other words, particularly, but not exclusively, where it had a comparative advantage in *vertical* intra-industry terms, where products were differentiated on the basis of quality) rather than seek to compete with the likes of China and India on price. Moreover, the argument was also that this objective was best served by pursuing multilateral trade policies, as these held the greatest potential to enable European producers to 'compete' at the international level. This distinctly neoclassical economic analysis led DG Trade – albeit cautiously, at this stage in the mid-1990s – to argue that requests for import protection or government support to affected groups should be resisted (see European Commission 1996a: 2); market disciplines were positive as they encouraged competition and a more efficient allocation of resources. In terms of the categories of the globalisation discourse literature, this was a view of globalisation as a positive, yet contingent outcome, with EU competitiveness as a desirable objective to be pursued.

After the departure of Sir Leon Brittan the emphasis on multilateralism was retained but recast by the new Trade Commissioner Pascal Lamy in terms of the doctrine of 'managed globalisation'. Deliberately vague in order to strike a consensual tone, there are those who suggest that it betrayed a certain *dirigiste* apprehension concerning the consequences of globalisation for state intervention in the economy – in contrast to American *laissez faire* neoliberalism (Abdelal and Meunier 2010). In this vein, the implicit view was that '[i]nternational institutions with muscle can work in managing globalisation only if their constraining rules apply to the largest possible number of countries' (Meunier 2007: 912).

Lamy's idea of 'managed globalisation', however, represents less of a discontinuity with previous ideas than some would argue (see also De Ville and Orbie 2013: 3–4). Even if he did seem to hold a view that the positive nature of globalisation was ultimately dependent on political choices – that is, on its appropriate 'management' via multilateralism in the international trading system – as Commissioner he still emphasised the ultimately desirable (but still contingent) nature of both globalisation and trade liberalisation (see, for instance, Lamy 1999). Lamy's views, in this sense, seemed to correspond to Hay and Smith's (2005: 130) additional category for globalisation discourses, where the process is cast as a 'political project which must be made defensible' (on the positive/negative outcome axis this is seen as dependent on political choices, while on the contingent/inexorable axis it is seen as contingent, see Chapter 2). But here, Hay and Smith (2005: 130–1) find that 'even where the contingent character of globalisation is acknowledged [...] the potential for positive externalities is [often] emphasised'. Thus, even if one interprets Lamy's espousal of multilateralism as having important consequences for trade policy in that it led Lamy to explicitly eschew preferential trade policies through a moratorium on new FTAs (Meunier 2007) it has to be situated within the wider neoliberal trajectory of EU trade policy. Exporter interests (such as the ESF) still had the ear of Commissioner Lamy when the aim was achieving market access gains at the multilateral level. Indeed, he appeared to have internalised the same ideas that were espoused in the 1996 'Market Access Strategy', which stated that boosting EU competitiveness in global markets depended on eliminating restrictions in third party markets for high-end EU exports. At the 2000 Market Access Symposium, Lamy (2000: 1, emphasis added) was to note '*que l'exportation est aussi un aiguillon pour l'amélioration conti-nuelle de la compétitivité de nos entreprises*'.[18] Moreover, the (exporter-oriented) multilateralist bent of EU trade policy predated his tenure; it emerged first during the Uruguay Round and was reaffirmed in the 1996 'Market Access Strategy' and in the actions of his predecessor, Leon Brittan, who sought to actively involve businesses in setting EU priorities for multilateral liberalisation.

This continuity in the neoliberal beliefs of trade officials and Commissioners does not, however, detract from the importance of the arrival as Trade Commissioner in November 2004 of Peter Mandelson. He marked not only a return to the less conditional faith in globalisation and trade liberalisation of the mid-to-late 1990s, but also an intensification of the emphasis on seeing liberal trade policies as drivers of economic restructuring. That is not to say that Mandelson's was the only imprint on DG Trade thinking; as shown above, officials in DG Trade already espoused neoliberal views before his arrival. His significance lies in that he brought a return to views of globalisation as unambiguously positive (rather than contingent upon political choices as under Lamy) and that he imbued these ideas with an aggressive activism that they had not possessed before.

The September 2005 'Issues Paper on Trade and Competitiveness' represented DG Trade's first major reflection on the conduct of trade policy during Mandelson's tenure. It therefore offers an interesting snapshot of the views of policymakers in this period. Its starting point was the economic analysis that the EU's largely open trade and investment regime had helped the EU's competitiveness. Beyond providing domestic producers with a source for 'cheap inputs' that helped them compete in international markets, the 'Issues Paper' argued that '[i]n many sectors (such as textiles or automotive), extra-EU liberalisation has been a major factor in reinforcing competitive disciplines in the EU economy' (European Commission 2005a: 3). In this it mirrored statements made earlier in the 1996 'Market Access Strategy' on the positive effects of marketisation and pursuant economic restructuring; as before, the position of the EU on world markets was argued to be good 'mainly due to its ability to sell upmarket products' (European Commission 2005a: 5). Ultimately, the challenge was to continue seeking this type of vertical intra-industry specialisation in its trade with emerging economies (as trade with them was still seen to be largely inter-sectoral); the EU's entire export model was premised on seeking gains for upmarket producers, reflecting a faith in the forces of vertical intra-industry specialisation. Combined with the hope expressed in the 'Issues Paper' that the EU's trade with emerging economies would eventually move in the direction of horizontal intra-industry specialisation, as had occurred within the EU with the Single Market, the argument was that broad intra-industry specialisation would allow the EU to maintain a large manufacturing base (see the discussion on neoclassical trade theory in Chapter 2; European Commission 2005a: 35–7).

However, such a form of horizontal specialisation – premised on trade in similar goods or services differentiated by variety – was dependent on a 'catch-up in living standards' between emerging economies and the EU. Unless this occurred, so the argument went, 'intra-industry trade is very likely to stagnate' as remaining differences in living standards were likely to 'limit horizontal intra-industry trade', while 'the narrowness of the market for EU upmarket products [was to] limit[] vertical intra-industry trade'; in such a situation '[i]nter-industry trade is then far more likely to develop', leading the EU 'to an extreme specialisation in high-technology products' (European Commission 2005a: 36). The Commission was thus acknowledging the limits to pursuing vertical intra-industry specialisation strategies, which in the long-run had the potential to become 'synonymous' with inter-industry adjustment (European Commission 2005a: 36). This is an issue I return to in more detail in subsequent chapters and in the conclusion to this volume. The importance of this discussion for my purposes here is that it adds grist to the mill to the argument that there was an awareness of the political contingency of trade liberalisation policies, as under Brittan and Lamy, given the (long-term) desire to minimise the costs resulting from adjustment.

This did not prevent trade policymakers, however, from pursuing their ultimate objective to reorganise European production around the principles of international comparative advantage. This was in the line with their faith in the forces of vertical intra-industry specialisation, which had, after all, allowed their upmarket exporters to fare quite well.[19] As a result, the aspiration expressed in the 'Issues Paper' was to minimise long-run adjustment *costs*, not to eliminate economic adjustment resulting from free trade, which was seen as inherently positive. In this respect, the 'Issues Paper' represented an important 'leap' when compared to previous thinking in DG Trade towards a more 'activist' form of neoliberal trade policy, underpinned by a decidedly positive view of globalisation. It argued that the European economy was already very open to world trade – save for a few exceptions in manufacturing and agriculture – in large measure thanks to the Single Market project.[20] The logical corollary, it concluded, was that it was precisely access to third party emerging markets that represented the greatest potential for boosting EU external competitiveness, despite the potential for high adjustment costs which policymakers themselves recognised. Trade policy was cast as the 'final frontier' of the neoliberal project of marketisation and economic restructuring. In this vein – and very importantly – it was suggested that the EU '[u]rge trade partners to open their markets, using our possibilities for movement on our trade protection as negotiating leverage' (European Commission 2005a: 6, emphasis omitted).

Whereas in 1996 policymakers had been rather coy about the prospect of 'resisting' protectionist pressures, in 2005 – following Mandelson's influence – they chose to confront them head-on in the interest of boosting EU competitiveness. It would be killing two birds with one stone by achieving market access gains for EU export-oriented sectors (in other words, 'competitive' industries) using a reduction in import duties as a bargaining chip, even though this was seen as a desirable outcome in itself! This was therefore not an espousal of 'mercantilism' – driven by a concern with maximising net exports – as some have argued (Raza 2007). Rather it corresponded to a neoliberal view of economic relations, as trade policy was to take a more 'activist' role in the restructuring of the European economy. In terms of neoclassical economic mantra, this was a case of the EU 'specialising' in upmarket exports (such as outward-oriented service suppliers) on the basis of its comparative advantage in this domain, redistributing productive capacity away from lower-end products (such as more basic manufacturing) which still enjoyed (economically sub-par) trade protection. As in 1996, globalisation was being portrayed as a positive and contingent outcome, but one in which competitiveness through market opening (particularly of third party economies) was a political objective that had to be pursued with greater emphasis.

The ideas voiced in the 'Issues Paper' plainly suggested the beginnings of a re-orientation of policy towards aggressively serving export interests at the expense of import-competing sectors that had traditionally enjoyed protection. From the economic analysis offered in the 'Issues Paper' – which focused on protectionist trends in sectors that served as inputs for downstream industries (the so-called 'pockets of protection') given the preoccupation with producer competitiveness – it was quite clear where the pain would be felt. Broadly, it argued that although most raw material and 'intermediary product' imports enjoyed relatively low duty rates, the same was not the case for 'finished products' (European Commission 2005a: 12). Of greatest significance, given future developments, were those 'finished products' of use to industry. Of the eleven tariff lines with applied tariffs in excess of 10 per cent – which were explicitly listed – no fewer than ten concerned motor vehicles and tractors (European Commission 2005a: 14). Mentioned earlier in the 'Issues Paper' as a specific example of the 'disciplining' effects of extra-EU liberalisation, it is clear that this sector was being singled out. Indeed, among EU trade policy insiders, the automobile industry was often derided for its opposition to multilateral liberalisation efforts and its persistent efforts to preserve levels of protection for its sector.

Although agricultural protectionism was the subject of a specific subheading in the 'Issues Paper' that considered its impact on the European food and drink industry, it was not one of the 'pockets of distortion' being targeted (European Commission 2005a: 17–24). No pressure to reform agricultural support systems would emanate from the 'Global Europe' strategy itself, in contrast to the pressure that had resulted from EU participation in the Uruguay and Doha Rounds and which, in the case of the former, had been accepted by the EU in part to satisfy its offensive trade agenda. This may be taken by some as suggesting a more prominent role for a material, interest group explanation of EU trade policy, given the widely acknowledged entrenched position of agribusiness in decision-making in this area (for an overview, see Rieger 2005). There is, however, a literature that suggests that this 'agricultural exceptionalism' is not just a product of the constellation of material interests but of the persistence of institutionally embedded ideas in the EU political economy, suggesting a role for a constructivist explanation (see Skogstad 1998; Daugbjerg and Swinbank 2009). Unfortunately, exploring this issue in detail goes beyond the scope of this study, especially given the low salience of the issue in the 'Global Europe' offensive trade agenda with South and East Asian economies. After all, the MERCOSUR talks, where agriculture has figured prominently as a barrier to agreement between both parties (see Jank *et al.* 2004), have not been the primary focus of 'Global Europe'. As a result, it is unsurprising that members of the European agricultural establishment were generally quite welcoming of the strategy; it promised market access gains for European agricultural exporters to offset the (limited) concessions the EU was expected to make on agriculture in the Doha Round. With South Korea, for example, the EU boasted an agricultural trade surplus (see Chapter 4), while negotiators on the EU side were keen to highlight that the EU and India had largely 'complementary' trading patterns in agriculture.

The internalisation of a neoliberal discourse might explain why policy-makers in DG Trade chose to pursue costly trade-offs in the context of its 'Global Europe' inspired FTAs and why they might have chosen to respond to interest groups' 'competitive threat' rhetoric, given that the prospects for an ambitious multilateral trade deal seemed increasingly off the table during Mandelson's tenure (more on which below). The question, however, remains of how they were eventually able to overcome the opposition of affected economic interests. In this vein, much as DG Trade championed the cause of the ESF, the car lobby had powerful allies not only among Member States, but also in the European Commission in the form of DG Enterprise and Industry, whose officials have traditionally seen themselves as the champions of European industry. Similarly, a 2006 report on the future of the automobile sector co-authored by DG Enterprise, the automobile industry and other stakeholders (the so-called 'High Level Group for a Competitive and Sustainable Automotive Industry') seemed to pre-empt the conflicts that would emerge over the EU–Korea FTA when it 'warned against any [trade policy] initiative [in the Doha Round] that may lead to the automotive industry being used as a bargaining chip for other sectors', while favouring similar FTA talks with ASEAN where its interests were less defensive (European Commission 2006a: 35).[21] As a result, in the next sub-section I seek to begin explaining how DG Trade – which, as was highlighted above, was fully cognisant of the political contingency of its trade liberalisation agenda – overcame this opposition by focusing on the use it made of Lisbon Agenda rhetoric to recast the politically *contingent* process of liberalisation as economically *necessary*.

Rendering the (contingent) process of trade liberalisation (discursively) necessary[22]

Launched at the Lisbon Summit in 2000, the stated aim of the Lisbon Agenda was to turn the EU into 'the most competitive and dynamic knowledge-based economy in the world, capable of sustainable economic growth with more and better jobs' by 2010 (European Council 2000). The Lisbon Agenda, however, did not produce a single, homogeneous economic discourse. For one, the first paragraph of the Lisbon European Council Summit Conclusions launching the strategy read that '[t]he European Union is confronted with a quantum shift resulting from globalisation and the challenges of a new knowledge-driven economy. These changes are affecting every aspect of people's lives and require a radical transformation of the European economy' (European Council 2000). At the heart of this emphasis on the external constraints faced by the European economy was a stress on the competitiveness problems faced by EU producers in the new globalised, knowledge-based economy. This represented the culmination of the neoliberal discourse of external constraint that had first appeared in an EU context around the time of the SMP. In a report on the completion of the Single Market, for example, the Commission was to underscore that 'with a slow-down in the world economy and in international trade, it becomes more and more important that the competitive edge of industry in the Community should be sharpened' (European Commission 1987: 1; see also Cockfield 1988). This is not surprising if one considers that the context of the Lisbon Agenda was the perceived slowing of market integration in Europe following the completion of the SMP and the increasingly poor economic performance of the EU vis-à-vis its main competitors, particularly the US (Wallace 2004). However, a potentially contradictory discourse stressing the malleable nature of globalisation, whose outcome was dependent on political choices, found its way into the very same paragraph: '[t]he Union must shape these changes in a manner consistent with its values and concepts of society' (European Council 2000).

Thus, although the Lisbon Strategy proposed that the EU's economic woes were to be remedied by pursuing policies of 'structural reform for competitiveness and innovation and by completing the internal market', this was to be accompanied by a process of 'modernising the European social model, investing in people and combating social exclusion' (European Council 2000). These comprised the so-called first and second 'pillars' of the Lisbon Strategy, with the third relating to establishing an 'appropriate macro-economic policy mix'. The question of whether the EU can reconcile its doctrine of 'social Europe' with efforts to boost competitiveness is largely beyond my remit in this book – although it does point to the broader conflict between tendencies towards neoliberalism and the 'social embedding' of markets (Caporaso and Tarrow 2009; see also Chapter 6; Scharpf 2002; Schiek *et al.* 2011). It also suggests the potential for a discursive battle at the heart of the EU political economy that commentators have been quick to pick up on, stressing, among other things, how Member States have sought to cast the Lisbon Agenda in different lights to justify their preferred course of action (Hay and Rosamond 2002). The 2005 mid-term review of the Lisbon Agenda, moreover, arguably emphasised the 'first pillar' at the expense of the 'second' (European Council 2005; ter Haar and Copeland 2010: 288). Even before, however, the Lisbon Strategy had been cast as an instance of communicative discourse used by policymakers to construct external imperatives for economic reform (see, for example, Hay and Rosamond 2002: 153).

It was the arrival of Peter Mandelson as Trade Commissioner in November 2004 that was the watershed for the Lisbon Strategy in EU trade policy. DG Trade explicitly seized upon its 'competitiveness pillar' to underwrite its arguments for a more aggressive trade policy. This new emphasis on 'competitiveness-driven' trade policy – which would ultimately culminate in the 'Global Europe' Strategy – became apparent from the start of Mandelson's tenure. From their inception, he participated in two *ad hoc* groupings that had been formed by incoming Commission President Jose Manuel Barroso to underscore his commitment to the Lisbon Agenda: the Lisbon Strategy Commissioner's Group, under the chairmanship of Barroso himself, and the Competitiveness Council Commissioners Group, under the leadership of Vice-President and Commissioner for Enterprise and Industry Günter Verheugen. Although these meetings institutionalised links between EU trade officials and competitiveness/industry policymakers working on the Lisbon Strategy who had previously worked quite separately, the groupings were largely perceived as ineffectual, producing little in the manner of concrete proposals.[23] There is, however, some value in highlighting Mandelson's involvement in these two initiatives, as they suggest the beginning of DG Trade's process of capturing discursive space within the EU for its agenda of liberalisation by explicitly drawing on the communicative discourse of Lisbon's 'first pillar'. Moreover, the re-launching of the Lisbon Strategy at the March 2005 Brussels Summit (and its emphasis on 'competitiveness pillar') appeared to add impetus to DG Trade's discursive strategy. 'Global Europe' stressed that its purpose was 'to set out the contribution of trade policy to stimulating growth and creating jobs in Europe', having previously referred to the 2005 mid-term review of the Lisbon Agenda and underscored the need to achieve its objectives (European Commission 2006g: 2; see Table 3.1).

Hay (2007) has therefore suggested that 'Global Europe' should be understood as part of a wider Commission agenda aimed at bolstering

Table 3.1 DG Trade's diverging discourses on competitiveness and trade liberalisation

'Trade and Competitiveness Issues Paper' (September 2005)	Globalisation (economic openness) as a **contingent** and **desirable** outcome. International competitiveness as a **contingent** and **desirable** outcome.	'Like the Single Market, the EU's ever greater openness to trade and investment has been a major "catalyst of growth" over the last two decades. [...] In many sectors (such as textiles or automotive), extra-EU liberalisation has been a major factor in reinforcing competitive disciplines in the EU economy [...] The aim of this paper is to show *how trade policy can* and indeed does, *contribute to competitiveness* and which policy levers *should be* used to maximise this contribution.' (European Commission 2005a: 3, emphasis added)
Coordinative Discursive Setting	Trade liberalisation as a **contingent** and **desirable** process.	'What can we do to add to EU external competitiveness? i) **Reduce our own protection in the few areas where it remains** [...] ii) **Urge trade partners to open their markets**, using our possibilities for movement on our own trade protection as negotiating leverage.' (European Commission 2005a: 6, emphasis in original)
'Global Europe: Competing in the World' (October 2006)	Globalisation (in the form of competitive pressures in East and South Asia) as an **external economic constraint.**	'In 2005, the renewed Lisbon strategy set out the steps we *must* take in Europe to deliver growth and jobs. [...] The purpose of this Communication is to set out the contribution of trade policy to stimulating growth and creating jobs in Europe. It sets out how, *in a rapidly changing economy,* we can build a more comprehensive, integrated and forward-looking external trade policy that makes a stronger contribution to Europe's competitiveness. It stresses the *need* to adapt the tools of EU trade policy to new challenges, to engage new partners, to *ensure* Europe remains open to the world and other markets open to us.' (European Commission 2006g: 2, emphasis added)

(continued)

Table 3.1 (continued)

	The Lisbon (**competitiveness**) objectives as a **necessary** outcome given this constraint.	'European exports are [...] less well placed than Japan and the US in rapidly growing markets, particularly in Asia.' (European Commission 2006g: 4) 'The Communication also addresses some of the links between the policies we pursue at home and abroad. *As globalisation collapses distinctions between domestic and international policies, our domestic policies will often have a determining influence on our external competitiveness and vice versa.*' (European Commission 2006g: 2, emphasis added)
Communicative Discursive Setting	Trade liberalisation as a **necessary** process to meet the Lisbon objectives.	'Europe must reject protectionism. [...] As our prosperity depends on trade, others' reciprocal obstacles would damage our economy. [...] **Our core argument is that rejection of protectionism at home must be accompanied by activism in creating open markets and fair conditions for trade abroad.**' (European Commission 2006g: 5–6, emphasis in original)

Source: Siles-Brügge (2011: 637), Table 1; reproduced with permission and slight changes.

the 'competitiveness' pillar of Lisbon. By 'provid[ing] a powerful stimulus for structural economic reform [...] trade liberalisation [as emphasised in 'Global Europe'] renders the – at this point, still *contingent* – Lisbon agenda *necessary*' (Hay 2007: 31–2, emphasis in the original). The argument presented in this volume, although owing a great deal to Hay's analytical insights, in essence puts this line of reasoning on its head, arguing that the Lisbon Agenda was a *means to an end* for policymakers in DG Trade, rather than the end itself. One should not overlook the fact that Lisbon predated 'Global Europe' by six years and was only appropriated as an ideational vehicle for EU trade policy following Mandelson's arrival in Brussels. Moreover, even though his arrival coincided with the Barroso Commission as a whole being more forceful on the Lisbon Agenda leitmotif of 'growth and jobs', the fact remains that DG Trade was in the driving seat when it came to linking trade policy to Lisbon. Particularly illustrative in this respect are the mechanics of the consultations held by DG Trade over the drafting of the 'Global Europe' strategy with the Member States in the Competitiveness Working Group, which handled issues relating to the Lisbon Agenda, over the course of 2005–06. These discussions did not play a major role in the shaping of the 'Global Europe' strategy as the latter – and the associated DG Enterprise and Industry in the Commission – were largely marginalised in the consultation process. DG Trade was far more concerned about the wishes of exporters. The institutionalisation of links between these two previously distinct and separate bodies did derive from the explicit attempt to link trade policy to the Lisbon Agenda competitiveness pillar, but purely for 'communicative' (rhetorical) rather than 'coordinative' (policy-setting) purposes. In sum, rather than subordinate trade policy to the imperatives of this wider strategy, that is, to see it as a *means to end* (as in Hay 2007), it was this wider strategy that was being used by DG Trade to legitimate its (neoliberal) agenda of market opening. Policymakers in the Commission have thus been keen to stress that 'Global Europe' was not a 'product' of the Lisbon Agenda, but rather that they 'used' Lisbon to further their own objectives.

In this vein, 'Global Europe' noted that 'as globalisation collapses distinctions between domestic and international policies, our domestic policies will often have a determining influence on our external competitiveness and vice versa' (European Commission 2006g: 2). DG Trade was thus, among other things, carving out a role for itself in domestic economic policymaking by stressing the links between internal and external policies that globalisation had rendered inexorable. This emphasis on the 'external dimension of (internal) competitiveness' translated, among other things, into an increased involvement in dialogues with other DGs over internal EU regulation, with the aim of promoting its neoliberal vision of economic restructuring premised on comparative advantage. Similarly, in the 'economic criteria' for FTAs – apart from being evidence of the influence of interest groups – policy-makers in DG Trade found a useful tool to establish their pre-eminence in trade governance. They had for long complained about the 'political' nature of trade agreements pursued in the past – that is, ones sought for geopolitical and/or other non-commercial reasons – and by stressing the importance of 'competitiveness-driven' trade policy they were recapturing the terrain for themselves (and commercial trade policy drivers). It is not too difficult to also see how this embodied the neoclassical economic theory such policymakers had internalised regarding the sources of protectionism; both 'political' FTAs and import protection were seen as products of sub-par *political* decision making, which went against the grain of *technical*, 'welfare-maximising' trade policymaking by experts. Although I could potentially accommodate such insights with an institutionalist account of the dynamics of bureau-aggrandisement, my wider argument in this book is that DG Trade's attempts to seize discursive space are best conceptualised as part of its ideational commitment to constructing a neoliberal order in the European political economy. In this vein, although the emphasis in this chapter (and in the book more broadly) is on the more important external trade policy dimension of 'Global Europe', one can see from the preceding discussion that the strategy had potentially wider ramifications for the conduct of European economic policymaking. More crucially, the explicit linkage between 'internal' and 'external' competitiveness was to underscore the Commission's discursive 'logic of no alternative' in the trade sphere and the increasing emphasis on regulatory liberalisation as part of the drive to open foreign markets.

The single most important aim of DG Trade's discursive strategy in 'Global Europe' was to repackage a political agenda centred on achieving external trade liberalisation (and trade-offs that were potentially costly for certain sectors) as a *necessary* step given the external economic constraint posed by globalisation. In other words, it was appealing to the Lisbon competitiveness pillar discourse to underscore that boosting EU competitiveness was no longer just desirable but imperative. This was a necessitarian form of neoliberalism in the sense that it advocated the inevitability of economic restructuring on the basis of the EU's 'competitive' sectors, where this was seen in terms of their ability to function within globally integrated markets on the basis of comparative advantage. In this vein, in Table 3.1 I note how in 'Global Europe', the

Lisbon Agenda was seen as an externally given set of objectives that the EU *must* achieve given the economic constraints posed by 'a rapidly changing [global] economy' in which the EU was strongly embedded. The corollary to this was that trade liberalisation was a necessary process to boost competitiveness, as it was the only means of achieving market access gains for exporting (read, *competitive*) industries; 'rejecting protectionism' (to serve those interests) was not so much a choice as a necessity as 'others' reciprocal obstacles would [*rather than could*] damage our economy' (European Commission 2006g: 5–6). The 'Global Europe' strategy was thus discursively rendering the potentially most controversial aspect of its trade agenda – trading pockets of protection for market access – *necessary* by appealing to the external constraint posed by globalising markets. Policymakers were especially keen to point to the competitive pressures exerted by the EU's major commercial rivals, particularly in East and South Asia. This is another reason as to why interest groups (and particularly services lobbyists) were so influential with their 'competitive threat' discourse.

To identify the strategic nature of the appeal to such constraints I draw on the analytical strategy I developed in Chapter 2 (in Figure 2.2) to contrast the 'Global Europe' document with its precursor, the so-called 'Trade and Competitiveness "Issues Paper"' (see Table 3.1). In contrast to the highly publicised 'Global Europe' document that explicitly situated itself in the broader public debate surrounding the Lisbon Agenda and thus clearly represented an instance of communicative discourse, the 'Issues Paper' can be considered to fall within a coordinative setting (see the Appendix). As such it was more suggestive of the actual beliefs held by the Commission. Rather than presenting trade liberalisation as a necessary process in light of the Lisbon objectives, which were themselves necessitated by external economic constraints, the 'Issues Paper' argued that these were *desirable* outcomes. These findings are summarised in Table 3.1, which leads to the conclusion that 'Global Europe's' invocation of external threats and economic imperatives was not reflected consistently in different discursive settings. My analytical strategy suggests that, as a result, DG Trade invoked these arguments *strategically* (or rhetorically) to serve its neoliberal agenda of market opening. This is underscored by the fact that the shift in discourse occurred during the tenure of a single Commissioner (and over little more than a year). There are clear parallels here to the approach of Trade Commissioner Leon Brittan who deployed a similarly necessitarian logic in his public pronouncements (see Rosamond 2000), while a more contingent view of trade liberalisation was evident in coordinative documents penned during his tenure, such as the 1996 'Market Access Strategy'. Thus, whereas it is true that the move from 'contingency' to 'necessity' arguments did imply a discursive 'depoliticisation' of trade policymaking – by subordinating such political processes to the supposed logic of economic necessity – that resembled a technical-rational version of neoliberalism (Hay 2004c), it is clear that Mandelson and his team did not so much internalise this discourse as draw on it instrumentally in order to silence political opposition to their liberalisation agenda. One should remember that in their coordinative pronouncements policymakers always acknowledged the strong possibilities for 'politicised' trade policymaking and were explicitly seeking to overcome this. In sum, the fact that they argued in a different discursive setting that trade liberalisation was politically contingent suggests that such actors were not only *strategically* invoking this discourse of external constraint but also believed they had good reason to do so.

The 'reflexive' dimension to business and Commission discourse: Exporters as both shapers of discourse and ideational resource[24]

So far I have shown the importance of ideas in shaping the agendas of DG Trade and exporters. I have not, however, explicitly considered the links between the discourse strategically deployed by business and DG Trade's neoliberal beliefs. Interest groups' rhetoric also came to shape trade policymakers' (internalised) discourse in the Mandelson years, illustrating the dialectical process of discourse construction and sedimentation addressed by the first side of the so-called 'reflexive' pathway in discourse analysis (see Figure 2.3). This is evident in the case of provisions made for the so-called 'external dimension of competitiveness' in 'Global Europe' which focused on the consequences of the 'global competitiveness challenge' for the EU's regulatory environment (European Commission 2006g: 9). Business (particularly UNICE) played a key role in pushing for the inclusion of this provision, the aim being mainly to prevent domestic regulations from hampering the international competitiveness of EU firms.

Crucially, in Mandelson and his DG the ESF and UNICE found a particularly forthcoming interlocutor. The Commissioner and his team's ideational perspective made them particularly amenable to the interests of those who were clamouring for more market access abroad via FTAs. For one, the regulatory nature of much of this liberalisation was a close fit with the wider neoliberal deregulatory project advocated by trade policymakers which had its origins in the SMP of the 1980s. Mandelson, for his part, imbued these long-standing neoliberal ideas with an aggressive activism that, in contrast to Lamy's 'managed' view of globalisation and his emphasis on multilateralism, appeared to be more concerned with 'trading pockets of protection' for market access. Although Lamy himself was also broadly committed to neoliberalism in trade and it is difficult to tell how he might have reacted to the increasingly poor state of the Doha Round (especially from 2005–06 onwards) – as he left the office of the Trade Commissioner in November 2004 – the fact remains that Mandelson's beliefs made him and his DG only too happy to act upon the lobbying efforts of exporters. Given a stalled Round, FTAs came to be seen by these trade policymakers as the most effective (and possibly the only) way of delivering the sorts of liberalisation gains that both they and their constituency of exporters were eager (and even anxious) to obtain. As a result, the 'reflexive dimension' to discourse also has a lot to tell about why Mandelson abandoned the multilateralist approach of his predecessors when faced with intense interest group lobbying.

As noted above, considering this 'reflexive' dimension to discourse has, so far, not provided any added insight when compared to a rationalist account in terms of explaining why the Commission listened to exporters rather than import-competitors while drafting 'Global Europe'. A rational choice explanation stressing collective action dynamics would (correctly) note that the latter never mobilised to pressure policymakers, arguing that these groups did not face an explicit threat to their interests as the strategy was pitched at a high level of abstraction. That being said, such rationalist explanations are unable to account for why the Commission would continue to favour exporters at the expense of protectionists when the latter mobilised in force against the EU–Korea FTA. In fact, the Commission went as far as to give such groups privileged access during the drafting of the 'Global Europe' strategy and, as will be shown in Chapter 4, in the negotiation of the EU–Korea FTA, it even went as far as to actively seek to involve exporters in its campaign to marginalise protectionists in the ratification of that agreement. This suggests not only that business shaped the beliefs of policymakers, but that policymakers themselves used exporters' pronouncements as an ideational resource to push their agenda of market opening (the second aspect of the 'reflexive' pathway to the study of discourse).

One can already see the roots of this in the 1996 'Market Access Strategy's' emphasis on engaging with exporters. It is now clear that this active engagement represented not just an internalisation of the notion that trade liberalisation was politically contingent but also served as a discursive resource to guard against protectionist interests seeking to limit liberalisation efforts. This role of exporters became most apparent in the case of 'Global Europe'. Firstly, DG Trade seized upon the ideas of an 'external dimension to competitiveness' – handed to it by business – in order to capture discursive space within the wider EU political economy. The emphasis on 'economic considerations' in FTAs – again emphasised by business – allowed DG Trade to capture the discursive terrain for trade policy, which had often been driven by non-commercial agendas and interests. Secondly, the economic criteria for FTAs that found their way into 'Global Europe' should not just be interpreted as evidence of DG Trade's ideational affinity for business' 'competitive threat' rhetoric but also as part of the Commission's discursive strategy. DG Trade found this discourse particularly useful in underscoring its own rhetoric of an 'external constraint' necessitating liberalisation. DG Trade would also deploy similar arguments to justify the (rapid) conclusion of the EU–Korea FTA, arguing that it served the key interests of exporters facing a competitive threat from the US. As a result, one can see that exporters' economic rhetoric did not just shape the ideas of policymakers but also became embedded in their discursive strategy.

Conclusion

My first aim in this chapter, after having provided a brief overview of the shift from 'embedded liberalism' to 'neoliberalism' in EU trade policy, was to show the important role that interest groups have played in shaping the EU's 'Global Europe' trade strategy. Rather than conceptualise lobbying behaviour in terms of externally given interest and rational choice assumptions, which do not paint an entirely accurate picture of the late (post-Cancún) mobilisation of interest groups in favour of preferential liberalisation, the aim has been to recast interest group activism in terms of strategically invoked economic discourse (or rhetoric). I focused in particular on the case of the so-called 'competitive threat' discourse, which was deployed particularly successfully by the services lobby; this particular grouping of sectors was especially concerned by the gains made by commercial rivals in the context of preferential liberalisation. This sensitivity came to be reflected in the EU's unique template for services and investment agreements, the 'Minimum Platform', drafted to ensure the EU achieved at least parity with its main competitors. I then turned to the neoliberal ideas internalised by trade policymakers on the intrinsic desirability of trade liberalisation. Recognising, however, that market opening was politically contingent – particularly the controversial objective of restructuring the EU political economy along the lines of comparative advantage by trading away 'pockets of protection' in exchange for market access for EU exporters – these policymakers anchored trade policy within the context of the Lisbon Strategy. In this way, they sought to legitimate potentially unpalatable (neoliberal) policy decisions by rendering them discursively *necessary*. In this sense, the 'Global Europe' communication represented the culmination of a discourse of external constraint which had its origins in the SMP of the 1980s, but it still was given a key push by Commissioner Mandelson. Finally, I commented on the so-called 'reflexive dimension' to discourse, which explains why certain business groups had the ear of DG Trade – which also appropriated some of their arguments for its own purposes.

The drafting of 'Global Europe', however significant, is only the beginning of the story. In the next chapter, which focuses on the negotiation and ratification of the first 'Global Europe' FTA with South Korea, I show the impact of 'Global Europe' in EU trade policymaking. The conflict with the potential *losers* of this new trade strategy was to come to the fore, as was the important role played by services lobbyists in shaping the EU's offensive trade agenda.

4
Resisting 'Protectionism': The EU–Korea Free Trade Agreement

In October 2009, after a series of controversial talks, the EU and South Korea initialled (provisionally signed) the FTA they had been negotiating for just over two years. The agreement was then approved by the Member States in October 2010, ratified by the EP in February 2011 and implemented in July 2011. The importance of the EU–Korea FTA lies in that it serves as the most visible expression so far of the 'Global Europe' communication and is widely held up as the EU's most ambitious trade agreement to date (see, for example, European Commission 2013c). As I noted in Chapter 3, 'Global Europe' emphasised negotiating bilateral trade agreements containing strong regulatory and services provisions with emerging East and South Asian economies. It also implicitly targeted Europe's few remaining pockets of protection, seeking reciprocal concessions where EU firms were competitive. In both of these respects, the EU–Korea FTA is a case in point, obtaining substantial gains for European service suppliers and investors in South Korea in exchange for a significant opening of the automobile sector, still reeling from the effects of the economic crisis.

The EU–Korea FTA poses a conundrum for much of the IPE literature stressing the domestic sources of trade policy. The acknowledgement of collective action problems – that the mobilisation of interest groups on an economic policy is more likely on the basis of losses, due to their more concentrated and immediate nature compared to the greater diffusion of and uncertainty regarding the benefits – has meant that trade policymaking has often been seen to be skewed to the advantage of import competitors. As a result, in the case of preferential liberalisation, the consensus in the literature has been that this was often preferred to multilateral trade-opening because it was more likely to be *partial*; in other words, it offered the possibility of key market access gains without the usual pain for import-competing sectors. Even those IPE models of regionalism relying on firm preferences for *discriminatory* liberalisation have internalised a similar Olsonian understanding of interest group mobilisation. Where policymakers are seeking to respond to the concerns of exporters they will still take the interests of protectionists into account (see, in particular, Dür 2010: 34), seeking preferential agreements based on vertical intra-industry specialisation and its lower adjustment costs for import-competing sectors (Manger 2012). Gains for service suppliers (and other beneficiaries of preferential liberalisation) are unlikely to be sought by policymakers at the (significant) expense of other sectors (in what could be called inter-sectoral specialisation trade-offs) – particularly if the latter mobilise in opposition to the agreement.

What this seems to indicate, *a priori*, is that more could be gained from much of the literature on EU trade policy that points to the institutional insulation of policymakers from protectionist pressures. This is the approach of Elsig and Dupont (2012), who use PA to emphasise the Commission's autonomy as an agent in negotiating the EU–Korea FTA. In my view, however, this is not a sufficient explanation of the EU–Korea FTA since import-competing interests enjoyed good access to key officials during the negotiation and ratification of the agreement – especially those who were hostile and had the power to block the agreement. Although the arguably more permeable EP (which, given the entry into force of the Treaty of Lisbon, had to give its assent) was the focal point of many of their high-profile interventions, defensive interests were also shown to have access to policymakers in Member States and the Commission itself, particularly DG Enterprise and Industry. This suggests that even in politically insulated policy structures decision makers cannot avoid the distributive politics of liberalisation. This point is rendered all the more significant by the advent of the 2008 Financial Crisis which galvanised opposition to the FTA, especially from the powerful automobile sector, but did not prevent the EU from signing and ratifying the agreement. In sum, as there was a strong mobilisation of protectionists with good access to policymakers this liberal policy outcome cannot be explained purely in terms of institutional insulation, nor can it be simply 'read off' from the material interests of (protectionist) societal actors. In the same vein, one cannot explain why exporters, in particular the services lobby, did appear to have truck with policymakers by simply considering material factors.

For one, there is the issue of explaining *why* the Commission chose to pursue the controversial (inter-sectoral) trade-offs envisaged by the 'Global Europe' strategy and put into action in the EU–Korea FTA and *why* it chose to listen to exporters (in particular service lobbyists) over import-competing sectors. In this chapter I build on the findings in

Chapter 3, arguing that the neoliberal ideas held by policymakers (derived from neoclassical trade theory and its faith in comparative advantage) led them to pursue the trade-offs foreseen in the EU–Korea FTA. I also find that this explains why the arguments presented by the ESF – which stressed the need for liberalisation in the face of competitive pressures – were so influential with policymakers, while calls for protectionism were not only routinely ignored but also deliberately marginalised. A second puzzle raised specifically by the advent of the trade agreement with South Korea is the question of *how* the Commission was able to overcome the major opposition mounted against it. I argue that this question is best explained by appealing to the power of strategically invoked discourses highlighted in my constructivist approach to EU trade policy. In Chapter 3 I showed how in 'Global Europe' the Commission consciously used such ideas to construct an ideational imperative for liberalisation. In this chapter I draw on these insights to show how DG Trade was able to legitimate the trade-offs inherent to the EU–Korea FTA. I should underscore that I am not saying that rationalist accounts of trade policy are unable to explain the EU–Korea FTA. Rather, my analysis suggests that ideas and language played an important (though overlooked) role in constructing economic narratives that enabled policy-makers to achieve free trade outcomes – even in the face of protectionist pressures (which in theory could, and in practice did, overcome policy insulation).

The remainder of this chapter is structured as follows. In the first section I provide a background to the distributive consequences and systemic context of the EU–Korea FTA, which informed the subsequent politics over its negotiation and ratification. In the second section I focus on the negotiation of the agreement itself, highlighting the important trade-offs at the heart of the agreement and the resultant market access gains for EU service suppliers (the main beneficiaries of the FTA). This led to a crucial discursive battle over the ratification of the agreement, which is considered in the third section. It resulted in a victory for the advocates of liberalisation in the Commission and among exporter groups. The consequences of this are then briefly discussed in the final section, which also serves as a conclusion to this chapter.

A background to the EU–Korea Free Trade Agreement: Its likely distributive consequences and systemic context[1]

Despite a similar allocation of production among sectors between the Korean and the EU economies, in 2004 trade with South Korea only accounted for 1.3 per cent of EU trade in services, compared to 2.4 per cent of total merchandise trade (Copenhagen Economics and Francois 2006: 14). According to a quantitative study commissioned by DG Trade on the effects of an EU–Korea FTA, this was only partly due to the presence of non-tradable services; rather, it was the (on the whole) significant trade barriers in Korean services markets that were largely responsible for the comparatively small size of EU–Korean services trade. The same study argued that the trade cost equivalent levels of import protection in South Korea for EU service suppliers (46 per cent) were almost double the average tariffs on agriculture and processed foods (28 per cent) and almost eight-fold the average tariff on manufacturing (6 per cent) (Copenhagen Economics and Francois 2006: 16–17). It is therefore not altogether surprising that the study argued that 'that most of the economic gains [from an FTA] are attributable to liberalising trade in services' – up to 70 per cent of the total according to one econometric estimation advanced by its author (Copenhagen Economics and Francois 2006: 4). Such views seem to be echoed in other, qualitative studies, which also underscored the EU's comparative advantage in a number of commercial service sectors, most notably in financial and business services (Kim 2005; Guerin *et al.* 2007). The EU's relative competitiveness was also reflected in the overall balance of services trade. In 2007 this was skewed in favour of the EU and more so than average at 3.15 billion euro, or about a quarter of total services trade between both parties. This was proportionally greater than South Korea's trade deficit in services with the world – a little under a sixth of its total services trade (author's calculation, using data from European Commission 2010d).

These findings are summarised in Table 4.1, which provides a more detailed overview of the sectoral output gains and losses calculated by the quantitative study of the EU–Korea FTA. The table also puts these figures into perspective by juxtaposing them with the sectoral balance of trade and existing levels of protection in the EU and South Korea. For those services sectors in which the EU was argued to have a particularly marked comparative advantage (financial and business services) output gains were estimated at 0.17 per cent and 0.66 per cent respectively (for a full FTA). Together, these two sectors comprised the equivalent of 144 per cent of the EU's (overall) surplus in services trade. Through Figure 4.1 – in which I summarise the quantitative study's estimates for the sectoral share of trade expansion arising from a partial FTA – I underline this finding by highlighting that even in the case of a more limited liberalisation of services trade, 22 per cent of the value of the EU's increased exports to South Korea would fall to business services, the largest single proportion of any of the sectors considered by the quantitative study.[2] Meanwhile, liberalisation gains for all services were calculated to

Table 4.1 The likely distributive consequences of the EU–Korea FTA

	Expected Output	Pre-FTA	Pre-FTA	EU Balance of Trade in 2006 (€ million)	EU Sectoral Balance of Trade as a Share of EU Surplus/Deficit in Services/Goods (%)
	Gains/Losses from a Full FTA	Level of EU Protection	Level of Korean Protection		
Main Winners					
Services		17.30%	46%	2701	
Transportation	0.15%	N/A	N/A	834	31
Communications	0.33%	N/A	N/A	32	1
Financial and banking	0.17%	N/A	N/A	231	9
Business services	0.66%	N/A	N/A	3048	113
Main Losers					
Manufacturing		4%	6%	–18631	
Motor vehicles	–1.74%	10%	8%	–5843	34
Electrical machinery	–1.68%	1.7%	1%	–2670	15
Non-ferrous metals	–0.96%	3%	4%	232	1
Iron and steel	–0.89%	7.4%	3%	–70	0
Textiles	–0.61%	8.6%	10%	–296	2

Sources: Eurostat (External Trade and Balance of Payment Statistics), EU–Korea FTA tariff schedules, Copenhagen Economics and Francois (2006).

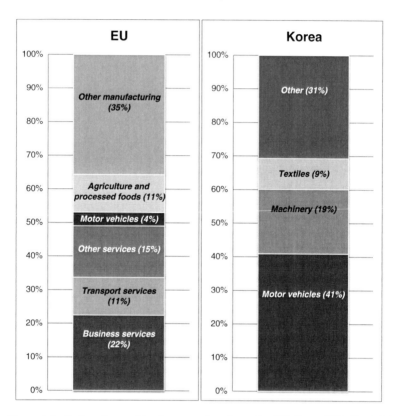

Figure 4.1   Sector share of trade expansion from the EU–Korea FTA (Partial 1 scenario)

Sources: Adapted from Copenhagen Economics and François (2006: 40), Figure 4.4. Also includes data from Table 4.15 (Copenhagen Economics and Francois 2006: 44).

comprise 48 per cent of the increased export value of the EU, or 9.2 billion euro (author's calculation using data from Copenhagen Economics and Francois 2006: 40, 44). Returning to the financial and business services sectors, it is also important to note that these comprised not only the bulk of EU mode 3 service suppliers, but also of EU total external FDI stocks, at 17 per cent and 63 per cent of the total respectively in 2005 (author's calculation using data from Eurostat 2008: 71). This made financial and business services the most important sectors likely to gain from liberalisation with South Korea. The EU's outward FDI stocks in South Korea of 28.4 billion euro in 2006 also dwarfed Korea's 7.4 billion euro of FDI stocks in the EU (European Commission 2010d: 1).

In sum, these statistics strongly implied that services and investment liberalisation was going to be of crucial importance to the EU in the negotiations with South Korea. The EU – a clear demandeur in the services talks, particularly for mode 3 – was facing a trading partner with significantly elevated barriers in services. This draws attention to the key role that regulatory liberalisation was to play for EU providers seeking to enter Korean services markets. The EU–Korea FTA was also unlikely to put the European agricultural establishment, usually seen as the protectionist *bête noire* of EU trade politics, under much pressure. The EU boasted a large surplus with South Korea in agricultural trade; in 2007 it exported 1.39 billion euro of agricultural commodities to Korea while importing only 399 million euro (European Commission 2010d: 8–9). Moreover, those European agricultural producers with an interest in the EU–Korea FTA largely saw it as an opportunity to increase their market share in Asia. Thus, in marked contrast to the failed negotiations with MERCOSUR – where EU defensiveness on agriculture was one of the principal stumbling blocks (see Jank *et al.* 2004; Doctor 2007) – agribusiness was strongly on-side in the case of South Korea.

In contrast, the same series of studies found the biggest losers in the EU from a full FTA with South Korea would be the motor vehicle (a total output loss of 1.7 per cent) and electrical machinery (–1.7 per cent) industries.[3] These were also the sectors where South Korea stood to gain the most. An FTA brought potential output gains of 28.8 per cent for automobile and 27.1 per cent for electrical machinery manufacturers as a result of the inroads that would be made by Korean producers into the EU market; the automobile and electrical machinery industries were estimated to respectively swallow 40.9 and 13.5 per cent of the total expansion of EU imports resulting from the FTA (Copenhagen Economics and Francois 2006; see Table 4.1 and Figure 4.1).[4] The study's conclusions were clear: these industries were argued to suffer from the biggest market penetration and (therefore) potential output drop because of the significant protection they enjoyed (see also Guerin *et al.* 2007). The behemoth automobile sector dwarfed any of the other potential losers from the FTA. In 2006 it accounted for approximately 1.5 per cent of the overall output of the EU economy and just over 1 per cent of total employment (Ward and Loire 2008: 2). What is more, trade in automobiles on its own accounted for 34 per cent of the total deficit in goods with South Korea (Table 4.1). To an extent, this was a product of the nature of the automobile markets targeted by producers from either entity. While Korean manufacturers exported smaller passenger cars in great volume and thus had a sizeable chunk of the European mass market, EU producers were largely confined to the markets for larger (and luxury) passenger vehicles, exporting only 29,404 cars to South Korea's 734,710 in 2006 (Guerin *et al.* 2007: 30–1).

Having considered the likely distributive consequences of the EU–Korea agreement, I now turn to consider the systemic context of these negotiations, in light of the IPE literature on the drivers of regionalism (and more specifically, firm preferences). This highlights the importance of 'strategic interaction effects' as such competitive pressures would strongly feed into the discursive pronouncements of interest groups and policymakers that I consider below. By the time it launched negotiations with the EU in May 2007 South Korea had already concluded FTA negotiations with Chile (2004), the European Free Trade Association (EFTA) (2006), Singapore (2006), ASEAN (2006) and the US (April 2007). It was also in the process of negotiating an agreement with Canada.

However, given the commercial importance of the US and the relatively significant level of regulatory liberalisation generally undertaken in its bilateral FTAs, it was the Korea–US (KORUS) FTA that was crucial in DG Trade's (and pro-FTA interest groups') efforts to present the agreement as indispensable. Although KORUS had not yet been ratified by Congress, with US policymakers expressing some doubts as to its future ratification at the time, the fact remains that the agreement was not completely dead. KORUS' prospects were revived when it was announced that the US and South Korea had renegotiated several key provisions that had been important stumbling blocks to ratification in Congress – including greater protection for the American automobile market – in December 2010 (ICTSD 2010). The agreement was subsequently ratified by the US Congress in October 2011 and by the Korean National Assembly in November 2011, entering into force in March 2012 (Sang-Hun 2011; Eun-Joo 2012). That being said, as will become apparent below, these developments took place just as the EU had, to all intents and purposes, concluded its debate on ratification of the FTA; the agreement had already been signed in October 2010 and an 'informal' deal to conclude ratification had been reached between the Commission and the EP. Thus, the renegotiation of KORUS did not translate into meaningful moves to reopen the EU–Korea FTA (see The Dong-A Ilbo 2010).

Negotiating the EU–Korea Free Trade Agreement

The statistics considered above suggest that South Korea was a very good target for DG Trade's agenda of seeking market expansion opportunities for its exporters (particularly the service providers it had developed a very close relationship with).[5] Moreover, the figures from the econometric studies also highlighted what became more apparent later: that the FTA was to exemplify the strategy of trading away pockets of protection first verbalised in the 'Issues Paper'. This was a clear reflection of the neoliberal ideas held by policymakers in DG Trade. They saw liberalisation as a desirable outcome and were thus particularly concerned with securing market access gains for their competitive exporters, as this would lead to a reorganisation of production around the principles of comparative advantage.

In the case of the EU–Korea FTA, this *quid pro quo* dynamic surfaced relatively early in the negotiations. European negotiators in the services talks submitted a substantial market access offer early on, hoping to elicit a reciprocal response from the Korean side. This, however, was not the case, as Korean negotiators made what was considered to be – amongst EU officials – a rather modest submission and rebuffed European requests for an improved offer. The perception amongst European services negotiators was that South Korea was blocking the EU's offensive agenda in services and investment (where South Korea was mainly defensive) until its offensive interests in automobiles – and to a lesser extent other sectors – (where the EU was defensive) were satisfied. It was only from around October 2008, approximately five months since the last set of formal negotiations, that the Korean side began to make concessions, with negotiations on services and investment moving forward rather swiftly from this point onwards. This change of tack came at a time when the EU first demonstrated a willingness to make concessions on electronics manufacturing and, principally, automobiles, as a result of decisions taken at the higher echelons of the DG Trade hierarchy. One can only speculate as to why this decision was not taken earlier, given the willingness displayed by DG Trade in the 'Issues Paper' to 'sell out' the EU's remaining pockets of protection. But it seems that doing so early on in the negotiations would have reduced the EU's negotiating leverage with South Korea; one should remember that the aim expressed in the 'Issues Paper' was to *trade* away this protection in exchange for movement on the EU's offensive interests. Such an interpretation of the negotiating dynamics is supported by the fact that the decision to make concessions in the EU's defensive areas was soon followed by reciprocal concessions from South Korea.

The importance of this trade-off is underscored by the substantial nature of the concessions ultimately made to Korean negotiators in the automobile sector. Apart from accepting an elimination of duties (following a transitional period) and other trade barriers in a sector in which it had a substantial trade deficit with South Korea – the automobile industry, it should be remembered, had traditionally enjoyed considerable protection – the EU ended up accepting Korean 'duty draw-back'. This meant that Korean producers would continue to be allowed to claim back import duties on parts used in the manufacture of automobiles for export. Duty drawback had traditionally been a 'red line' for EU officials in FTA negotiations with emerging economies and was an area of clear offensive Korean interest, so much so that Korean negotiators had refused to compromise on the issue. The EU's FTAs with newly industrialised economies – notably with Mexico, Chile and with Mediterranean countries – had so far prohibited the use of duty drawback after a short transitional period (Estevadeordal and Suominen 2006: 87–8). This was also noted in a Commission report on the practice compiled after the completion of the EU–Korea negotiations: '[i]n a **preferential environment**, the EU has traditionally followed a practice of prohibiting DD [duty drawback] in many of its free trade agreements' (European Commission 2010b: 2, emphasis in the original).[6]

In this report, moreover, the EU stressed that there are 'good reasons in favour of seeking, as a matter of general policy, to prohibit DD in free trade areas'. The potential for unbalanced competition, it was argued, damaged the prospects of domestic industry. 'However, since the prohibition of DD may also create problems in its application for our partner countries, some *limited concessions to this general policy line* may be considered in exchange of adequate concessions from the other party and on the condition that "rules of origin" [...] would fulfil the needs of the EU industry' (European Commission 2010b: 7, emphasis in the original). The experience of the EU–Korea FTA, therefore, led to a further codification of the principle of trading away protection (however insignificant a ban on duty drawback may have been in individual circumstances) in exchange for market access, in this case, in the ambit of rules of origin. There is no space here to go into a substantive debate about whether the EU–Korea FTA's provisions did 'fulfil the needs of EU industry' in the sense of protecting it from 'unfair competition', to use DG Trade's turn of phrase.[7] Rather, the point is that the EU did make, in the context of the trade negotiations, an important concession to South Korea in order to obtain what amounted to a relatively substantial liberalisation of Korean services markets.

Before turning to this issue, however, it is worth briefly considering the nature of this trade-off. Although the decision and the distributive politics underpinning it were clearly inter-sectoral – as policymakers knowingly traded away liberalisation in a sector in which EU industry was generally defensive for market opening in a series of sectors where the EU was generally offensive – it is interesting that officials in DG Trade felt that economic gains from the FTA could accrue from vertical *intra-industry* specialisation. They believed that EU carmakers at the higher-end of the production chain (large and luxury vehicles) would gain from increased trade with South Korea, given their comparative advantage in this area and the perceived maturity of the Korean market (certainly when compared to other emerging economies). This highlights the neoclassical economic faith attached by Commission policymakers in the 2005 'Issues Paper' to the potential for intra-industry specialisation between more developed economies (see Chapter 3) – and which Manger (2012) has postulated drives PTA formation.

Key market access gains in services[8]

The degree of influence – and privileged access – enjoyed by the ESF and other services lobbyists within the EU's trade policymaking is reflected in the services and investment provisions of the FTA itself. In Table 4.2 I provide an overview of the key concessions sought by various European service sectors and the extent to which these were reflected in the final FTA text as a result of pressure from EU negotiators. The fact that both columns in the Table bear a striking resemblance to one another not only indicates that services lobbyists were quite effective at influencing EU decision makers, but also points to the importance of the concessions made by the EU in the automobile sector; the evidence above has suggested that it is unlikely South Korea would have yielded to European requests in services unless they gained ground in their areas of offensive interest. Similarly, the contentiousness of these concessions within the EU highlights the importance that DG Trade attached to the EU's bilateral services and investment agenda (as best exemplified by the 'Minimum Platform').

Manger's (2009: 44–8) two propositions regarding the importance of liberalisation in services and investment for incumbent service operators and potential entrants cast some light on the results illustrated in Table 4.2. His hypothesis concerning the role of regulatory liberalisation and 'first-entry' is particularly pertinent, as the FTA included significant provisions for the liberalisation of establishment in financial and business services – two sectors which represented the bulk of EU mode 3 suppliers and a major part of the total market access gains. Moreover, these were often unmistakably discriminatory provisions, which at times not only matched US gains, but exceeded them. This was the case, for instance, in legal and financial services (Table 4.2). In the case of the former, the ability of lawyers to use their home title and establish an

Table 4.2 Requests from services lobbyists compared against key gains in the EU–Korea FTA

Requests from Service Industries (mostly based on ESF 2007c: 2–4)	Key Gains in the EU–Korea FTA (as initialled October 2009; where I directly cite the text of the agreement, emphasis has been added)
GATS Modes 1 and 2 (cross-border supply and consumption abroad)	**GATS Modes 1 and 2**
Improvement on Korean WTO offer (in brackets) sought for all sectors mentioned below.	Accounting, auditing, bookkeeping and taxation services: bound liberalisation in mode 2 for qualified public/tax accountants.
For both modes 1 and 2, improved offers sought for accounting, auditing, bookkeeping services (mode 2 unbound), taxation (modes 1 and 2 unbound for reconciliation and representative services), insurance (modes 1 and 2 unbound for direct insurance, brokerage, auxiliary insurance services) and banking and securities (modes 1 and 2 totally unbound).	Computer services: additional liberalisation in modes 1 and 2.
	Courier services: full liberalisation for express delivery services.
	Insurance services: bound liberalisation for brokerage and auxiliary insurance services.
	Banking and securities: some bound liberalisation.
For mode 1, improved offers sought for, amongst others, computer and related services (no commitments), courier (restricted to air and sea), postal (exclusive rights for the Korean Postal Authority), distribution (limited market access for pharmaceuticals and medical goods) and telecommunication (*restrictions on satellite broadcasters*) services.	*Telecommunication services: satellite broadcasters can operate directly in South Korea without having to liaise with a local operator.*
GATS Mode 3 (commercial presence) Status quo in brackets.	**GATS Mode 3**
Accounting, auditing, bookkeeping and taxation services: public liberalisation sought of qualification requirements (only Korean qualified professionals were allowed to set up practices/firms).	Accounting, auditing, bookkeeping and taxation services: public accountants certified in an EU Member State allowed to invest in Korean firms (49% foreign equity cap). EU tax accountants allowed to establish an office.

Legal services: Full liberalisation sought (the establishment of foreign lawyers was not permitted).

Telecommunication services: Parity sought with KORUS FTA, with 100% foreign equity cap (49% at present). Complicated licensing.

Financial Services:

For financial services, expansive terminology was sought (particularly by the United Kingdom [UK] financial services industry) to cover all financial service suppliers (for example, Thomson Reuters and Lloyd's of London).

Insurance services: *Stress on the removal of restrictions on data-sharing.* Numerous other restrictions to be addressed (among them: nationality and residence restrictions on personnel and company offices for brokering; non-transparent regulatory process; interference by the regulator in product pricing and ranking of providers).

Banking: *Stress on the removal of restrictions on data-sharing.* Numerous other restrictions to be addressed (among them: discriminatory regulations; lack of regulatory transparency and use of non-internationally recognised approaches to regulation; nationality and residence restrictions; outsourcing restrictions)

Securities: Stress on improving licensing process and moving towards best international practice in regulation.

Legal services: *Law firms established in the EU allowed to set up a branch in South Korea and form partnerships with Korean firms. EU lawyers allowed to use home title.*

Telecommunication services: 100% foreign equity cap.

Financial Services:

For financial services, the agreement uses the more expansive term 'financial service supplier' was used, rather than just 'financial institutions' as in the KORUS FTA.

Insurance services: *Elimination of restrictions on data-sharing.* Limited liberalisation for insurance brokerage (2 employees per branch).

Banking: *Elimination of restrictions on data-sharing.*

Securities: *Elimination of restrictions on data-sharing.* Article 7.24 provides that '[e]ach party shall, to the extent practicable, ensure that internationally agreed standards for regulation and supervision in the financial services sector [...] are implemented and applied' including 'the *Objectives and Principles of Securities Regulation* of the International Organisation of Securities Commissions'.

(continued)

Table 4.2 (continued)

Other Issues	Other Issues
Strong MFN clause (ESF 2007a: 2).	MFN clause present in the FTA. MFN exemption wording (Article 7.14, paragraph 2): 'Treatment arising from a regional economic integration agreement granted by either Party to establishments and investors of a third party shall be excluded from the obligation in paragraph 1, *only if this treatment is granted under sectoral or horizontal commitments for which the regional economic integration agreement stipulates a significantly higher level of obligations than those undertaken in the context of this Section as set out in [the schedule of specific services commitments].'*

Sources: ESF (2007a,c), EU–Korea FTA (October 2009).

office in South Korea was restricted to those based in an EU Member State. Even more significantly, the EU–Korea FTA's chapters on financial services referred to 'financial service suppliers', rather than the more restrictive 'financial institution' used in the KORUS FTA. It was a provision that EU negotiators fought especially hard to include, responding in large measure to pressure from the UK and its financial services industry. A particular concern was that providers of financial services such as Thomson Reuters or Lloyd's of London (a City-based insurance market) that were not 'financial institutions' would not otherwise be covered by the (non-discriminatory) regulatory liberalisation already undertaken by South Korea in the context of the KORUS FTA. Thus, although the list of commitments in financial services was very similar to that achieved by the US, it covered a greater list of suppliers.

In other cases, liberalisation in line with (discriminatory) US gains was all that was sought. In the case of telecommunications services, the foreign equity cap that existed for investments was raised to match the KORUS FTA level of 100 per cent. Similarly, a persistent gripe of the (UK) financial services industry had been the data transfer restrictions imposed by Korean authorities, which had legally prohibited the transfer of customers' data outside of South Korea without individual consent. Such firms would have been required to establish a data processing centre in South Korea in order to operate a branch, severely undermining the competitiveness of foreign-based financial service suppliers in the Korean market. The KORUS FTA would lift these restrictions for US-owned financial institutions and so a resolution of the issue was of paramount concern to EU-based interests. In the end, a similar outcome was achieved via Article 7.43 of the EU–Korea FTA, which allowed for the transfer of information outside of South Korea by financial service suppliers 'for data processing, where such processing is required in the ordinary course of business'.

It is thus clear that some of the most significant concessions sought (and obtained) by the EU were in sectors where regulatory provisions had previously severely restricted or even outright prohibited the establishment of European service suppliers (for example in financial, legal and telecommunications services) and where there was a risk of the US making 'first entry'. The 'competitive threat' discourse deployed by the ESF was thus clearly important in shaping the provisions of the EU–Korea FTA. The agreement often mirrored the discriminatory clauses of the KORUS FTA agreement to serve the interests of potential new entrants 'threatened' by US market access gains. The importance of this dynamic is underscored by the MFN clause found in the agreement, which, to a great extent, mirrors the 'Minimum Platform's' restrictive MFN exemption for regional economic trade agreements (Table 4.2). Incumbent service operators, however, also played an important role during the negotiations; European banks with a presence in South Korea, for instance, were amongst the most vocal supporters of the deal, sensing new opportunities for expansion. What is more, some provisions sought by the EU in the FTA were non-discriminatory in nature, addressed other modes of supply and were not formulated with the KORUS FTA in mind. This included, most notably, market access for the cross-border supply of satellite broadcast transmission services in telecommunications, which had previously not been able to operate in the Korean market. EU negotiators cited this as one of the key concessions extracted from the Korean side.

In principle, the role of incumbents and non-discriminatory liberalisation is something that Manger can (and indeed, does) accommodate within his model. That being said, the framework is not without its problems. An important part of the requests coming from the services lobby concerned the binding of liberalisation already undertaken autonomously by South Korea – with an improvement being sought by business on the modest commitments 'bound' by Korea in the GATS negotiations. This was particularly relevant in the case of GATS modes 1 and 2 for professional services (such as accounting, auditing, bookkeeping and taxation services) as well as for certain financial services (banking and insurance), where improved commitments were obtained from the Korean side in the FTA (Table 4.2). This is partly related to the nature of multilateral negotiations for the liberalisation of trade in services, which are often concerned with simply 'binding' autonomous liberalisation – more so than in the case of tariff negotiations for goods. In the absence of much progress in the Doha Round of services negotiations – which, as one will remember from Chapter 3, was a factor in driving the ESF to push for FTAs in the first place – European service providers sought additional legal security by binding commitments bilaterally (rather than multilaterally). Their efforts were given greater weight by the onset of the Financial Crisis and the fear that states might adopt protectionist measures. One representative of the services lobby, for example, was to remark that there was an increasing concern with securing core markets, rather than expanding into new ones.

As a result, the ESF's pronouncements are best thought of as a contingent economic rhetoric, and the internalisation of particular 'as if' rationalities, rather than just the externalisation of materially given interests. In this respect, the notion of a 'competitive threat' discourse introduced in Chapter 3 is particularly useful. This was deployed strategically by the ESF and other interest groups in the run-up to 'Global Europe' in order to pressure the Commission into pursuing preferential trade policies with a strong emphasis on regulatory liberalisation. Its continued prominence and success in the case of the EU–Korea FTA negotiations is illustrated by the specific gains obtained by the services sector. The ESF's rhetoric referred specifically to the 'first-mover' advantages created by FTAs for mode 3 service suppliers in tightly regulated sectors, that is, Manger's second proposition. In the case of the EU–Korea FTA, the 'threat' was embodied by the KORUS FTA agreement. Underscoring the constructed nature of this discourse, however, is the fact that the FTA did not serve potential first entrants in competition with the US only. The discourse of 'external threat' itself was a useful tool to expedite negotiations and also reflected service lobbyists' interests in preferential regulatory liberalisation. But it obscured other, broader market access objectives that were less compelling arguments to use when seeking to pressure policymakers.

Recasting interest group pressure in terms of a constructivist ontology is useful at highlighting why the ESF's arguments about market access were so influential with policymakers – in contrast to defensive interests, which were deliberately marginalised. Without extensively repeating arguments stated elsewhere, it is clear that the espousal of neoliberal ideas – which emphasised the desirability of market openness to serve export competitiveness, for the purposes of economic restructuring premised on comparative advantage – made such officials amenable to the competitive logic discursively deployed by the ESF. Put quite simply, the former's construction of commercial 'facts' chimed with DG Trade's neoliberal beliefs (while the latters' did not). Moreover, these arguments themselves became a useful ideational resource for policymakers trying to face off opposition to the agreement (together, both of these elements comprise the so-called 'reflexive pathway' to the study of discourse). Thus, although it does offer an insight into the role and preferences of services lobbyists, Manger's theoretical framework needs augmenting with a constructivist ontology.

The discursive battle over the EU–Korea Free Trade Agreement

Economic rhetoric was an important part of DG Trade's strategy when it came to the approval of the agreement by the Council and the EP.[9] In both of these bodies, opposition to the EU–Korea FTA's provisions for the liberalisation of the automobile sector – and other negatively affected industry groupings such as textiles – was brewing. The European automobile industry, in particular, perceived the agreement as providing a significant (and unfair) advantage to Korean producers at a time where the sector was experiencing severe economic strain following the onset of the Financial Crisis. Although there were some cleavages within the automobile sector between large/luxury and small- to medium-sized car producers – the former being more likely to gain from the FTA in light of the EU's export patterns (Natarajan 2011) – on balance the industry was strongly against the agreement. Its otherwise highly influential supranational lobbyist, the European Automobile Manufacturers' Association (known by its French acronym, ACEA), was vehemently anti-FTA, while significant national auto industry federations, including that of Germany which counted amongst its members a number of important large/luxury car manufacturers, were also opposed (Elsig and Dupont 2012: 501, 503–4). The substantial market size asymmetry between the EU and South Korea was an issue that was repeatedly raised by such actors. Even under a partial liberalisation scenario, the EU's increase in export value (760 million euro) was dwarfed by the market expansion of Korean auto manufacturers in the EU (5.2 billion euro) (author's calculation, using data from Copenhagen Economics and Francois 2006: 40). In this vein, one of the Commission's impact studies of the FTA was to note that 'the size of [the Korean] market [...] is limited and the development of the market is rather sluggish' while at the same time highlighting how Korean manufacturers had already managed to expand their market share in the EU (Guerin *et al.* 2007: 98–9).

The car industry as a whole was rather sensitive over the relaxation of any rules of origin provisions, as had been illustrated by an earlier dispute in the negotiations between the EU and South Korea over whether products produced in Kaesong industrial complex in North Korea should be covered by the FTA's content requirements (Bounds and Fifield 2007). Of these provisions, the duty drawback practised by Korean manufacturers was particularly worrying as it raised the spectre of indirect imports of car parts from China. In response to this and other grievances with the text – including a concern with the provisions on NTBs, which, it was argued, allowed South Korea significant leeway to continue discriminating against EU exports – ACEA mounted a concerted lobbying campaign targeting Member States and the EP. The former had formal power to veto what was ultimately a 'mixed agreement' – incorporating areas that were still shared competence (Bungenberg 2011: 133) – while under the Lisbon Treaty's new provisions on trade policy, the EP was granted the power to ratify the EU–Korea FTA.[10] DG Enterprise and Industry, the traditional champion of industry within the Commission, also had qualms about the deal (see a report co-authored with ACEA, European Commission 2008b: 42).

At first, the opposition campaign appeared to pay dividends when several prominent Member States voiced concerns over the implications of the FTA for their automobile sectors, including France, Italy and Germany (Goldirova 2009). But these concerns were put largely to rest at a July 2009 meeting of the Article 133 Committee of Member State trade representatives, where recalcitrant Member States were given the option of clarifying provisions on a safeguard clause for automobiles without re-opening the negotiations with South Korea. This would allow for the imposition of temporary duties if there was evidence of injury to domestic industry. As a result, the EU and South Korea initialled the agreement on 15 October 2009.

How did DG Trade manage to convince the Member States to agree to the provisions of the FTA, including the principle of allowing 'duty drawback', when it was facing the opposition of the behemoth car industry? The answer is that, in a sense, it had already won the battle, by recasting liberalisation (in the 'Global Europe' strategy) as a *necessary* process, both because of the external constraint posed by globalisation and also the 'competitive threat' from overseas rivals, particularly in Asia. This latter argument, although not stated openly by Mandelson, was repeated time after time by officials within DG Trade (and ostensibly also in their discussions with Member States and rival DGs). The agreement itself and the urgency with which it was pursued also reflected the desire to seek at least parity with KORUS, particularly in the key area of services and investment. What is more, this discourse was a reflection of the content of the 'Minimum Platform', which was largely justified in terms of matching US liberalisation gains. The ESF, for its part, was more candid, underscoring that the 'proper balance of the benefits of the agreement' had to be appreciated, 'including the enormous potential for the various services sectors [...] that desperately need further market access abroad so as to allow our companies to maintain their competitive advantage' (ESF 2009: 2).

This begs the question of whether such appeals were indeed strategic or rather simply represented the heartfelt beliefs of policymakers and interest groups. Although KORUS had been languishing in Congress since 2007 (when the EU started its internal debate on the EU–Korea FTA) the fact remains that the passage of this FTA was potentially possible in the foreseeable future (it was ratified by both parties in late 2011).

In the case of the services lobby's (and others') appeals, these mirrored their language during the debates surrounding the drafting of 'Global Europe'. Here, external constraint rhetoric was found to be more persuasive (given its urgency) as a device to seek market access gains, rather than arguments about multilateral dysfunction (see Chapter 3 and above). Moreover, their appeals to an external economic constraint can be interpreted in light of the constructivist theory of interest group pronouncements advanced in Chapter 2, which paints the language of lobbyists as intrinsically strategic regardless of whether they believe in the existence of a competitive threat.

In the case of DG Trade, one has to be more cautious about whether one imputes a strategic motive to their appropriation of the 'competitive threat' discourse with reference to South Korea. However, one should not forget that KORUS' fortunes were really only revived in December 2010 after the EU had concluded its internal debate on the FTA and the agreement was all but ratified. As a result, it is not too surprising that Elsig and Dupont (2012) have made a similar argument to the one being advanced here; in their view, the Commission created a 'focal point' centred on the notion of exporter discrimination to 'buil[d] an informal coalition with the parts of the industries [...] that were receptive to their arguments' and 'to build buffers against criticism from import-competing interests' (Elsig and Dupont 2012: 492). Although they work from a PA perspective that emphasises the autonomy (read insulation) of the Commission – which does not entirely correlate with the considerable political pressure that existed against the FTA – they accord an important explanatory role to what is ultimately the 'competitive threat' discourse by another name. What is more, the fit of the services lobbyists' 'competitive threat' discourse within DG Trade's broader rhetoric of external constraint suggests that it is reasonable to assume that DG Trade was appropriating it for strategic purposes (rather than simply because it believed it to be a true threat, although the two are not exclusive, see Figure 2.1).

That being said, the more general point about the use of external constraint rhetoric by the Commission to justify the conclusion of the FTA is not dependent on claims about the KORUS FTA. DG Trade appealed more generally to the need to resist protectionism in an age of globalised markets and simply drew on the rhetoric of interest groups to bolster this argument. The arguments made by officials within DG Trade have to be situated within the Commission's wider strategy of linking trade policy to the Lisbon consensus on the wider macroeconomy. The Financial Crisis itself was even harnessed on occasion in order to bolster the argument that liberalisation was a necessary response to external economic pressures. As Mandelson's successor as Trade Commissioner, Catherine Ashton, was to note in an EP plenary debate in September 2009:

> I make no apology for putting forward to this Parliament what I believe is a serious, 21st century free trade agreement of enormous benefit across the economy of the European Union. I especially make no apology for doing it at a time of economic crisis because, if ever there was a time when my responsibility was to provide as much support for the businesses and the workers of Europe, I believe that time is now and that is what this deal does.
>
> European Parliament (2009)

Overcoming opposition from Member States, interest groups and the European Parliament[11]

In the EU Council of Ministers this consensual doctrine would pay considerable dividends. Indeed, the Member States had practically agreed unanimously upon 'Global Europe', with one official noting how surprised he was at the level of favourable consensus shown by Member States in response to the strategy. What is more, this discourse continued to be a powerful argument following the advent of the Financial Crisis and in the context of debate over the EU–Korea FTA. The sentiment behind the pledges of government support made to several struggling automobile manufacturers – while the FTA negotiations were still ongoing – was to be quickly forgotten (see, for example, Benoit 2008). Although initially those Member States with significant automobile industries, most notably Germany, France and Italy, did show some reticence vis-à-vis liberalising trade in automobiles, they all eventually came around to supporting the agreement. In the case of Germany, initial opposition to the FTA gave way to support after the outcome of regional elections favoured Chancellor Angela Merkel and her ruling party. The opposition to the FTA and its provisions for the automobile industry was, in all likelihood, prompted by, among other things, short-term electoral concerns in several key *Länder* (German states), rather than any fundamental opposition to the notion of substantial liberalisation in the case of the EU–Korea FTA. The case of Italy is discussed in more detail below, but at this stage I can note that it also went from opposing the deal to supporting it, following pressure from its peers in the Council. France for its part, which did have some serious reservations about the FTA and the principle of liberalisation as implied in 'Global Europe', was isolated in the Council, as other Member States were not receptive to its calls for greater emphasis on 'reciprocity' in trading relations. This is underscored in the case of automobiles by a March 2009 meeting of the Competitiveness Council, which 'insist[ed] on the need to refrain from protectionism and discriminatory measures in the global car market' (Council of the EU 2009: 5).

A similar dynamic also came to the fore in the EU Council of Ministers when the Member States had to definitively approve the agreement. After the Member States had agreed to initial the agreement back in July 2009, Italy, under strong pressure from its automobile industry, underwent a *volte face*, threatening to oppose the final approval of the FTA and causing some consternation among Members of the Council. The Italian Trade Minister went as far as to threaten to veto the agreement at the Council meeting held to approve (the signature of) the FTA held on 10 September 2010 (Korea JoongAng Daily 2010). At a meeting held a few days later, the Italian delegation was still refusing to approve the agreement, initially asking for a one-year delay in implementation of the FTA, a demand which it soon reduced to six months following isolation in the Council (Deutsche Presse Agentur 2010). This isolation is underscored by the fact that Italy backed down relatively quickly and agreed to the FTA at the next Council meeting held on 16 September. This allowed the agreement to be signed according to plan at the EU–Korea summit on 6 October 2010 (Reuters 2010). The fact that opposition to Italian demands was spearheaded by not only the UK, traditionally seen as a free-trading nation, but also Germany and France (Deutsche Presse Agentur 2010), which had previously resisted aspects of the FTA for fear it might threaten domestic producers, is also testament to the success of DG Trade's discursive strategy. Member States' acceptance of this discourse on the necessity of liberalisation was also reflected subsequently in the conclusions of the October 2010 European Council, which 'emphasise[d] the need to continue keeping markets open […]' and 'the need to avoid all forms of protectionism' (European Council 2010b: 3).

The most interesting measure of the success of this strategy was that even the automobile industry (and some of its supporters in the EP, among Member States and in DG Enterprise) spoke in terms of ensuring equitable (or 'reciprocal') *liberalisation* rather than invoking defensive arguments *per se*. Such arguments had already featured previously in the debates between the Commission in Council over 'Global Europe'. France had expressed some ambivalence regarding the Commission's neoliberal agenda of liberalisation 'at any cost' by emphasising the need for 'reciprocity' in trading relations (see Council of the EU 2006: 2). In this context, such views were suggestive of a more mercantilist view of trade (that national welfare was best served by maximising net exports) that made France, in particular, more amenable to what amounted to support for import protection in some of the EU's more defensive sectors. In this it had the support of the automobile industry. In a report co-authored with DG Enterprise in 2006, ACEA noted that in the Doha Round 'there should be no reduction in EU import duties on automobile products unless it is fully compensated' by a series of market access gains (European Commission 2006a: 35). Thus, reacting subsequently to the initialling of the FTA with South Korea in October 2009 ACEA noted that '[t]he automotive industry supports the EU in seeking trade liberalisation in a fair and balanced way. The current agreement with South Korea, however, is not in the interest of Europe's citizens' (ACEA 2009). Rather than calling for the maintenance of protection as such, the automotive lobby sought to address several issues left outstanding by the FTA that hampered EU market access into South Korea, including the continued existence of several NTBs such as unstandardised emissions testing (ACEA 2010; this concern was also reflected in the safeguards regulation approved by the EP, see below). Only on the issue of duty drawback did ACEA appear to voice concerns about its effects on EU producers in their domestic environment, but the argument was phrased so as to stress the economically 'distorting' effects of such a practice, which amounted to 'unfair competition' (ACEA 2009). As if to further underscore this point, EU automobile lobbyists went on to pressure the EU to match the potential gains obtained by the US on these standards in its December 2010 renegotiation of KORUS (Chosun Ilbo 2010). In sum, these demands not only illustrated that such actors had reservations about the EU–Korea FTA, but also that they felt that they had to tread carefully by not making explicitly protectionist arguments.

The Commission, for its part, publicly stressed, in line with its belief that the FTA was desirable because it allowed for vertical intra-industry specialisation, that 'EU car exporters will gain from duty elimination in Korea' (European Commission 2009a: 1); it was referring of course, to the upmarket producers of luxury and larger vehicles which had a comparative advantage, but the necessitarian logic being invoked was that its overall economic benefits justified the conclusion of the FTA 'as soon as possible'. Given the substantial imbalance in trade in cars between the EU and South Korea noted above, it is doubtful whether liberalisation in this mould will bring about the benefits claimed; after all, the quantitative study of the effects of the FTA referred to above made allowances for the elimination of NTBs (Copenhagen Economics and Francois 2006). In fact, of the three FTA liberalisation scenarios foreseen by the study, the European automobile industry was calculated to contract most under full liberalisation.[12] Thus, even if vertical intra-industry specialisation does bring some gains for upmarket EU car producers (as officials in DG Trade are keen to point out, see above and European Commission 2010i: 4), these are likely to be outweighed by the costs of inter-sectoral economic adjustment. Small cars, where Korean manufacturers have a comparative cost advantage (which is likely to be heightened by the FTA's elimination of duties and acceptance of duty drawback), represent the bulk of automobile trade between the EU and South Korea (Guerin *et al.* 2007: 30–1, 98–9); in turn, high-end services suppliers are likely to gain the most on the EU side from the EU–Korea FTA. This highlights the limitations of the Commission's faith in vertical intra-industry specialisation, which were raised in the 2005 'Issues Paper'. The document had, after all, argued that vertical intra-industry specialisation could lead to inter-sectoral adjustment (European Commission 2005a: 36).

Returning to the automobile industry's position, it is clear that this amounted to a tacit acknowledgement of the discourse of economic constraint advanced by the Commission in its 'Global Europe' communication: the EU faced competitive pressures to which it *had* to respond by pursuing trade liberalisation policies. Whether it had truly internalised DG Trade's discourse on the 'necessity' of liberalisation or simply felt compelled to invoke it in order to oppose the agreement is difficult to tell, but in either case it becomes evident that these ideas had served DG Trade's purposes well. As Krebs and Jackson (2007: 36) note, the purpose of rhetoric can be seen as coercive in that it is irrelevant whether an idea has been internalised; all that matters is that 'the claimant's opponents have been talked into a corner'. Indeed, in order to challenge ACEA's argument that the FTA did not *liberalise sufficiently*, all DG Trade had to do was retort that the FTA 'has real economic value and opportunity for both sides. This deal will create new market opportunities for EU business, including the car sector. European companies in industrial production, agricultural sectors and services are very keen that we conclude these negotiations as soon as possible' (European Commission 2009a). The Commission was thus able to isolate ACEA by arguing that the agreement served all European economic interests. In fact, the Commission's discourse on the necessity of liberalisation was so powerful that ACEA was often dismissed by other European interest groups as a protectionist hangover that had failed to adapt to the changing nature of the global economy.

Getting the agreement signed, however, was only the first hurdle. Another potential obstacle was the ratification of the agreement. Here the EP played a key role – following the entry into force of the Treaty of Lisbon – in having to give its assent to the agreement. As a result and because of the ease of access to policymakers, this is where most of the lobbying efforts of the opposition were concentrated following the conclusion of negotiations with South Korea. A consistent fear voiced by DG Trade officials was that the EP would scupper the agreement, although this idea was possibly being strategically invoked in order to mobilise supporters of the agreement. There was some evidence of supporters of the FTA trying to hurry along ratification – lest the agreement be compromised by protectionist special interests! – by invoking external economic constraints, in particular the so-called 'competitive pressures' already noted above. In a hearing held in June 2010 in the EP's Committee on International Trade (INTA) the representative of the services industry was to stress the agreement's supposed 'benefit of "first-mover" [...] provided that the FTA is provisionally implemented by end 2010' (ESF 2010: 10). As cited above, DG Trade was to underscore this by noting that most sectors of the EU economy were 'keen that we conclude these negotiations as soon as possible' (European Commission 2009a), drawing on business statements as an ideational resource to help isolate opponents to the FTA. This strategy was largely successful. Despite some last-minute hiccups the agreement was not wrecked by the EP.

This is most evident in the case of the safeguard regulation for the agreement (dealing with the implementation of the safeguard clause discussed above) which needed to be ratified by the EP before the final vote on the agreement. INTA approved its version of such a regulation in June 2010 (European Parliament 2010b); the scheduled plenary vote on the measure, however, was postponed in October 2010 in order to pressure the Council into accepting its proposed changes (Brand and Vogel 2010). These included provisions that would have allowed the EP and industry associations to launch safeguard investigations – under the original Commission proposals this would have been the exclusive prerogative of the Commission and Member States – which ostensibly made it easier to restrict imports in automobiles from South Korea. That being said, the EP was not proposing to make significant amendments to the conditions under which it would be possible to invoke such measures. Crucially, the Commission had proposed that such measures be allowed only in circumstances where there was a case of 'serious injury' or a 'threat of serious injury' to domestic producers, a definition which was retained in the EP's amended regulation (European Commission 2010a; European Parliament 2010a). This was in contrast to EU anti-dumping legislation, whose threshold for action was the requirement of 'material injury' or 'threat of material injury' (Council Regulation [EC] No. 384/96). Rather tellingly, the EP was also seeking to modify the Commission's safeguard proposals to ensure they could also be invoked in cases where South Korea did not meet its *liberalisation* obligations under the FTA in NTBs (European Parliament 2010a). This is a provision that owed its existence to ACEA's lobbying efforts – given onerous Korean environmental regulations and other automotive standards which were supposedly scrapped in favour of mutual recognition in the FTA. It points to the success of DG Trade in seizing the discursive ground with its liberalisation rhetoric even in the case of 'protectionist' sabre rattling.

A compromise out of this supposed 'impasse' was reached relatively quickly in December 2010. This informal deal between concerned Members of the European Parliament (MEPs) and the Council 'paved the way' for ratification of the agreement in early 2011 (EurActiv 2010). Even though the EP mostly got its way in the compromise agreement approved at the January 2011 session of INTA (European Parliament 2011a) this victory was largely pyrrhic. Safeguard clauses have only been invoked by the EU in extremely rarely instances – probably as a result of the more onerous burden of establishing 'serious injury' when compared to more lax provisions under anti-dumping regulations (see Hindley 2007). More importantly, although the disagreements over safeguards meant a delay in ratification of the FTA, as the EP flexed its political muscles over competences, this did not lead to a wrecking of the agreement. The EP did not have the power to amend the actual text of the agreement, and, following the momentum created by Member State approval, the December 2010 informal deal on ratification was to be expected.[13] The formal hurdle was then officially cleared in the EP's plenary session of 17 February 2011 (Stearns 2011) with the FTA entering into force in July 2011.

Conclusion

In this chapter I have focused on explaining the content, negotiation and ratification of the EU–Korea FTA, which represents the most tangible embodiment of the 'Global Europe' project so far. In this respect, I have built on some of the themes first explored in Chapter 3 to argue that despite their considerable insight into the politics of trade agreements, rationalist accounts emphasising collective action dynamics do not tell the full story when it comes to the EU's agreement with South Korea.

I have focused on the related issues of *why* DG Trade chose to pursue politically contentious liberalisation in the context of its agreement with South Korea – where market access for European service exporters was obtained in exchange for a liberalisation of trade in automobiles and other manufactured goods – and *how* it was then able to achieve this outcome despite the opposition of a major industry with powerful backers inside the EU policymaking machinery. After providing some background to the agreement in terms of its likely distributive consequences and systemic context, my constructivist approach, focusing on the strategic and reflexive dimensions of discourses of economic constraint, has been able to account for these two developments while also providing an insight into the importance attached by the EU to bilateral services and investment liberalisation.

My findings in this chapter also have wider implications for IPE scholarship, where several authors have remarked on the 'strange non-death of neoliberalism' during the present crisis (Crouch 2011; see also Schmidt and Thatcher 2013). In a similar vein, I have underscored the continued purchase that neoliberal understandings of socioeconomic order hold in trade policymaking circles despite the onset of the Financial Crisis and the power wielded by invoking discourses of external economic constraint. On the first issue, policymakers in DG Trade showed a remarkable faith in the forces of comparative advantage. They believed that, in spite of the EU's overall defensiveness in automobiles, its upmarket producers in this sector could gain from the vertical intra-industry specialisation that would result from a trade deal with what was perceived to be a more mature emerging economy. Secondly, they were able to rhetorically frame this in such a manner as to neutralise any opposition to liberalisation and the potentially costly (and ultimately inter-sectoral, given that the car sector is likely to contract and services likely to expand) adjustments implied. However, it remains to be seen whether in future it will be able to legitimate such a strategy, particularly if the crisis continues biting and if emerging economies move up the value chain. This will threaten the EU's upmarket producers – for whom the EU underwent a painful adjustment process in the first place – which is an issue I return to in Chapter 6.

For now, however, it would be interesting to see whether the neoliberal ideas internalised by policymakers and the discourses invoked strategically to legitimate their agenda have made their mark beyond the EU's 'commercial' trade agenda with emerging economies. In this sense, the EU's longest standing preferential trade arrangement, its relations with the ACP group which are currently being reorganised under the umbrella of so-called EPAs, provide an interesting case. Although seemingly driven by different imperatives, promoting the 'development' of the EU's partners rather than the EU's own 'commercial' gain, the neoliberal paradigm in EU trade policy has also shaped EU policymaking practices in this domain. This development and its broader implications are considered in the following chapter.

5
'Global Europe' and the Economic Partnership Agreements

In 'Global Europe' the Commission was careful to distinguish between Europe's 'main trade interests', predominantly in East and South Asia, and its trade agreements with the ACP – seen as the flagship of its development policy – which supposedly served 'development objectives' (European Commission 2006g: 10–11). Since 'Global Europe' – and although arguably this is not an entirely novel development as commercial considerations have played a role in EU–ACP relations in the past – it has become increasingly difficult to disentangle the EU–ACP relationship from the EU's wider 'commercial' trade relations. After a period of relative neglect under Lamy, Mandelson's DG Trade strongly insisted for the new EPAs being negotiated with ACP states – what amount to 'asymmetrical'[1] FTAs featuring a development assistance component which replace the EU's previous Lomé regime of non-reciprocal trade preferences – to feature 'WTO-plus', regulatory liberalisation provisions; this is notwithstanding the fact that the original justification given for these agreements was one of WTO compliance, as Lomé was judged to be in contravention of multilateral trade rules (see Heron 2013: Ch. 2). These provisions, in turn, have borne a striking resemblance to the texts of several of the EU's 'Global Europe' FTAs.

What is interesting here is that a similar demarcation between 'commercial' and 'developmental' policy has also found itself into much of the existing scholarly literature on EU–ACP relations, which has often worked within a rational institutionalist framework similar to that used to study EU trade policy more generally. While such authors may have recognised that the EU–ACP relationship has not been immune from commercial considerations, the focus of their accounts has been on the *functional* differentiation existing between two different sets of bureaucracies (DG Trade and DG Development) with divergent interests and involved in embittered 'turf wars' (Stevens 2000; see also, amongst others, Elgström and Pilegaard 2008; Faber and Orbie 2009; Holland and Doidge 2012). Thus, while this body of work may have identified the recent entwinement of EU trade and development policy during the EPA negotiations, this has been seen as the product of bureaucratic reorganisation (the shifting of responsibility for negotiating EU–ACP trade agreements from DG Development to DG Trade). This, however, does not explain either the timing of the current EPA agenda (which came after DG Trade assumed responsibility for EU–ACP trade in 1999); the fact that policymakers in DG Development and DG Trade share similar (neoliberal) ideas about trade-led development or that the content of the EPAs ultimately reflected these policymaking priorities. Although those developing a critical/neo-Gramscian approach to the study of EU–ACP trade relations have emphasised the role of these neoliberal discourses in shaping EU policy towards the ACP (for instance, Hurt 2003; Nunn and Price 2004), these accounts are embedded in a historical materialist framework that tends to overstate the hegemony of such ideas (as they are seen to originate with the dominant transnational capitalist class). This is hardly consistent with the widespread (and largely successful) resistance to the EPAs, with only one region so far (the Caribbean) signing a full agreement with the EU.

In this chapter I therefore recast the study of EU–ACP trade relations in terms of a constructivist IPE perspective. The aim is not to offer a holistic account of the EPAs but rather to explain a series of interrelated developments: why WTO-plus liberalisation has been sought so strenuously by the Commission from these agreements; why these provisions have been so similar to those sought in the EU's commercial FTAs and why this development has coincided with the turn towards bilateralism, with the EPAs becoming 'part and parcel' of the EU's preferential trade strategy. My framework allows me to focus on the distinct role played by particular actors and neoliberal ideas in the EPA negotiations; as a result, I can also accommodate the fact that, despite the strategic invocation of the same discourse that allowed it to overcome opposition to the EU–Korea FTA, the EU has been less than successful in its efforts to achieve significant 'behind-the-border' liberalisation in ACP countries. The broader objective of situating EU–ACP trade relations within the wider context of EU trade relations is also very important. For one, it illustrates the all-encompassing nature of the neoliberal coordinative discourse that has shaped both 'Global Europe' and the EPAs (and allowed interest groups to play a prominent role in influencing policymakers on both) and the rhetoric of external constraint invoked in defence of both sets of agreements. This is particularly relevant in light of Commission attempts to label 'commercial' and 'developmental' trade agendas as distinct and separate developments. For another, the failure of DG Trade's discursive strategy in this instance is analytically significant for the future conduct of EU trade policy.

The rest of this chapter is organised as follows. In the first section I begin by providing the historical background on the EU–ACP relationship before charting the more recent convergence of the EU's 'commercial' and 'developmental' trade agendas. In the second section I consider this issue in more detail by comparing the services and investment provisions of the EU's EPA with the Caribbean region to those in its 'Global Europe' FTAs. The determinants of this convergence, interest group activism and, more importantly, the Commission's internalised neoliberal discourse, are considered in the third section. In the fourth section I focus on the rhetoric deployed in defence of the EPAs and consider its relative failure. The implications of this development for the future conduct of EU trade policy are briefly considered in the final section, in which I also bring the chapter to a close.

Charting the convergence of the EU's 'developmental' and 'commercial' trade agendas

The story of the EU's relations with developing countries begins with the Treaty of Rome, which saw the French successfully spread the burden of maintaining their colonial relationship with (largely) African territories.[2] The Treaty granted the 'Associates' duty-free access to the European market behind the protective wall of the common external tariff as well as financial assistance in the form of the European Development Fund (EDF). These arrangements lasted until 1962 – by which time most of France's former colonies had gained independence – when they were succeeded by the Yaoundé Conventions that foresaw a continuation of reverse preferences (in other words, the Associates had to continue reciprocating EU preferences) and the EDF (Ravenhill 1985: 48–57).

The true watershed in the EU's relationship with the developing world would not arrive until the First Lomé Convention of 1975, signed for an initial period of five years (and subsequently renewed three times, in 1979, 1984 and 1989, in the latter case for a period of 10 years). It saw the expansion of the EU's preferential arrangement to include a further 46 African, Caribbean and Pacific states, leading to the formation of the group of the same name. More importantly, non-reciprocity replaced the reverse preferences of Yaoundé and a series of (for the ACP) extremely profitable commodity protocols for key agricultural products were established, guaranteeing prices above world market rates as a result of being tied into the market-distorting CAP (Ravenhill 1985). Ultimately, Lomé represented an important exception to the liberal (and GATT-oriented) regime of the CCP (much like the CAP) in that it was not compliant with Article XXIV (which had provided an exemption from MFN for free trade areas) or the emergent principle of 'special and differential' treatment (because it discriminated between developing countries). That is of course not to say that Lomé was impervious to EU commercial considerations – in particular a concern with maintaining old colonial economic relationships and a steady supply of raw materials (Gibb 2000: 461–2) – but rather that it represented a distinct and separate trading arrangement.

It is clear that Lomé – albeit reflecting greater bargaining power on behalf of the ACP in the 1970s context of 'commodity power' and calls for a New International Economic Order (Ravenhill 1985; Gibb 2000) – did not eliminate the inherent asymmetry of the relationship; it was based on EU largesse in bestowing non-reciprocal trade preferences on recipient countries. By the 1990s granting one-way trade preferences and development assistance to Third World nations seemed far less strategically pressing in a post–Cold War setting (Crawford 1996: 514–15). More importantly, the principle of non-reciprocal trade preferences seemed to jar with the increasing neoliberal and multilateral orientation of EU trade policy following the completion of the SMP. EU support for the judicialisation of the trading system put it on collision course with those WTO members opposed to the discriminatory Lomé import regime. This was most visibly the case for the banana protocol, where a series of unfavourable rulings at the WTO's strengthened Dispute Settlement Body dogged EU policymakers. Although it is worth remembering that the origins of this dispute actually lay in the application of Single Market legislation (Alter and Meunier 2006), the repercussions of these rulings were largely felt in the context of EU–ACP relations. They were, in fact, the immediate cause behind a Commission policy U-turn on non-reciprocal trade preferences. In the seminal 1996 'Green Paper on Relations between the European Union and the ACP Countries' – considered a turning point in trade relations between both parties (Holland and Doidge 2012: 65–8) – the Commission argued that these rulings had 'undermined the principles underpinning Lomé trade preferences, in particular those on non-reciprocity and stability' (European Commission 1996b: 10–11).

A number of authors, from a (largely) critical IPE tradition, have argued that WTO compliance only became an issue for the EU–ACP relationship in the 1990s because the EU wanted it to, as it *could* have sought another waiver to exempt the ACP trade regime from compliance with the GATT/WTO principle of non-discrimination (for example, Gibb 2000; Hurt 2003). However, regardless of whether the EU could have resisted WTO pressure, it is clear that the recalibration of EU–ACP trade relations not only coincided, but was also significantly driven by the EU's turn to multilateralism in its commercial relations (see also Heron 2013: Ch. 2). The parallel is also apparent in the 1996 'Green Paper', which was very sceptical of the record of trade preferences under Lomé. It noted that they had failed to promote export growth or diversification and plumped for 'differentiated reciprocity' in EU–ACP trade relations. In other words, the 'Green Paper' called for free trade between both parties (albeit on the basis of 'asymmetrical' liberalisation commitments) in order to better 'integrate' the ACP into the world economy (European Commission 1996b). The Commission thus pushed to replace Lomé with the Cotonou Agreement in 2000 – rather than seek a renewal of the waiver at the WTO. This agreement foresaw the creation of a series of reciprocal EPAs between the EU and separate ACP 'regions', six of which were subsequently identified by the Commission: the Caribbean, the Pacific, West, Central, Eastern and Southern, and Southern Africa.[3] The EPAs were meant to be completed by December 2007, when the EU's transitional waiver for non-reciprocal trade preferences expired.

What is particularly interesting at this juncture is that these EPAs, albeit having been brought about by the shift towards multilateralism, were largely subordinated to the EU's broader multilateral strategy in the Doha Round, much as the Lomé principle of non-reciprocity had fallen by the wayside when it became politically contentious in the WTO. Commissioner Lamy reportedly showed little interest in negotiating the EPAs. This was reflected in the fact that the talks – lacking a significant push from the EU side – were extremely slow-moving during this period, with the specific regional EPA negotiations only having commenced with all regions by 2004 after a series of 'all-ACP' framework talks (ECDPM 2006: 1). Similarly, Lamy (albeit inadvertently) undermined the basis of EPAs by offering least-developed countries (LDCs) duty-free and quota-free access to the European market under the 'Everything But Arms' (EBA) initiative. The intention here appears to have been to strengthen the EU's hand in the ongoing multilateral trade talks in two ways. Firstly, it showcased the EU's developmental credentials in an effort to get developing countries to support the launch of the Doha

Round (van den Hoven 2004: 264). It also contributed to 'constructing' an 'imperative for reform' of the (heavily protected) EU sugar market to 'make it compatible with its wider [multilateral] trade agenda' (Richardson 2009: 675). EBA, however, also removed an incentive for such states to sign an EPA, as preferential market access to the EU market was guaranteed without the need to make (any) reciprocal concessions.[4]

Lamy's attitude was also reflected in the modest content of the EPA agenda under his tenure. In contrast to the EU's ambitious wish-list for Doha – which saw the EU struggle against developing country opposition to include the Singapore Issues in the Doha agenda – the EU barely touched upon these WTO-plus issues in its first two years of talks with ACP countries. Investment, competition policy and government procurement were not even on the table at this stage, while in both Cotonou and the EPA mandate (approved by Member States in June 2002) the EU stated that it 'should be prepared to further postpone the start of negotiations [in services]' (European Commission 2002: 5). Thus, in the first phase of all-ACP negotiations (2002–04) the EU was principally concerned with resisting the inclusion by the ACP of GATS mode 4 (the supply of a service through the presence of natural persons) in the negotiations rather than pushing an offensive agenda. The outcome of this first round of talks was that services liberalisation was to be 'adapted to the level of ACP countries and their sectors and specific constraints and underpinned by principles of [special and differential treatment], asymmetry and positive regional discrimination' (te Velde 2004: 4).

The Economic Partnership Agreements and the shift towards bilateralism[5]

What is particularly interesting, therefore, is that at the beginning of Mandelson's tenure (in late 2004) EPA negotiations not only picked up speed but that WTO-plus issues began to feature prominently in the EU's negotiating strategy. Crucially, the EU's changed approach to negotiating the EPAs coincided with the rise of the 'Global Europe' agenda of regulatory liberalisation. By strongly pushing for the inclusion of WTO-plus issues in its negotiation with the ACP, DG Trade was going beyond the Cotonou Agreement and exceeding the original negotiating mandate that had been set back in 2002 (see European Commission 2002). This approach – closely associated with Commissioner Mandelson – was the subject of vociferous complaints from the ACP states and numerous NGOs (which mounted a relatively successful campaign in opposition to the EPAs), even attracting criticism from some EU Member States such as the UK (Beattie 2006; for more on these developments, see below).

The increasing controversy surrounding the EPA negotiations was naturally only in part driven by concerns related to the inclusion of WTO-plus issues. Issues such as transition periods, standstill and MFN provisions for goods were similarly, if not more, polarising, as they were of direct relevance to ACP commodity exports. What is more, many LDCs, which were already in receipt of non-reciprocal trade preferences under EBA since 2001, had little incentive to liberalise their trade with the EU or with non-LDC ACP states.

This being said, the WTO-plus agenda has been as central to the EPA talks for both parties as it has been to the FTA negotiations initiated under the 'Global Europe' strategy. For one, the serious difficulties encountered have not deterred DG Trade from strongly pursuing regulatory liberalisation in the context of EU–ACP trade relations; for another, most ACP countries have until now resisted considerable pressure from the Commission to incorporate these issues into the agreements. Thus, as the December 2007 deadline for the completion of full EPA talks loomed – and only negotiations with the Caribbean region were nearing completion – the Commission devised a system whereby it would continue to offer non-LDC ACP members (which were not covered by EBA) market access (under a new instrument known as the 'Market Access Regulation'; see European Commission 2007d) in exchange for signature of 'goods-only' interim EPAs (IEPAs). Crucially, the IEPAs that the EU did sign included, more often than not, rendezvous clauses for both services and investment (under a single chapter, as in the 'Minimum Platform') and a number of other Singapore Issues. These included, in many cases, public procurement, which had not even been mentioned in the Cotonou Agreement. The clauses set the parameters for future negotiations on a 'full EPA' to include such regulatory provisions and were still largely perceived as an imposition by a significant number of ACP countries.[6] As a result, only some (mostly preference-dependent commodity exporting non-LDCs) have to this date either signed or initialled an IEPA with the EU, with many of these delaying their signature of the agreements and application of reciprocal trade preferences (see Table 5.1). Moreover, the deadlines stipulated in a number of rendezvous clauses have all been missed; in the case of Cameroon, this deadline even *preceded* its signature of the agreement! Since then, the ACP's footdragging has continued, as no negotiation for a full EPA had been concluded at the time of writing (September 2013), save with the Caribbean region. In sum, the opposition encountered by Commission negotiators and their persistence in pursuing the WTO-plus agenda only highlight the centrality of the issue to the EPA negotiations in the post–'Global Europe' context.

Table 5.1 Services, investment and other Singapore Issues in IEPAs

	Status of Agreement (as of September 2013)	Rendezvous Clause for Services and Investment	Rendezvous Clause for Competition	Rendezvous Clause for Public Procurement
Central Africa IEPA	Only Cameroon (initialed Dec 2007, signed Jan 2009).	Yes, specific 'services and establishment' rendezvous clause (deadline: 1 Jan, 2009)	Yes (deadline: 1 Jan, 2009)	Yes (deadline: 1 Jan, 2009)
Western Africa IEPAs	Separate agreement with Ghana (initialed Dec 2007, signature pending).	Yes (deadline: end of 2008)	Yes (deadline: end of 2008)	No
	Separate agreement with Cote d'Ivoire (initialed Dec 2007, signed Nov 2008).	Yes (no deadline, but the parties are 'encouraged' to conclude a full EPA covering this issue by 'end 2008')	Yes (no deadline, but the parties are 'encouraged' to conclude a full EPA covering this issue by 'end 2008')	Yes (no deadline, but the parties are 'encouraged' to conclude a full EPA covering this issue by 'end 2008')
East African Community (EAC) IEPA	Initialed Nov 2007, signature pending.	Yes (no deadline)	Yes (no deadline)	Yes, but only transparency (no deadline)

Eastern and Southern Africa IEPA	Ratified and provisionally applied by Madagascar, Mauritius, the Seychelles and Zimbabwe (May 2012; signed Aug 2009; initialed by all Nov–Dec 2007). Signature pending from Comoros and Zambia.	Services but not investment (no deadline)	No	No
Pacific IEPA	Ratified and provisionally applied by Papua New Guinea (May 2011, signed July 2009); signed by Fiji (Dec 2009). Originally initialed in Nov 2007 by both countries.	No	No	No
Southern African Development Community (SADC) (minus South Africa) IEPA	Signed by Botswana, Lesotho, Mozambique and Swaziland (June, 2009, initialed by all Dec 2009) Signature pending from Namibia.	Yes (deadline: 31 Dec, 2008)	Yes, but only cooperation (no deadline)	Yes, but only cooperation (no deadline)

Sources: The texts of various agreements and European Commission (2013e).

While the dominant institutionalist perspective would attribute the changed approach to the EPAs to a reshuffle of competences for EU–ACP trade that cemented DG Trade's hold in the Commission bureaucracy (Ravenhill 2004: 130–1; Holland and Doidge 2012: 104, 130), the Commission unit responsible for trade with the ACP had already been transferred from DG Development at the beginning of Lamy's tenure and at his insistence. Much as for the 'Global Europe' strategy, there was no institutional catalyst sufficient to explain the policy shift. In contrast, I argue in the remainder of this chapter that these developments represented a convergence between the EU–ACP trade negotiations and the EU's much wider 'Global Europe' strategy – which spawned a generation of FTAs with a very strong regulatory component. The shift towards seeking bilateral market opening (with a strong regulatory dimension) meant that the EPAs were no longer subordinated to potentially incompatible multilateral trade aims (for example, offering EBA in order to get developing countries to support the Doha Agenda), but rather could (and did) become part and parcel of the EU's preferential trade strategy.

Services and investment provisions in the EU–Caribbean Forum Economic Partnership Agreement[7]

The EPA negotiations with the Caribbean Forum (CARIFORUM) – the EU's interlocutor in the region, representing the Caribbean Community (CARICOM) in addition to the Dominican Republic – were completed in December 2007, with all countries (save Haiti) signing the agreement by October 2008. It has been provisionally applied since 29 December 2008 (except for Haiti, which only signed in December 2009) and includes chapters on services and investment, competition and government procurement. This is the first and only 'full' EPA signed by the EU to date with any of the ACP regions and thus provides a useful insight into the drivers of the EU's EPA strategy, especially into the implementation of the EU's services and investment agenda. As has become apparent in previous chapters, this is a key component of the EU's 'Global Europe' strategy – in particular the drive to seek to match (and, if possible, exceed) the gains obtained by commercial rivals. As a result, I compare these provisions to those found in the commercially oriented 'Minimum Platform' and the 'Global Europe' FTAs which are based on this template (the EU–Korea FTA and draft mandates for negotiation with India and ASEAN dating from early 2007).

The first point to note about the CARIFORUM EPA services and investment 'Title' is that it very closely follows the template of the 'Minimum

Platform'. As a result, it mirrors the EU–Korea FTA in many respects. Firstly, 'Title II' of the EPA covers provisions for 'Investment, Trade in Services and E-Commerce', following the EU practice established by the 'Minimum Platform' of including services and investment under a single rubric. Secondly, the agreement includes a review clause for services and establishment provisions that opens the door to a future upgrading of liberalisation commitments. Most importantly, the CARIFORUM EPA includes an MFN clause for establishment in Article 70, with a restrictive exemption for regional economic integration agreements for the CARIFORUM Signatory Parties. All of these provisions – which are derived from the 'Minimum Platform' – are also to be found in the EU–Korea FTA and in the draft mandates for the EU–India and EU–ASEAN FTAs (European Commission 2007a,b).

Despite these similarities, officials in the European Commission are keen to highlight a supposedly key difference between the EU–CARIFORUM EPA and the EU's more commercially minded FTAs which, in their eyes, distinguishes the EPA from the EU's 'Global Europe' FTAs. Unlike in the 'Minimum Platform', the EU–Korea FTA and the draft mandates for FTAs with India and ASEAN, the MFN and the review clause in the EU–CARIFORUM EPA are to be supposedly applied with a view towards respecting the 'special and differential' needs of the ACP signatories. Firstly, while in the EPA the EU offered full MFN treatment – without even an exemption for regional economic integration agreements as found in the EU–Korea FTA – the Caribbean signatories were only required to offer the EU MFN in the case of an agreement they signed with a 'major trading economy' (Article 70, paragraph 1b). Secondly, even if a Caribbean ACP state were to sign a relevant agreement with such a state this would not necessarily trigger the application of MFN automatically (as in the EU–Korea FTA); rather, it would lead to consultations between the EU and CARIFORUM as to whether MFN treatment should be extended to the European party (Article 70, paragraph 5). These provisions owe their existence to the spirit voiced in Cotonou of offering 'special and differential' treatment to ACP service suppliers and (albeit subsequently, as investment did not feature in the Cotonou Agreement as an area for negotiation) investors. Finally, the review clause for the EPA is not as onerous as the one for the EU–Korea FTA, as it does not include a provision to address outstanding 'obstacles to investment' (Article 7.16 in the EU–Korea FTA; Article 74 in the EPA).

That being said, this contractually enshrined asymmetry – which advocates of the EPA are eager to stress – is less significant than first meets the eye. In other words, it does not detract from the argument that the services and investment provisions in both the EU–CARIFORUM EPA and EU–Korea FTA are driven by similar commercial imperatives. The EPA's caveat that MFN treatment is only to be applied by the ACP parties in the case of an agreement with a 'major trading economy' is still designed to address a perceived threat from the EU's major competitors for markets. The definition of the former encompasses not only any developed country, but any state (or even group of states acting collectively as part of a customs or other economic union) accounting for a meaningful percentage of world merchandise exports – 1 per cent in the case of single states, 1.5 per cent in the case of economic unions. A United Nations Economic Commission for Latin America and the Caribbean (ECLAC) study found that this threshold includes most emerging economies with rapidly growing services markets such as China, Brazil (as well as the wider MERCOSUR) and ASEAN (ECLAC 2008: 32). As if to underscore this point, officials in the European Commission have justified the inclusion of the MFN clause for services and investment by stressing that they do not want the EU to be at a competitive disadvantage as a result of having signed EPAs.

Similarly, the non-automaticity of the MFN clause and the less onerous review clause are in themselves not as generous concessions to the ACP as some would suggest. Although it would in principle give Caribbean states some leeway in their discussions with the EU when either clause was invoked, it remains to be seen to what extent the ACP will be able to resist EU pressure to extend MFN treatment or liberalise investment further given the power asymmetries inherent in the EU–ACP relationship (Heron 2011; Bishop *et al.* 2013). These asymmetries have arguably been heightened by the fragmentation of the ACP group during the EPA negotiations, which has deprived the ACP of a collective voice in its talks with the EU (see Babarinde and Faber 2005). Underlining this is the fact that Korean negotiators, unlike their Caribbean counterparts, were able to dilute the EU's desired MFN exemption; the EU–CARIFORUM EPA MFN exemption more narrowly conforms to the wording of the 'Minimum Platform' than that found in the EU–Korea FTA. It is more restrictive, exempting fewer potential agreements from an invocation of the MFN clause (the EPA refers to an exemption for regional economic integration agreements creating an 'internal market' or 'requiring the parties thereto to approximate their legislation' [Article 70, paragraph 2], whereas in the EU–Korea FTA, any agreement with a 'significantly higher level of obligations' is excluded [Article 7.14, paragraph 2]). What is more, it is clear that the MFN and review clauses are unlikely to serve the interests of the ACP signatories by allowing them to benefit from the concessions the EU might make to third parties. Crucially, they do not apply to the main area of offensive interest in services for the CARIFORUM signatory parties, namely mode 4 (the presence of natural persons), where the EU had defensive interests during the negotiations. In sum, despite the EU's supposed commitment to 'special and different' treatment for the ACP, the EU–CARIFORUM EPA was tailored to further the commercial objectives embodied by the 'Minimum Platform', namely, ensuring at least parity with its most significant competitors in (mode 3) service delivery.

The drivers of convergence: Interest groups and neoliberal economic discourse

The dominant institutionalist paradigm in EU trade policy has difficulty in accounting for the growing convergence between the EU's 'commercial' and 'developmental' trade agendas as this did not occur against the backdrop of any significant shift in policymaking competences between DGs in the European Commission.[8] Instead, I trace this increasing convergence to the rise of 'Global Europe', suggesting common drivers for both sets of agreements. In Chapter 3 – building on IPE models of interest group activism – I highlighted the importance of EU service suppliers in driving the wider 'Global Europe' agenda as well as the more specific bilateral services and investment agenda embodied in the 'Minimum Platform'. Similarly, in the case of EPAs, it was clear that in the wake of the 'failure' of the EU's 'multilateralism-first' strategy, the ESF found itself drawn to the potential market access gains offered by preferential liberalisation with the ACP. Thus, in a February 2007 position paper on FTAs, it

> dr[ew] attention to [among other FTA negotiations in progress] [...] the talks under way to create economic partnership agreements (EPAs) with the African, Caribbean and Pacific (ACP) countries. [...] *To the extent that the Doha Round does not yield the early and significant results on services which ESF would like to see, this range of negotiations should provide an alternative means of making progress.*
>
> ESF (2007a: 3–4, emphasis added)

As the December 2007 deadline for the conclusion of EPA negotiations approached without any deal in sight, the ESF addressed a number of letters to Mandelson in which it underscored its interest in a successful outcome to the talks on services. The first, dated April 2007, 'note[d] that the negotiations to establish economic partnership agreements [...] are now reaching a crucial phase. ESF fully supports these negotiations and is of the view that they should also include substantive liberalisation commitments for services' (ESF 2007b). With the deadline looming in November 2007, the tone of the ESF's subsequent letter to the Commissioner was even more insistent. It noted that the

> interim agreements can in no way be seen by the negotiating partners, or by industry in Europe, as a satisfactory result. To unleash the potential of trade to create employment and growth in the private sector of the EPA regions, ESF encourages the continuation of the negotiating process so that the EPAs can be concluded within a reasonable deadline and that the outstanding issues such as services and intellectual property rights can be satisfactorily resolved.
>
> ESF (2007d: 1)

In this vein, it specifically requested that the Commissioner 'ensure that the interim agreements contain binding commitments to continue negotiations' as '[e]xperience has shown that a review clause does not always fulfil its purpose' (ESF 2007d: 2).

Recent scholarship in this area has underscored the role of this services lobby in explaining the convergence between the EU's 'developmental' and 'commercial' trade agreements, basing itself on a similar (albeit less detailed) examination of their respective services and investment provisions (Heron and Siles-Brügge 2012). This work's argument, which I have expanded upon and refined above, largely draws on the rationalist IPE models of preferential liberalisation that I have considered in Chapter 2. Although it is not too far a jump from the emerging markets emphasised in such models to the ACP, there are still a number of open questions. Most significantly, there is the puzzle of why the Commission, and more specifically DG Trade, would not only heed the arguments of services lobbyists but also go as far as to provide them with a platform – a set of regional trade workshops organised to promote the EPAs (see ESF 2008a,b) – to make their case, especially when negotiating agreements that fulfilled 'developmental' rather than 'commercial' objectives. I should underscore at this stage that the Commission had strongly argued for a distinction between such agreements (the EPAs) and the 'commercial' FTAs negotiated under the auspices of the 'Global Europe' agenda. 'Global Europe' made only a passing reference to the EPAs, noting that Europe's economic interests lay elsewhere. Moreover, in describing the CARIFORUM EPA, the Commission was to note that

[b]y explicitly taking into account the development objectives, needs and interests of the CARIFORUM region the EPA is very different from every other trade agreement negotiated up to now between developed and developing countries. This comprehensive approach is what constitutes the development dimension of the EPA and all the provisions of the EPA are designed to support it.

European Commission (2009b: 1)

This demarcation between the EU's supposedly 'developmental' and 'commercial' trade agendas has also been repeatedly stressed by EU trade policymakers. As a result, one needs to turn to the realm of ideas – and specifically those ideas internalised by policymakers (and which manifested themselves as coordinative discourse) – to understand why the Commission was so forthcoming to interest group arguments that stressed the need for WTO-plus liberalisation. Here one also finds further evidence of the convergence between the free-trade discourse underpinning 'Global Europe' and DG Trade's vision of trade-led development.

The entwined neoliberal discourses of 'competitiveness' and 'development'[9]

It is clear that there was a common (coordinative) discourse underpinning both agendas that one can trace back to the harbinger of change in EU–ACP relations, the 1996 'Green Paper' authored by officials in the trade unit in DG Development. As I noted earlier, this has been seen by many authors to mark the beginning of a neoliberal reorientation of the EU's relations with ACP countries. If one examines the document somewhat more closely, one finds that its pronouncements largely correspond to the coordinative discourse emerging at around the same time in the context of the EU's broader commercial relations and which was epitomised by the 1996 'Market Access Strategy' (see European Commission 1996a; for more on the selection and coding documents in this section, see the Appendix). Trade liberalisation was a *desirable* objective to pursue to enhance competitiveness (in this case of the ACP), but this was an outcome that was ultimately *contingent* on political factors. In this vein, although the 'Green Paper' identified a number of possible future options for the EU–ACP relationship (including the Lomé *status quo*), it was plumping for the principle of 'uniform reciprocity'. This would 'require all ACP countries to extend reciprocity [...] after a common transitional period, to EC exports' (European Commission 1996b: 65). The 'Green Paper' argued that this would help maintain, even enhance, the security and predictability of the preferences and by opening and 'locking in' the import regime of the ACP countries it will lend credibility to their trade policies in the eyes of domestic and foreign investors. As a consequence an enhanced pull on FDI can be expected, as well as a further impulse from domestic investors.

European Commission (1996b: 65c)

The main problem in the eyes of the drafters of the 'Green Paper' in DG Development was not the principle of reciprocity itself but rather the 'feasibility' of having *'all ACP countries agree* on a single "plan" and "schedule" [...] which takes into account their [differing needs]' (European Commission 1996b: 65c–d, emphasis added). This explains the 'region'-based approach to the negotiations eventually adopted in Cotonou. Moreover, there was recognition of the fact that 'many ACP countries lack the human skills and the administrative capability to engage in free trade negotiations with the EU' (European Commission 1996b: 65c). Although there was no mention of regulatory liberalisation as such, policymakers working on 'developmental' trade agreements in DG Development shared a similar assessment of the benefits of trade liberalisation as their counterparts working in DG Trade, who had authored the 1996 'Market Access Strategy' at around the same time. For one, this suggests that arguments stressing inter-institutional conflict between both DGs are overblown, given the shared neoliberal paradigm. For another, it highlights the discursive roots of the future convergence of the EU's developmental and commercial trade agendas.

WTO-plus issues would not figure prominently in the EPA negotiations until the arrival of Peter Mandelson. That is not to say that Commission officials dismissed the value of negotiating such issues with developing countries (including the ACP) in the multilateral context. DG Trade was to underscore the value of WTO-plus liberalisation for 'sustainable development' in a 1999 communication on EU objectives for what was then still known as the 'Millennium Round' (European Commission 1999). It was also to subsequently pursue such regulatory liberalisation in the context of its ambitious Singapore Issues agenda for the Doha Round. However, with the multilateralist discourse dominant, the EU–ACP relationship was subordinated to the EU's commercial (and developmental) objectives in Doha. At this point in time, the EU saw ambitious regulatory liberalisation in a multilateral context as inherently more desirable (both in terms of promoting sustainable development and serving its commercial interests) than in a bilateral (or, in the case of the ACP, 'bi-regional') context (see European Commission 1999, 2002).

The arrival of Peter Mandelson meant a more activist neoliberal turn in the EU's trade discourse. This was first spelt out in the September 2005 'Trade and Competitiveness Issues Paper', which represented a 'leap' when compared to previous discursive statements – in particular the 1996 'Market Access Strategy' (see Chapter 3). Rather than simply advocate free trade policies to serve EU competitiveness – seen as the ability of its high-end producers of goods and services to compete on global markets – the 'Issues Paper' crucially called for the EU to kill two birds with one stone by trading away Europe's remaining 'pockets of protection' in exchange for market access for its upmarket producers. This more activist view vis-à-vis the 1996 'Market Access Strategy' (and its multilateralist commercial strategy) regarding the desirability of pursuing trade liberalisation was mirrored in developmental trade discourse by a similar 'leap' in Commission thinking in relation to the 1996 'Green Paper' (and its multilateral development strategy). As will become more apparent below, this marked the convergence of DG Trade's competitiveness-driven 'commercial' and 'developmental' trade discourses.

In this vein, officials in Mandelson's DG Trade – which was now responsible for setting EU–ACP trade policy – shared the 1996 'Green Paper's' positive-sum view of free trade. The discourse, however, was more activist in that whereas the 1996 'Green Paper' had stressed 'feasibility' issues in negotiating free trade with ACP countries – which it argued could 'not be expected' to 'meet the conditions' or be 'capable of, or [be] willing to enter into, FTA negotiations with the EU' (European Commission 1996b: 65d) – DG Trade was now stressing that these capacity issues deriving from poor economic governance arrangements *should* be addressed through the EPA negotiations; the argument was that the EU should promote regional integration as a first step towards negotiating agreements covering regulatory liberalisation with the EU. In this context, DG Trade argued in an internal working paper in November 2005 that the EPAs were

> part of the overall effort to build up the economic governance framework, the stable, transparent and predictable rules necessary to lower the costs of doing business, attract fresh domestic or foreign investment and make ACP producers more diversified and competitive.
>
> European Commission (2005c: 6)

The importance of this shift in outlook was stressed by actors in DG Trade themselves. Foremost among them, Commissioner Mandelson publicly spoke of the need for 'a new focus' in EU–ACP relations so that 'their development focus is strengthened'; in other words, they needed to become 'a tool of "progressive trade opening"' (Mandelson 2005a: 1). Regulatory liberalisation was now seen as central, while EPAs needed to 'be comprehensive, dealing with all the rules and issues that concern private investors and traders' (European Commission 2005c: 30).[10] This was indeed new as the 1996 'Green Paper' had not mentioned WTO-plus liberalisation in the context of the EPAs (which also took a backseat during the multilateralist period). It also mimicked the emphasis placed in the 'Issues Paper' on promoting the competitiveness of EU producers by ensuring the appropriate (de)regulatory environment, which it argued had been strongly facilitated by the pan-European Single Market.

This latter point highlights another important discursive parallel between both agendas that began emerging around this time, namely the increasing emphasis placed on facilitating deregulatory regional integration in the EPAs as an outcome rather than simply seeing it as a pre-requisite for negotiations to proceed. As noted above, the 1996 'Green Paper' had stressed not the particular *desirability* of regionally 'differentiated reciprocity' but rather its *feasibility* given disparities between ACP countries in both capability and the desire to liberalise. In this vein, Article 35 (2) of the Cotonou Agreement stated that 'economic and trade cooperation [between the EU and the ACP] shall build on regional integration initiatives of ACP States' while Article 37 (5) noted that 'negotiations of economic partnership agreements will be undertaken [...] taking into account the regional integration process within the ACP'. Following Mandelson's arrival, however, promoting regional integration among the ACP itself became one of DG Trade's principle aims in the EPAs. WTO-plus liberalisation was to play a key role here. In response to the resistance offered by members of the Southern African Development Community (SADC) negotiating group to the inclusion of these issues DG Trade was to remark that

> it should also be made very clear [to SADC] that to base the future EPA on market access provisions only, and leave aside all references to regulatory supply-side commitments *(e.g. Services, Investment; Government procurement; trade facilitation; IPR, environment, labour and Competition)*, is not an acceptable option. These issues are the essence of the EPA sustainable development package.
>
> European Commission (2006i: 8, emphasis in the original)

In response to arguments that the region lacked sufficient capacity to address these issues, DG Trade was to remark that the EU 'should therefore be looking to a solution by which common rules [for the SADC customs union] in these areas would also help to build-up [sic] capacity and assistance, as this would ensure effective implementation' (European Commission 2006i: 8–9). The difference in emphasis when compared to Cotonou is thus quite plain to see. Rather than wait for regional integration to occur before broaching 'new generation issues' – that is, seeing the lack of regional integration as a factor limiting the ability of the ACP to negotiate on such issues – the Commission adopted a more activist approach in pushing for regional integration, seeing regional deregulatory liberalisation as part and parcel of a broader trade agenda. This new emphasis on achieving regional deregulation explains why Commission negotiators pushed so hard for the controversial 'regional integration' clause in their negotiation with the ACP – which would have obliged ACP countries to offer each other any new liberalisation commitments they undertook with the EU (see Meyn 2006: 7–8). In this vein, the document cited above noted menacingly how if 'the region [...] ch[ose] not to make an effort in addressing these issues [...] the EC would find it difficult to improve SADC access to its market' (European Commission 2006i: 8). There was even some talk in Brussels that DG Trade had actively encouraged EAC to break away from the Eastern and Southern African (ESA) region to form its own customs union and negotiate separately with the EU because it represented a successful example of regional integration. The parallels to the neoliberal discourse on the desirability of regional deregulation through the Single Market (as highlighted in the 2005 'Issues Paper') are difficult to overlook. Similar views were also echoed in internal publications written by DG Development, where it underscored the importance of addressing 'supply-side constraints' and the fact that 'the Commission is convinced that the EPAs can play a role in sorting out, reinforcing or accelerating existing [regional] integration efforts' (European Commission 2007d: 27, see also 26–8).

The internalisation of this discourse explains how the Commission's previous agenda of WTO-compatibility in the EPAs became one of ensuring WTO-plus liberalisation instead. As Peter Mandelson and Louis Michel (the Development Commissioner) were to state in a joint memo to fellow Commissioners, 'the [WTO] constraint we face has only been part of the reason for negotiating EPAs. The more important part is the **opportunity** EPAs offer [...] [in terms of] the progressive integration of the ACP into the international economy' (European Commission 2007e: 2, emphasis in the original). Trade liberalisation was thus seen as a *desirable* outcome in the Commission's coordinative discourse throughout the period following the publication of the 1996 'Green Paper', but only under Mandelson did it become part of a wider discursive project centred on the need to ensure competitiveness through bilateral regulatory liberalisation. Turning one's attention to the specific tools of trade policymaking, the emphasis on multilateralism that had marked Lamy's and his predecessor Brittan's tenure was also giving way to an espousal of preferential liberalisation as a legitimate trade policy option, which meant that the EPAs and the EU's commercial trade agenda were no longer antithetical to one another. This was reflected in the EU's 'developmental' agenda, which experienced a flurry of activity on WTO-plus issues after Mandelson's arrival. The discursive parallels I have highlighted between DG Trade's pronouncements on EU–ACP trade relations and the 'Issues Paper' naturally beg the question of whether this truly represented a convergence of DG Trade's coordinative 'developmental' and 'commercial' trade discourse; in other words, one needs to ask whether in addition to seeing regionally coordinated regulatory liberalisation in the ACP as good for *their* development, Commission policymakers also perceived it as an objective to be pursued for the sake of EU *competitiveness*. My argument in this book is that the common *positive-sum* view of free trade served as a discursive bridge between both agendas. Although actors within DG Trade were always careful to stress the benefits from liberalisation to the ACP, which one can assume was a belief *truly* held by such policymakers, there was also an *implicit* acceptance that this would also be of benefit to EU competitiveness.

The idea that development policy could also serve the competitiveness of the EU economy was also explicitly raised in the 2005 'Issues Paper'. This noted the importance of addressing the 'institutional deficiencies' of its 'emerging country partners' by 'ensuring inclusive development'; the rationale was that this would minimise long-term trade adjustment costs in Europe that would result from a situation in which such countries failed to develop and would simply engage in inter-industry trade with the EU (see European Commission 2005a: 35–7). Even more suggestive of the entwinement of the Commission's 'developmental' and 'commercial/competitiveness' discourses was the timing and content of the EU's EPA agenda during Mandelson's tenure. For one, the emergence of an ambitious (de)regulatory agenda in the EPAs coincided with the rise of the 'Global Europe' agenda and its associated coordinative discourse regarding the benefits of trade liberalisation. For another, the parallels between the EU's 'commercial' FTAs and the specific provisions sought from the EPAs are hard to overlook. Here, the only way to reconcile the Commission's stated aim of negotiating a 'development-friendly' agreement, with its insistence on an MFN clause in services and investment to protect itself from the gains of potential competitors (as in the EU–CARIFORUM EPA, following the mould of the 'Minimum Platform'), is by noting how the discourses of development and EU competitiveness have been combined into a single discourse on the shared benefits of trade liberalisation. This faith in neoclassical economic mantra is reflected in the fact that Commission officials dismiss the distributive consequences of liberalisation in such areas as services and government procurement – where EU firms are clearly better placed to compete – by simply invoking the law of comparative advantage. Their argument is that such countries will benefit from having access to top-notch service providers and regionally integrated markets. In the case of the Caribbean, moreover, they went as far as to argue that services liberalisation would even be beneficial for autochthonous suppliers (particularly in mode 4). Crucially, such ideas persisted after the departure on Peter Mandelson, suggesting the important 'staying power' of the 'Global Europe' agenda (see, for example, European Commission 2010e, 2012b).

In sum, I have shown that despite rhetorical attempts to differentiate between both agendas, the EU's 'commercial' and 'developmental' trade discourse was underpinned by a similar neoliberal emphasis on free trade and the importance of regulatory liberalisation. This explains why the EU sought, following the consolidation of the neoliberal paradigm under Mandelson, to pursue WTO-plus rather than just WTO-compatible agreements with the ACP. Returning to the puzzle I raised above, this coordinative discourse also explains why the Commission was not just amenable to the arguments of business groups which pushed for WTO-plus liberalisation, but also actively encouraged their involvement in the EPA negotiations. This points to the important 'reflexive' dimension to economic discourse, specifically how interest groups came to be influential with Commission trade policymakers and how their discursive constructions came to shape the rhetoric of policymakers themselves. Interest groups invoked the same specific arguments as Commission policymakers on the need to attract foreign investors and integrate into the global economy; the ESF (2008a: 7), in particular, argued that services and investment liberalisation would be 'sending a strong signal to foreign investors [...] [reassuring them of the] legal security of investments' while also making a 'contribution to the integration of the [ACP] in the world economy'. This suggested DG Trade's affinity for the message of these lobbyists. In this vein, the fact that the Commission actively encouraged European business to share its perspective at a series of regional workshops is evocative of the concerns first expressed in the 1996 'Market Access Strategy' with mobilising business (specifically exporters) in support of trade liberalisation in the face of potential political opposition. DG Trade even went as far as to actively encourage the formation of a pro-EPA Business Trade Forum for EU–Southern Africa to co-opt African business leaders (Corporate Europe Observatory 2009; see also Langan 2011). Secondly, much as during the drafting of 'Global Europe' and the ratification of the EU–Korea FTA, exporters' pronouncements on the necessity of liberalisation were used as an ideational resource in defence of the EPAs, underscoring DG Trade's strategically invoked discourse of 'no alternative'. This is discussed in more detail in the next section.

Responding to the critics: Economic rhetoric and the Economic Partnership Agreements

The parallels to the EU's 'commercial' trade agenda are not just limited to the internalised, coordinative discourse of the Commission. Much as trading away 'pockets of protection' in the EU–Korea FTA provoked the ire of, among others, the automobile industry, the WTO-plus agenda in the EPAs was resisted by a large number of opponents, predominantly from the community of development-oriented NGOs. The beginnings of their response to the EPAs can be traced to late 2002 and early 2003 when the first critical reports on the negotiations were published (Dür and De Bièvre 2007: 89). The movement gained strength when many of these organisations – which included a number of influential civil society groups from both EU and ACP countries – eventually coalesced around the common banner of the 'Stop EPA' campaign (for membership of this organisation, see EPA Watch 2013). This was founded in April 2004, publicly launched in Europe in October 2004 (in December 2004 for Africa) and gradually gained substantial traction among critically minded NGOs (Dür and De Bièvre 2007: 89–92; Del Felice 2012: 9). Faced with an increasingly activist EPA agenda focused on WTO-plus liberalisation after Mandelson's arrival as Trade Commissioner, one of the key demands of this campaign was that the EU, through its Member States, 'withdraw demands for reciprocity and the negotiation of the Singapore Issues' (EcoNews Africa and Traidcraft 2005: 50). In their eyes such liberalisation had the potential to damage the development potential of such countries while undermining their negotiating position at the WTO (Christian Aid *et al.* 2004: 3).

DG Trade was acutely aware of the increasingly prominent interventions of this group of organisations when it acknowledged in its November 2005 working paper on the EPAs that 'Non State Actors (NSA) have also taken an active interest in EPAs' (European Commission 2005c: 31). It responded with its own high-profile information campaign and process of engagement with NGOs – as exemplified by the Civil Society Dialogue. Although the Commission initially adopted a more conciliatory tone – stressing the need to strengthen the 'developmental' aspect of the EPAs – this position soon hardened (Dür and De Bièvre 2007: 91), most likely in the face of an increasingly influential 'Stop EPA' campaign. Henceforth, Mandelson's DG sought to paint the EPAs and in particular their WTO-plus liberalisation provisions, as *necessary* for the development of the ACP given the *external constraint* posed by globalised markets that such countries had no choice but to integrate into. Thus, for example, in response to the argument from the NGO side that the EPAs represented an EU imposition, DG Trade not only argued that 'this is not true [as] [t]he EU has never said that it would insist on these issues being covered by EPAs', but also stressed

> that there are good development reasons why they should be. Services like telecommunications, banking and construction are the backbone of a growing economy and most ACP countries desperately need to attract foreign investment in these sectors and others. Every ACP investment report published says that breaking the dependence on basic commodity exports requires a transparent secure, rules-based investment climate.
>
> European Commission (2008a: 2)

In the face of global pressures – including 'falling far behind the rest of the developing world in attracting the foreign investment that is vital for development' – opponents of the EPA were simply 'closing the door to investment that Africa [and the other ACP regions] urgently, urgently need[]' (Mandelson 2006a: 2–3). Such arguments would be repeated time after time by officials in DG Trade (see Table 5.2, in which I provide an illustrative selection under the 'communicative discourse' heading). What is particularly interesting to note at this stage is that this rhetoric echoed the competitiveness-based discourse deployed in 'Global Europe' in defence of the Commission's neoliberal commercial agenda of trading away pockets of protection, only that here it was ACP (rather than EU) competitiveness that was being held hostage by external constraints (the need to attract foreign capital). Much like protection in Europe was painted as harmful to the overall competitiveness of the European economy (see European Commission 2006g), commodity-dependence, which in the Commission's discourse had been bred by reliance on market distorting preferences (see European Commission 1996b), 'had seen [Africa] fall far behind the poverty reduction and economic growth of Asia and Latin America'. As a result 'calling for an end to EPA negotiations when there is no credible alternative' to gearing up the ACP economies for competition in the global economy was portrayed as 'playing poker with the livelihoods of those we are trying to help' (Mandelson and Michel 2007). In Mandelson's words, 'there [was] no plan B' (Trade Negotiations Insights 2007: 1). Such arguments were underscored by interest groups such as the ESF and BUSINESSEUROPE (UNICE's new name since 2007), which were given a platform at several regional workshops by DG Trade to extol the virtues (and ultimate necessity) of liberalisation of trade in services (see ESF 2008a,b; Corporate Europe Observatory 2009). Thus, despite its efforts to discursively differentiate between the EPA and 'Global Europe' agendas, the Commission's use of a similar communicative discourse (drawing on business pronouncements as an ideational resource) strongly suggests that both were driven by the same, broad neoliberal commitment to trade liberalisation.

Having taken the first step towards identifying a potential discursive strategy – by locating a communicative discourse of external constraint – the analytical strategy introduced in Chapter 2 suggests that I now need to contrast this communicative discourse to the actor's coordinative discourse. In Table 5.2 I bring this information together to contrast the EU's discourse on WTO-plus liberalisation in the EPAs in these two discursive settings. This shows that there are inconsistencies between the Commission's 'coordinative' and 'communicative' discourses. In the former, while EPAs were 'part of the overall effort to build up the economic governance framework [...] necessary to lower the costs of doing business, attract fresh domestic or foreign investment and make ACP producers more diversified and competitive' this was seen as 'the responsibility of the ACP themselves' albeit with the help of donors and the international community (European Commission 2005c: 6). Similarly, while stressing that SADC negotiators agreed on the importance of regulatory liberalisation, the Commission highlighted that 'its lack of capacity would make the implementation of these commitments more difficult' (European Commission 2006i: 8). Moreover, this justified a potential turn towards 'differentiated solutions between what is applied inside the region, and linked to SADC [sic] state of harmonisation, and what can be further defined at bi-regional level' (European

Table 5.2 Contrasting coordinative and communicative discourse on WTO-plus issues in EPAs

Coordinative Discursive Setting	
Regulatory trade liberalisation in the EPAs as a highly **desirable**, yet politically **contingent**, process which enhances ACP competitiveness.	Commission staff working document (November 2005): '*Capacity constraints remain a challenge. Negotiating a development-oriented EPA is a new experience and ACP regions have to adapt to this scenario.* EPA negotiations go well beyond the traditional focus on ACP market access to include the elements of a regulatory framework conducive to private sector development. The technical and institutional capacity of regional and national institutions and non-state actors, along with political commitment at all levels, are essential ingredients for successful EPAs and the Commission is giving all possible attention to reinforcing them.' (European Commission 2005c: 30, emphasis added)
	Commission staff working document (November 2006): 'In the last EC–SADC Senior Officials meeting SADC underlined that "none of the EC arguments on the importance of trade-related rules is disputed, in substance". *However its lack of capacity* would make the implementation of these commitments more difficult.' (European Commission 2006i: 8, emphasis added)
	Memo from Peter Mandelson and Louis Michel to members of the Commission (December 2007): 'But the constraint we face [in terms of WTO compatibility] has only been part of the reason for negotiating EPAs. The more important part is the **opportunity** EPAs offer. They bring the opportunity to support the progressive integration of the ACP into the international economy and to make sure that the unparalleled *ACP access to the EU markets brings real trade growth and broad-based economic development*.' (European Commission 2007e: 2, emphasis in the original)

(continued)

Table 5.2 (continued)

Communicative Discursive Setting	
Regulatory liberalisation in the EPAs as a **necessary** outcome given the external constraint posed by globalising markets.	Speech by Mandelson (October 2006): '*Africa is trapped by barriers* to inward investment, nationalised industrial fiefdoms and fractured regional markets. [...] Those who dismiss the EU's position in these negotiations as "forcing open" these markets to unwanted EU investment, or accuse the EU of "peddling a corporate agenda" not only misrepresent the EU's intentions, but are wilfully misrepresenting the economic evidence. The only force being applied is by those closing the door to *investment that Africa urgently, urgently needs*.' (Mandelson 2006a: 2–3, emphasis added)
	Opinion piece in The Guardian newspaper by Peter Mandelson and Louis Michel (October 2007): 'Africa's dependence on a few basic commodities has seen it fall far behind the poverty reduction and economic growth of Asia and Latin America. Calling for an end to EPA negotiations *when there is no credible alternative* is playing poker with the livelihoods of those we are trying to help. Of course, there should be debate over EPAs. But those who suggest that they are a danger to development are not only wrong. They also undermine those in Africa and other ACP countries who are seeking to work constructively for economic reform and a new trade and development relationship with Europe.' (Mandelson and Michel 2007, emphasis added)
	Speech by Peter Mandelson (April 2008): 'Increased services trade, measures to support investment and rules of good economic governance are not in my view optional extras but development basics.' (Mandelson 2008: 1)

Sources: European Commission (2005c, 2006i, 2007e), Mandelson (2006a,b, 2008) and Mandelson and Michel (2007).

Commission 2006i: 9). In sum, although desirable for the competitiveness of the ACP, regulatory liberalisation was not only politically contingent – dependent on the ACP for implementation – but also severely hampered by capacity constraints. Moreover, these potentially necessitated a differentiated approach to liberalisation.

This contrasted with the Commissioner's subsequent public statements that despite protests from several regions the Commission '[would] continue arguing the need to provide stable, predictable and transparent rules in sectors where investment is needed to diversify the economy' (Mandelson 2006b: 2). More stark is the contrast between the statement made by Mandelson and Michel to fellow Commissioners in a memo, stating that 'the constraint we face [in terms of WTO compatibility] has only been part of the reason for negotiating EPAs [...] [while] [t]he more important part is the **opportunity** EPAs offer' (European Commission 2007e: 2, emphasis in the original), and in their opinion piece in *The Guardian* a few months earlier where they had stated that 'there is no credible alternative' to the EPAs (Mandelson and Michel 2007). *Communicatively*, the Commissioner was thus stressing that there was no viable alternative to the agenda of regulatory liberalisation it was specifying in the EPAs, whereas in a coordinative setting it had been less prescriptive about the policy tools necessary to boost ACP competitiveness. Given these discrepancies between discursive statements in both settings, it is reasonable to conclude that the Commission was invoking these external constraints strategically.

The limitations of economic rhetoric[11]

This discursive strategy serves to further highlight the entwinement of the Commission's 'Global Europe' and EPA agendas. It underscores the importance of WTO-plus liberalisation in both the EPAs and the EU's 'commercial' FTAs and the common commitment underpinning both sets of agreements to construct a neoliberal order in the EU's trade relations with third parties. Moreover, it also provides an example of a discursive strategy that has been largely unsuccessful – at least to the extent that most ACP countries have so far resisted signing an agreement with the EU (and seem unlikely to do so in future). This serves as an interesting counterfactual to the success of a very similar discursive strategy in the case of the EU–Korea FTA. For another, it highlights the need for constructivist explanations of trade policymaking that go beyond the emphasis on rationalist 'collective action' dynamics. Such explanations have been deployed to stress why NGOs are unable to mobilise the resources necessary to 'threaten or enhance political actors' chances of re-election or re-appointment' and thus lack any meaningful clout in EU trade policymaking (Dür and De Bièvre 2007: 79). Whereas it is true that the Commission did not take their views on board, this is not so much a product of their failure to mobilise material resources effectively as Dür and De Bièvre (2007) suggest. Rather, actors in DG Trade had internalised their own neoliberal discourse which did not chime with the arguments presented by such groups. Moreover, and going to the heart of the rationalist argument about the lack of influence of non-business actors, the above analysis of the Commission's strategy suggests that such groups did hold political power in the EPA negotiations, a point not lost on a number of scholars marrying insights from constructivism and the transnational activism literature (see, for example, Del Felice 2012; Hurt *et al.* 2013; Trommer 2013). NGOs not only put DG Trade on the defensive but even appeared to win the discursive battle; Commission officials themselves concede that they have failed at 'communicating' the benefits of EPAs to not only such groups, but also, on the whole, to their ACP partners. This is a point I return to below.

Before doing so, however, I should clarify that I am not arguing that the Commission's EPA agenda has failed exclusively because of its failure to seize this discursive terrain. Clearly the lack of a strong material incentive to sign a full EPA with the EU was a crucial factor.[12] This included both the existence of EBA in the case of LDCs – which enjoyed duty- and quota-free market access to the EU without the need to reciprocate – and the supposed stop-gap of the 'market access regulation' for non-LDCs which agreed to 'goods-only' IEPAs. Similarly, I am not saying that the only successfully completed EPA – that with CARIFORUM – is purely attributable to the success of DG Trade's discursive strategy. Heron (2011) convincingly argues that CARIFORUM subscribed to a raft of WTO-plus liberalisation measures as an acceptable concession within a highly asymmetrical bargaining context in order to ensure continuity of market access. Hanging on to regulatory tools was seen to be unnecessary given 'the widespread perception in the region that the islands possessed neither the resources nor the capacity to affect a state-led development strategy' (Heron 2011: 350). However, for the Caribbean side, WTO-plus liberalisation was not just an undesirable feature of the negotiations. Rather, one can observe a high degree of ideational affinity between the coordinative discourse of officials in DG Trade and Caribbean negotiators and other elites on this issue. As Heron (2011: 342) has again highlighted, the latter 'perceived EPA not only as a necessary step to arrest the progressive erosion of the value of traditional preferences but also to improve access to the EU market in areas like services and investment', particularly mode 4. This is another issue I will revisit shortly.

For now, suffice to say that my caveats do not detract from the importance attached by all actors (both pro- and anti-EPA) to ideas and more specifically the use of economic discourse as a tool to exercise political power. In the case of those Caribbean nations which signed an EPA, there is ample evidence that local elites mimicked DG Trade's rhetoric to legitimate the agreement to a set of critical domestic and regional actors; indeed, the EPA was very contentious domestically and among Member States of CARIFORUM. Broadly speaking, disagreements surfaced between advocates of greater integration of the Caribbean into the global economy (such as Barbados, Jamaica and the Caribbean Regional Negotiating Machinery [CRNM], the supranational entity linked to CARICOM which had negotiated the EPA on behalf of the region) and those favouring a more gradualist approach (smaller Caribbean states which feared the consequences of preference erosion); Guyana even initially refused to sign the agreement (see Jamaica Gleaner 2008; Bishop *et al.* 2013: 95–101). Thus, in responding to critics of the agreement within the Caribbean, Jamaican Prime Minister Bruce Golding – one of the most vocal, but by no means the only, advocate of the EPAs in the region – was to note, for instance, that Caribbean nations had to adapt to the competitiveness challenges posed by global markets:

> Our economies cannot survive on their own. Our economies cannot grow if the economic space within which they are to grow is limited to what we have in the region. We have to strengthen our legs. It is time for countries of the Caribbean to stand up on those legs like grown men and women and be prepared to walk into the future.
>
> Cited in The Eleutheran (2008)

Such arguments were repeated by the CRNM in a public briefing published around of the time of the conclusion of the negotiations. Here, the CRNM (2007: 4) noted that '[g]iven the Caribbean's declining eligibility for international aid and the decline of preferential market access, for the small developing countries of the Caribbean few avenues [other than the EPA] remain to support the process of diversifying their economies and developing in a sustainable way'. Moreover, it continued by underscoring that '[i]f new as well as established local industries take advantage of the many measures and opportunities negotiated to date in the EPA, they will be in a position to competitively develop, produce and sell high quality CARIFORUM goods and services on international markets' (CRNM 2007: 5). Crucially, it appears that such actors had *strategic* motives to invoke such discourses of external constraint. Barbados and Jamaica, for instance, had offensive interests in services liberalisation, which they had aggressively pursued during the negotiations. For its part, and as I briefly suggested above, the CRNM had internalised a neoliberal discourse that underscored the developmental benefits of the EPAs; much as their counterparts in DG Trade, such officials believed that the future economic success of the region depended on its ability to restructure their economies towards competing at the higher end of the value chain (particularly in the key area of services) (Bishop *et al.* 2013: 94–7).

What is also significant for the purposes of my argument is that in marked contrast to the case of the Caribbean, most other ACP countries were (more or less) successfully resisting the efforts of the Commission in spite of the marked (material) power asymmetries underpinning the relationship. This underscores the need for a focus on ideational factors. Here, a role was played by NGO involvement – especially through the 'Stop EPAs' campaign – and its somewhat successful challenge to the *necessitarian* argument deployed by Commission actors. Specifically, such groups sought to paint alternatives to the process that were more attuned to developing country needs. For instance, the influential NGO Action Aid was to make a series of alternative proposals – such as expanding the scope of EBA (see Action Aid 2005: 21–6) – that did not include 'the controversial and unwanted Singapore Issues. There is no WTO requirement for regional trade agreements to include these – they are on the table purely at the insistence of the EU' (Action Aid 2005: 14). For its part, Oxfam (2006a: 12), another major civil society organisation, was to recommend in September 2006 that a 'range of alternatives to EPAs is examined, in compliance with Article 37.6 of the Cotonou Agreement. This must include arrangements without reciprocal market liberalisation, without Singapore Issues and without WTO-plus provisions, particularly in relation to TRIPS.' This was a direct riposte to the Commission's discursive and diplomatic inflexibility; a December 2006 Oxfam report on the EPAs was tellingly entitled 'Slamming the Door on Development' in response to the Commission's supposed unwillingness to countenance alternatives to regulatory liberalisation and other provisions in the context of the Pacific region EPA (Oxfam 2006b).

This discursive activism on the part of anti-EPA activists had principally two intended audiences: EU Member States and the ACP. In the case of the former, NGO activism seemed to be rewarded as early as March 2005 when the UK government, after having previously supported the Commission's EPA strategy, came out to criticise the EPAs. At the launch of the Commission for Africa Report, Gordon Brown, then Chancellor of the Exchequer, was to note that '[o]urs is the first official report to call for lasting and deep-seated trade justice that would mean [...] [that among other things] we tackle [...] the much-criticised Economic Partnership Agreements' (cited in Action Aid 2005: 10). The Report, which had the clear endorsement of the UK government, instead underscored that 'development must be the priority in all trade agreements, with liberalisation not forced on Africa' (Commission for Africa 2005: 255), a clear allusion to the perceived bullying tactics of Mandelson and his DG. This was followed in April 2005 by an unsympathetic report from the International Development Committee of the House of Commons on the EPAs (see International Development Committee 2005: 14) – which was very critical of the discourse of no alternative being deployed to defend the EPAs – and a letter in October 2006 from the UK government to the Commission urging it to abandon the emphasis on WTO-plus liberalisation (Beattie 2006).

NGO activism may have also had its effects on the ACP side, as the EU's supposed partner countries have appeared to become increasingly sceptical of the supposed *need* for the EPAs. This is most apparent in the case of West Africa, where scholars have pointed to the success of the 'discursive practices' of NGOs in leading the region to resist EU moves towards a comprehensive EPA (Del Felice 2012; Trommer 2013). This is a particularly interesting case because there are also arguably clearer material incentives to sign an EPA, even for LDCs in the region. As Trommer (2013: 3) has argued, given Ghana and Cote d'Ivoire's potential future implementation of an IEPA, the commitment to regional integration (and cohesion) of the members of the Economic Community of West African States could only be accomplished if all parties signed up to an agreement with the EU. Although the status of both these IEPAs is still in doubt (as neither Ghana nor Cote d'Ivoire has yet ratified their agreement), the fact remains that the region ended up going from what appeared to be an initial acquiescence to Mandelson's negotiating parameters (European Commission 2005d) to prevarication and resistance to the signature of full EPAs over the course of the NGO campaign (Ablordeppey 2007; Murphy 2007; Del Felice 2012: 16–18). Other regions, moreover, have also had a similar experience. In the case of the Pacific, in October 2005, negotiators were anxious to conclude talks with the EU, stressing the need to be 'proactive' and not fall behind other regions. They were even willing to countenance negotiations on services and investment (AFX News 2005). By May 2007, one and a half years after the launch of the 'Stop EPA' campaign, one of the Pacific's Chief Negotiators noted that 'for an EPA to be beneficial to Pacific ACP States [...] it has to offer better preferences than in the alternative options *and assured terms and conditions*' (cited in Pacific Islands Forum Secretariat 2007, emphasis added). Since then, only IEPAs have been concluded with Papua New Guinea and Fiji (and implemented only in the case of the former) while other Pacific countries have shown little interest in a full agreement. Turning to other regions, Table 5.1 illustrates the full extent of this trend as a number of states at first initialled or even signed an agreement, only to stall over taking the next step towards implementation (respectively, signature or ratification of the agreement).

As noted previously, I am not saying that this turn of events is not also the product of reduced material incentives to sign an EPA with the EU, given the security of having contractually enshrined market access commitments in the case of those countries having an IEPA[13] or benefitting from EBA. This probably explains why the Commission sought to amend the market access regulation in September 2011 to suspend market access to those ACP countries not taking the 'necessary steps' towards ratifying or implementing their IEPAs by January 2014 (European Commission 2011d). Although in the wake of this move most of the ESA region ratified and provisionally applied its IEPA (in May 2012), the fact remains that there has been no suggestion (so far) of suspending market access in the future if countries do not move towards a full EPA (as opposed to ratifying and implementing their IEPA). Moreover, as a sign that a number of actors within the EU itself were unhappy with this Commission decision to pressure the ACP into signing EPAs, the EP has sought to extend the deadline in the amendment to the regulation (Duddy 2012), with the final regulation as approved by the EP containing a later deadline of October 2014 (EU–Africa Chamber of Commerce 2013). At the time of writing (September 2013) it is too early to tell how this dynamic will play out among the many ACP countries that are still stalling after many years of (for the EU) fruitless negotiations. These developments, moreover, do not detract from the importance of discursive factors, as these countries had been happier to countenance WTO-plus liberalisation before the intervention of NGOs; even the Commission has become, according to one official, a lot less militant in its approach to the negotiations about the need to include such issues in future agreements. In sum, one can say that the involvement of critical non-state actors – and especially that of the high-profile 'Stop EPA' campaign – may have played a role in shaping the increasing reticence of ACP states to sign (particular types of WTO-plus) agreements (even if those vulnerable to losing EU market access end up signing up to a goods-only IEPA).

That being said, how this particular discourse of external constraint was successfully deconstructed while a similar rhetoric persists in the related domain of commercial trade policy is still an area that warrants considerable further exploration.

Conclusion

My aim in this chapter has been to situate the EU's supposedly 'developmental' trade policy towards the ACP – often presented as separate by policymakers to more commercially minded foreign economic decision-making arenas – within the wider context of its developing neoliberal trade agenda. I began by providing a brief historical overview of the development of EU–ACP trade relations, highlighting how the EU's 'commercial' and 'developmental' trade agendas have increasingly converged following the EU's turn to bilateralism. I then proceeded to highlight how this is most visibly manifested in their shared emphasis on regulatory liberalisation. I focused specifically on the services and investment provisions in the recent EU–CARIFORUM EPA, which bore a striking resemblance to those negotiated in the context of the EU's commercial FTAs under the aegis of the 'Minimum Platform'. I then deployed my constructivist framework to show how this is underpinned by the same drivers as the 'Global Europe' agenda: interest group activism combined with the sympathetic ear of DG Trade policymakers, which have internalised an increasingly activist neoliberal trade paradigm. This has led them to see regulatory liberalisation in the context of regional integration as positive for *both* the development of ACP countries as well as EU exporters. Moreover and in spite of its attempts to rhetorically differentiate between its commercial and developmental agendas, the Commission has also deployed a 'Global Europe'-esque discourse of external constraint to counter mounting opposition to the EPAs from non-traditional trade actors – in particular to defend the need for regulatory liberalisation in its agreements with the ACP.

In contrast to its success in isolating opposition to the EU–Korea FTA, this discursive strategy has not been as effective in the case of the EPAs. Aside from the Caribbean, no region has signed a full EPA with the EU, while only a few countries and one region have implemented an IEPA. Whereas I underscored in this chapter that there are very significant material disincentives that explain this development, it is also important to note how the Commission's discursive strategy has met widespread opposition. This has included non-traditional trade actors in the EU, in particular development NGOs, which are not only less amenable to the neoliberal rhetoric of actors in DG Trade, but have been able to translate their opposition into what appears to be some meaningful influence during the negotiations. Interestingly, almost all of the EU's future 'commercial' FTAs are with developing countries. The EU's commercial and developmental trade relations have thus remained intertwined, even as the EPA agenda has stagnated. This is an issue I return to in the next chapter.

6
'Global Europe' during the Crisis: Reciprocity and the Political Limits to Liberalisation

Earlier in the book, I provided a glimpse into the EU's trade policy after the start of the Financial Crisis by focusing on the signature and ratification of the first 'Global Europe' FTA, signed with South Korea in 2010. The aim in this chapter is to provide more detailed analysis of how the 'Global Europe' offensive trade agenda of free trade negotiations has developed in what many consider the most significant economic downturn since the Great Depression. In the aftermath of the 2008 Financial Crisis and given the unfolding Eurozone Crisis, the greatest perceived threat in the eyes of EU trade policymakers has been the potential for protectionist tendencies to develop, as these threaten not only the EU's offensive trade agenda but also the liberalism of its import policies. This has been rendered all the more significant by the rise of the EP as an actor in the EU trade policymaking machinery as, in the eyes of some, it might contribute to politicising a previously 'insulated' EU policymaking arena (for example, Woolcock 2008: 5).

In spite of these developments, the WTO's 2011 trade policy review of the EU noted that it had 'maintained the overall openness and transparency of its trade and investment regime' (WTO 2011a: vii). Moreover, under the leadership of Karel De Gucht, who took over as Trade Commissioner in February 2010, there has been a move towards consolidating the EU's offensive 'Global Europe' agenda in the November 2010 'Trade, Growth and World Affairs' strategy. This has become the new overarching Commission statement on trade policy. Serving the EU's high-end export interests through ambitious FTAs – and doing so at the potential expense of 'pockets of protection' – is still DG Trade's goal. A new emphasis on 'reciprocity' in trading relations – a discourse traditionally associated with mercantilist-inspired protectionism in EU trade policy – seems to be aimed at improving the EU's offensive trade negotiating leverage while minimising the threat of protectionist fallout. That being said, it also betrays a sense of the EU's growing frustration with the slow pace of its FTA negotiations with emerging economies, who have been less forthcoming than it would like.

As in previous chapters, this raises the question of *why* and *how* DG Trade has pursued this course of action. Rationalist collective action theories would argue that prevailing economic conditions favour protectionist interests; likewise, the increased powers of the EP in trade policymaking suggest that policymakers are less insulated from societal pressures than before, precluding an institutionalist explanation. As before, my answer is to offer a constructivist perspective of events, emphasising the role of particular trade discourses. These have been both internalised by actors and otherwise deployed by them strategically in order to legitimate a neoliberal agenda of market opening. I find continuity in the beliefs held by policymakers in DG Trade between Mandelson's and De Gucht's periods in office, with a greater recognition under the latter of the political contingency associated with trade liberalisation. This informs the turn to reciprocity as an instrument of leverage and also suggests that recent appeals to globalisation as an external constraint – being framed in terms of the successor of the Lisbon macroeconomic consensus, 'Europe 2020' – should be interpreted as strategic. Whether such arguments will continue to hold weight, however, is an open question; the Commission's continued strategy of putting all of its eggs in the basket of further trade liberalisation (as new initiatives such as a transatlantic FTA suggest) may become politically unsustainable, especially as it may fail to deliver the promised outcome of 'growth and jobs'.

The remainder of this chapter is structured as follows. In the first section I discuss how the key element that distinguishes 'Trade, Growth and World Affairs' from 'Global Europe' is an emphasis on 'reciprocity' in trading relations. This 'new' agenda is driven by the same concern with achieving market access gains for exporters, seeking to improve the EU's waning negotiating leverage with emerging economies. The discursive drivers of these developments are discussed in the second section. The focus here is on the Commission's coordinative and communicative discourses since the start of the crisis; I ultimately find continuity between Mandelson's and De Gucht's periods in office in terms of the beliefs of policymakers and the rhetorics they use to legitimate free trade. In the penultimate section, I turn to the problems the Commission's trade and discursive strategies might face going forward. In the final section I conclude and offer some thoughts on the EU's newest flagship initiative: an FTA with its main trading partner, the US, which has only recently entered the scene and may be suggestive of growing a frustration with emerging economy partners.

Reciprocity: Improving the EU's waning leverage

The Commission's 'Trade, Growth and World Affairs' communication of November 2010 represented continuity with rather than a break from 'Global Europe'.[1] In a Commission staff working document accompanying the strategy, policymakers were to remark that 'Global Europe provided a clear vision for the role of trade policy in promoting the EU's global competitiveness' (European Commission 2010k: 21). 'Trade, Growth and World Affairs' itself emphasised continuing the ambitious liberalisation agenda set in 2006 – either by 'completing' the work carried out on existing initiatives (in the area of bilateral trade negotiations for instance) or by improving existing tools to better achieve unchanged objectives (European Commission 2010j). In the latter case, I am referring to the very visible institutional changes wrought by the Treaty of Lisbon – that came into effect in December 2009 – which granted the Commission (new) exclusive competence to negotiate all investment agreements and thus eliminated the last area of shared competence in trade (Woolcock 2010b: 385; see Figure 1.1). In practice this meant that the Commission could now move beyond the competence for pre-establishment liberalisation of investment granted by the 'Minimum Platform' (see Chapter 3) to negotiate post-establishment investment protection, which had previously been within the exclusive purview of Member States through BITs. Rather than change the shape of the EU's 'Global Europe' services and investment agenda, however, the evolving application of the new investment competence appears to be driven by the same objective of achieving ambitious market access for European service suppliers.[2]

Returning to 'Trade, Growth and World Affairs', the only significant variation with respect to the 2006 communication was in terms of the new emphasis placed on 'reciprocity'. When discussing its 'context and basic orientations', the strategy was to note that 'for an open trade policy in Europe to succeed politically, others – including both our developed and emerging partners – must match our efforts in a spirit of reciprocity and mutual benefit' (European Commission 2010j: 4). The broader context for this increased emphasis on reciprocity is the perception that the EU's 'power *in* trade' (Meunier and Nicolaïdis 2006: 906, emphasis in the original), or more specifically, its ability to use access to its market as a tool to exact concessions from trading partners, is waning. This is largely seen to be result of a changing balance of power in the global trading system, where emerging economies (in particular) are constraining the influence of the EU and US (McGuire and Lindeque 2010; Young 2011). Although this has been most acutely felt in the context of the multilateral WTO, the EU's 'Global Europe' FTA agenda has also proceeded at a slower pace than many actors within the EU (both officials and business groups) would have hoped. Of all the partners targeted by the communication in 2006 (including MERCOSUR, with whom negotiations had been ongoing beforehand), at the time of writing (September 2013) the only agreement in force is with South Korea, while negotiations have also been concluded with Singapore (European Commission 2013d).

The more specific problem faced by the EU, as diagnosed by the Commission, is that its largely 'open market can reduce the EU's leverage in negotiations as it reduces partners' appetite to reciprocate' (European Commission 2010k: 23). As a result, I argue that although the term 'reciprocity' has often been equated with mercantilist-inspired protectionism in EU trade policy (see Chapter 4) – and no more so than since the start of the crisis – this particular embodiment of the notion is consistent with DG Trade's wider neoliberal objectives in trade policy. As the Commission itself has stated, the 'concept of reciprocity aims at opening third countries markets, not closing ours' (European Commission 2013a: 7, emphasis omitted). In other words, reciprocity is ultimately about ensuring that the EU possesses sufficient *leverage* in ongoing trade negotiations; indeed, as became apparent in earlier chapters, leveraging protection has been one of the key ingredients of the EU's strategy to serve its export interests. One of the logical corollaries of the 2005 'Issues Paper's' argument, that the EU's trade and investment regime was already largely open, was that the EU had little left to give and therefore had to use 'movement on [EU] trade protection' as an instrument to exact concessions abroad (see European Commission 2005a: 6). In this vein, the reciprocity agenda points to the constraints the EU faces in terms of 'trading pockets of protection'. It has therefore led to the introduction of two key innovations seeking to address this perceived problem. First of all, the Commission has successfully brought about a series of reforms to the GSP for developing countries – aimed at increasing EU leverage in its FTA negotiations with emerging economies. Secondly, a new instrument to push for market access in government procurement – the 'horizontal' trade issue where the EU's negotiating leverage is perceived to be weakest – is being proposed (although it faces stiff opposition from a number of actors within the EU).

The new GSP regulation

All of the emerging country FTA partners originally identified by the 'Global Europe' communication – with the exception of South Korea and Singapore – are current GSP beneficiaries. The existence of this scheme of non-reciprocal trade preferences offered by the EU to developing countries – which is authorised under the WTO's Enabling Clause – has been seen by officials in DG Trade to create a serious disincentive for such countries to sign FTAs, as market access for many of their commodity exports is already guaranteed without the need for reciprocal liberalisation. India, for example, is said to 'enjoy[] relatively good market access for goods to the EU under the GSP [...] [while also] maintain[ing] fairly high tariffs and some peaks in areas particularly important to EU industry (such as cars, wines and spirits) and significant non-tariff barriers in other sectors important to EU exporters' (European Commission 2010k: 8).

It is within this context that we have to understand the recent reforms of the GSP scheme, which come into force in January 2014. These will see *all* high income and upper-middle-income countries – using the World Bank's income criteria – as well as any country having signed an agreement with the EU – 'which provides the same tariff preferences as the scheme, or better, for substantially all trade' (Regulation (EU) No 978/2012, Article 4) – become ineligible for GSP. Moreover, simultaneous changes to the graduation principle for GSP imports will make it easier to render specific product 'sections' (or categories of similar goods) ineligible for preferences. The impact of this measure was originally estimated by the Commission to render 5.3 billion euro worth of imports – spread among only six countries (China, India, Indonesia, Nigeria, Thailand and Ukraine) – ineligible for preferential access under the scheme (European Commission 2011b: 115); the first list of graduated products (for the period of 2014–16) closely matches these earlier estimates (Commission Implementing Regulation (EU) No. 1213/2012). Moreover, the Overseas Development Institute (ODI) also found that two other countries (Iraq and Vietnam) had the potential to have products graduated (ODI 2011: 7).

DG Trade's stated rationale for these changes is to 'focus the GSP preferences on the countries most in need' (European Commission 2011b: 2) – in their eyes LDCs and so-called 'vulnerable economies' lacking product diversification and being poorly integrated into the world economy (European Commission 2011c: 11). There are, however, clear grounds for doubting DG Trade's stated aims in this respect. If the primary driver of the EU's reform of the GSP is to help those 'most in need' by improving the value of their non-reciprocal preferences, then why is it seeking elsewhere to put trade relations with LDCs and 'vulnerable' economies on a contractually reciprocated basis in the form of the EPAs and other FTAs (such as those with Central American and Andean nations)? Similarly, how could the Commission reconcile what amounted to be an espousal of non-reciprocal trade preferences as a development model – a model, one should remember, it had renounced in the 1996 'Green Paper' on EU–ACP relations (see Chapter 5) – with its clear preference for contractually enshrined free trade?

As a result, I argue instead that the GSP reform has to be understood as part of the move towards improving leverage in ongoing trade negotiations. For one, the more likely beneficiaries of the changes are not LDCs or 'vulnerable' economies, but rather higher income countries, who may well benefit from trade diversion effects as emerging economies lose trade preferences (ODI 2011: 12–13). The new regulation has a much clearer impact on the EU's 'Global Europe' FTA partners; Argentina, Brunei, Brazil, Malaysia and Uruguay will lose all of their non-reciprocal trade preferences, while India is likely to lose preferences on 2.81 billion euro worth of trade, or about 11.1 per cent of its total goods exports to the EU (author's calculation, using data from European Commission 2011a; Eurostat 2013b)! Moreover, for India and a number of other emerging economies, these changes also affect exports that undoubtedly benefit from such preferences: in India's case, for instance, 44.8 per cent of GSP exports likely to be affected by the measures face MFN tariffs of 5 per cent or more (the equivalent figures are 27.6 for Thailand and 76.1 for Vietnam) (author's calculation, using data from ODI 2011: 10). DG Trade, in appraising the GSP changes, unsurprisingly argued that they 'ha[d] nothing to do with other [commercial] trade negotiations', but it was quick to point out that they 'might still have the unintended consequence of providing more advanced developing countries with a greater incentive to enter into and conclude reciprocal trade negotiations with the EU' (European Commission 2011c: 15). Moreover, there is strong evidence to suggest that the GSP reform not only had the support of exporters, but was also significantly driven by their lobbying action, with changes made to the instrument closely reflecting their preferences, as expressed during a public consultation exercise (European Commission 2010h).

The quest to open public procurement markets[3]

Public procurement markets have been seen for a long time as a source of 'untapped potential' from DG Trade. Here, emerging markets 'are expected to increase significantly and are likely to become important future business opportunities in sectors where EU industry is highly competitive' (European Commission 2011a: 11). Servicing these high-end exporters through ambitious procurement liberalisation negotiations, however, is rendered difficult from DG Trade's perspective by two factors. Firstly, only fourteen countries are parties to the WTO's plurilateral (and thus non-compulsory for WTO members) Government Procurement Agreement (GPA). This functions much like the WTO in that countries undertake to bind liberalisation commitments in particular sectors (see Anderson and Arrowsmith 2011). Secondly, the EU's openness on government procurement – both in terms of GPA-committed and autonomous liberalisation – far exceeds that of its trading partners. While DG Trade as a whole sees this trade openness as something positive – improving the efficiency of procurement markets – 'the EU's relative openness to foreign bidders [...] [also implies that] its leverage in trade negotiations on access to foreign public procurement markets is reduced' (European Commission 2011a: 11).

This issue is not entirely new. The problem was already identified in the 'Global Europe' strategy, which proposed an instrument to open the procurement markets of those trading partners that did not 'reciprocate' EU openness by 'introducing carefully targeted restrictions on access to parts of the EU procurement market to encourage [the EU's] partners to offer reciprocal market opening' (European Commission 2006g: 14). Although such an instrument was subsequently proposed to Member States, it was rejected in the face of opposition from the liberal wing of the Council which feared a turn to protectionist trade measures. In this sense, the fact that such a proposal is in the offing again suggests that the balance of interest in the Council has shifted in the changed economic climate. There does appear to be a fair amount of political pressure in Member States surrounding the awarding of public contracts to non-European contractors (see, for instance, Wiesman 2010). But although such developments may have facilitated the current proposals, the fact remains that they are very much driven by DG Trade's current neoliberal 'reciprocity' agenda, which aims to improve the EU's leverage in negotiations rather than erect barriers to foreign market entry. As shall become apparent when I turn to analyse the proposed options, DG Trade's position suggests that it wished to create an instrument to serve the interests of its exporters while guarding against market closures at home.

The Commission's proposed regulation was presented in March 2012, having been jointly drafted by DG Trade and DG Internal Market (European Commission 2012c). DG Trade's preferred option was to establish a new 'centralised' 'legislative initiative' for procurement not covered by the EU's international commitments, which was to be used as a bargaining chip to obtain market access gains. This would establish an instrument at the EU level allowing the Commission to carry out its own investigations into restrictive practices in third countries and, if subsequent consultations with an offending country '[do] not lead to satisfactory results within 15 months' the Commission would have had the power 'to adopt implementing acts to limit the access of goods and services originating in [said] country' (European Commission 2012c: 24). DG Trade fought hard to include this procedure in the proposals during its consultation process with DG Internal Market and unsuccessfully opposed the inclusion of the 'decentralised mechanism' which its counterpart had insisted on. This would allow individual procuring entities 'to decide to exclude third country goods, services and companies' for non-covered procurement, subject to *ex ante* notification of the Commission to ensure policy consistency across the EU. Under this so-called 'decentralised' procurement instrument, the Commission could not object to this market closure in cases where there is 'a lack of substantial reciprocity in market opening between the Union and the third country concerned' (what is also called the 'reciprocity test') (European Commission 2012c: 20–1).

DG Trade's positioning in the internal debates on the procurement mechanism is interesting in the sense that it strongly suggests that officials in that DG are keen to *minimise* protectionist fallout and *maximise* the ability of the instrument to yield leverage in trade liberalisation talks. As noted by one official in DG Trade, a centralised instrument yields greater predictability of outcome in two senses. On the one hand, it ensures that the Commission could credibly threaten and target those guilty of offering the EU sub-par market access with a closure of parts of the EU market without having to rely on the more haphazard decentralised procedure, where Commission discretion would be insufficient to exercise meaningful leverage. On the other hand, it ensures that the Commission is able to assess whether such measures are desirable given the wider trading context of the partner in question, avoiding the threat of potentially damaging retaliation. Moreover, by controlling this process DG Trade could also minimise the threat of succumbing to rent-seeking behaviour by import-competing firms and maintain a satisfactory *de facto* level of openness in public procurement. To an extent, one could say the same of the 'reciprocity test' for the decentralised mechanism, which provides a degree of control of the process to the Commission (as notifications have to be *ex ante* and the Commission can refuse the procuring entities' request for the exclusion of third country providers if there are no reciprocity issues). The inclusion of this 'test' might therefore explain why DG Trade ultimately acceded to a compromise that included both centralised and decentralised options.

In sum, one can see that for DG Trade this instrument is about maximising its leverage in offensive trade negotiations and minimising protectionist pressures. Its wishes for the design of the instrument betray the sentiments expressed in a staff working paper that '[a]ny strategy to encourage trading partners to make further concessions (for example by threatening to temporarily reduce the EU's level of openness) would need to be designed carefully, to avoid precipitating overall protectionist tendencies and welfare losses' (European Commission 2010k: 23). It must be said that nothing is yet set in stone. There are a number of issues that remain unresolved (such as the exact comitology procedure to be used to invoke the 'centralised' instrument), while considerable uncertainty surrounds the future of the proposals. These have yet to be approved by the Council and the EP, where they currently face substantial opposition from more liberal-leaning actors. Business groups (including exporters), for their part, are also divided between those which favour a more assertive approach to market access in government procurement and those which are opposed to the Commission proposals. Unlike for the GSP proposals, this aspect of the EU's strategy of trading pockets of protection also faces opposition from parts of DG Trade's core constituency.

The discursive drivers of EU trade policy since the crash

The 'Trade, Growth and World Affairs' strategy embodied the wider aims of the 'Global Europe' agenda of seeking market access gains for upmarket exporters at the expense of import-competing interests; the new emphasis on 'reciprocity' as an instrument for leverage in trade liberalisation talks, moreover, serves to underscore this agenda for market opening (even if it does point to the problems the EU faces trying to realise its objectives). Such a turn of events is not entirely expected given the onset of the Financial and Eurozone Crises. After all, in this context one might expect increased protectionist pressure among actors within the EU political economy. The emergence of the EP as an actor in the EU trade policymaking machinery following the Treaty of Lisbon, moreover, has increased access for such interests to policymaking. In Chapter 4, I showed how both of these developments played a role during the negotiation and ratification of the EU–Korea FTA. As in that chapter, therefore, one has to show *why* DG Trade has continued to pursue the ongoing 'Global

Europe' agenda – including the new place accorded to a particular understanding of reciprocity – and *how* it continues to legitimate these measures.

DG Trade's coordinative discourse under De Gucht[4]

To begin to understand *why* DG Trade has stuck to its particular offensive trade agenda, my analysis must turn to the private understandings (or beliefs) held by policymakers under De Gucht. The emphasis on trading away 'pockets of protection' that lies at the heart of the reciprocity agenda suggests that policymakers' views did not change dramatically from Mandelson's time. This, however, requires some empirical substantiation by focusing on the 'coordinative' discourses of such policymakers. In this vein, I focus on the contributions made by leading figures in DG Trade's Chief Economist's unit – in charge of developing the 'Trade, Growth and World Affairs' strategy – to an online debate organised by the 'policy portal' VoxEU.org – henceforth 'Vox' (Vox 2010; for more detail on Vox and on the selection and coding documents in this section, see the Appendix).

One of the lead commentaries kicking off this process – authored by the then Chief Trade Economist himself, Lucien Cernat – was tellingly entitled 'Shaping the Future of EU Trade Policy: How to Maximise the Gains from Trade in a Globalised World', already suggesting a positive-sum view of trade liberalisation. Specifically, Cernat (2010: 14, emphasis in the original) referred to the orthodox, neoclassic literature in trade economics to argue that 'promoting trade liberalisation brings a **triple benefit** that can underpin [economic] progress in the EU', namely 'economic growth', 'consumer benefits' and 'labour effects'. This was nothing new. The emphasis on 'economic growth' and 'labour effects' betrayed a continued faith in the forces of economic restructuring, with officials in DG Trade still espousing the view that the EU's competitiveness was dependent on its ability to export high-end products. It suggested continuity with the faith expressed in the 2005 'Issues Paper' that vertical intra-industry trade will result from the EU's market-opening initiatives with emerging economies (see Chapter 3). 'Consumer benefits', meanwhile, were surmised to stem from a 'wider range and variety of products and services' likely to result from intra-industry specialisation more broadly. More interestingly, and given the context of the economic crisis and the slowing of economic growth in Europe, the principal plank in Cernat's argument (and hence DG Trade's thinking) was that '[w]ith subdued domestic demand in the EU, trade is going to become an important driver of growth' (Cernat 2010: 13). In sum then, trade liberalisation was still seen as a desirable objective – contributing to the 'Europe 2020' agenda of economic recovery premised on boosting competitiveness – while globalisation was also still perceived – as under Mandelson – as an unambiguously desirable process to be actively embraced. Crucially, as subsequent analysis will show, both this competitiveness objective and the globalisation process were similarly still seen to be ultimately politically contingent in the context of the economic crisis.

This is most obvious if one turns to further contributions made by Cernat and other DG Trade officials to VoxEU discussions. The argument made in these pieces was that EU Member States had to resist the forces of 'murky', behind-the-border protectionism that were spreading through the international economic system following the Financial Crisis (Cernat and Susa 2010; Cernat and Madsen 2011). Regulatory liberalisation, moreover, promised the greatest market access gains according to Cernat and Madsen (2011) given that this was where most of the trade partners' protectionism was concentrated. In Cernat and his colleague Susa's (2010) words, 'this crisis might put an additional strain on those areas where the absence of clear WTO rules offers unbounded "protectionist policy space"'. Free trade (as well as further liberalisation), then, was seen to be far from inevitable as it depended, to a large extent, on the political will of participants in the international trading system to be maintained. Moreover, it was also seen to be increasingly contingent on domestic political pressure. The belief among policymakers in DG Trade was that the lack of reciprocity in trading relations with emerging economies – which were developing into keen competitors of the EU – risked turning EU public opinion against trade liberalisation (see Table 6.1; Cernat and Madsen 2011; see also O'Sullivan 2010).

There was indeed a real fear amongst trade policymakers that the public as well as political actors' understandings of trade policy were largely mercantilist, that is, focused on the gains to exporters from liberalisation rather than the gains from imports (in the form of cheaper consumer prices and so forth). The implication of this was that in the absence of countervailing gains for exporters (that is, where countries did not reciprocate EU openness), such actors would instead focus on the concentrated adjustment costs from trade liberalisation. The significance for my purposes of such internalised ideas – beyond highlighting that DG Trade's views continued to be neoliberal rather than mercantilist – is two-fold. For one, it highlights the importance increasingly attributed in DG Trade to communicating the benefits of free trade, and, in particular, of imports in line with the neoclassical economic view that this leads to a more efficient allocation of resources through specialisation based on comparative advantage. This is a point I return to below, where I discuss DG Trade's discursive strategy (or rhetoric). For now, I turn to the implications that ideas raise for the Commission's 'reciprocity' agenda in the sense that it was felt that a lack thereof threatened the liberal foundations of EU trade policy.

'Reciprocity' of course, has long been a code word in Brussels for mercantilist-inspired 'protectionism', having been appropriated by actors (for example, France) critical of the Commission's neoliberal market opening initiatives. However, DG Trade had not deviated from its long-held neoliberal paradigm by acknowledging the (political) necessity of reciprocity in trading relations. If one carefully examines DG Trade's previous pronouncements it becomes clear that it had always acknowledged the potential for opposition to liberal, technical-rational and (therefore) welfare-maximising trade policies amongst political actors. After all, there is a recognition of these dynamics among neoclassically trained economists and their following among political scientists, which have postulated theories of how to overcome these political dynamics prompted by collective action problems; apart from the advocacy of 'insulated' trade bureaucracies (see, for example, Destler 2005), the strategy of pursuing 'reciprocity' in trade negotiations has often been seen as a way of mobilising exporters to offset protectionist pressure (Bailey *et al.* 1997; Gilligan 1997). Indeed, this was the logic behind the 1996 'Market Access Strategy's' emphasis on mobilising business in favour of trade liberalisation. Similar feelings are also likely to be at the heart of DG Trade's preference for intra-industry specialisation to emerge in its trading relationship with emerging economies, as perhaps most explicitly stated in the 2005 'Issues Paper'. The hope is that this is likely to allow the EU to pursue free trade policies in the long term with a reduced adjustment (and hence political) burden (which of course has not prevented DG Trade from confronting defensive sectors, as the ultimate aim is still economic adjustment). The economic crisis, of course, has rendered these pressures increasingly relevant, explaining in part the emphasis on a more concrete political 'limitation' to the optimum outcome of unfettered trade liberalisation; the emphasis on reciprocity was a greater recognition than ever before of the political contingency of liberalisation, but this was not unexpected given the advent of the crisis. Underscoring its ideational lineage, reciprocity in Commission discourse was therefore ultimately about mobilising support *in favour* of trade liberalisation (by making this more achievable), rather than against market opening.

In this vein, reciprocity has become the newest embodiment of the Commission's agenda of neoliberal market opening in which the EU's trade protection is traded against market access further afield – as noted in the 2005 'Issues Paper'. Although there is more than just the potential for the introduction of increased trade protection, the main thrust of the Commission's strategy is ultimately to make market access gains without sacrificing the EU's openness. Given DG Trade's views that unrecipro- cated liberal trade was potentially politically unsustainable, the new stress placed on 'reciprocity' is an evolution in thinking that does not diverge too greatly from Mandelson's own neoliberal coordinative dis- course. Much as his agenda of trading away remaining 'pockets of protection' was about killing two birds with one stone – by obtaining market access gains for exporters while simultaneously reducing import protection (both of which were seen as desirable)[5] – De Gucht's reciprocity agenda is aimed at achieving two very similar and complementary objectives: obtaining, as before, ambitious market access gains for exporters while, simultaneously, rendering liberal trade policies politi- cally sustainable in the long-run.

In sum, then, the coordinative discourse in DG Trade has not changed significantly following the advent of the Financial and Eurozone Crises. The emphasis on reciprocity belies the continued emphasis placed on the economically desirable agenda of achieving market access gains for exporters on the basis of trading away protection. The ideational drivers of EU trade policy have remained fairly constant. In this vein, although DG Trade privately concedes, arguably more than before, the ultimately contingent nature of liberalisation, publicly it continues to invoke necessitarian arguments to discursively render trade liberalisation polit- ically legitimate in its 'Trade, Growth and World Affairs' strategy. In order to appreciate this, one must first turn to the 'Europe 2020' macro- economic policy document on which this strategy draws.

The 'Europe 2020' agenda

The 'Europe 2020' macroeconomic strategy was a direct response to the wider economic effects of the 2008 Financial Crisis. It was formally pro- posed by the (second) Barroso Commission in March 2010 and approved by the Member States at a European Council summit in Brussels in June 2010. Although ostensibly replacing the previous Lisbon Agenda – whose ambitious target (of making the EU 'the most competitive and dynamic knowledge-based economy in the world' by 2010) the eco- nomic crisis has definitively put to rest – the parallels are difficult to ignore. The rationale for 'Europe 2020' – as in Lisbon – was still Europe's (relative) economic decline, with the crisis (and the pain it was causing in Europe) adding increased urgency to plans for long-term economic reform *rather* than dashing them. The responses to these challenges were the three 'mutually reinforcing' objectives of delivering 'smart growth' (developing the knowledge economy), 'sustainable growth' (promoting greater resource efficiency, environmental awareness and competitiveness) and 'inclusive growth' (delivering high employment and social cohesion) (see European Commission 2010c). These translated into a set of five headline targets to be achieved by 2020. In sum, 'Europe 2020' sought not only to 'help Europe recover from the crisis' but also, in Lisbon fashion, to enable the EU to 'come out stronger, both internally and at the international level' by the new deadline of 2020 (European Council 2010a: 2).

'Europe 2020' was therefore not so much a reinvention of the EU's strategic macroeconomic goals as an updating of the Lisbon Strategy's so-called 'three pillars' to reflect changes in the European political economy (see Chapter 3). For one, the emphasis on the competitiveness challenges faced by the European economy still persisted; in fact, the crisis had added urgency to the need to respond to the external constraint posed by globalisation. Thus, in its justification of 'Europe 2020', the Commission was to note that '[t]he crisis has wiped out years of economic and social progress and exposed structural weaknesses in Europe's economy. In the meantime, the world is moving fast and long-term challenges – globalisation, pressure on resources, ageing – intensify' (European Commission 2010c: 5). At the same time, the objective of ensuring 'inclusive growth' corresponded to the need to preserve the European social model, the 'second pillar' of the Lisbon Agenda. The potential for conflict between both pillars thus persisted. The emphasis on 'sustainability' was new – a product of the growing profile of environmental issues in political and economic discourse in the EU – but interestingly this was also linked to the wider competitiveness agenda given the emphasis on sustainable *growth*.

This continuity in discourse is important for my argument, as will become more apparent below. For now, it is important to highlight that, unlike Lisbon, 'Europe 2020' directly embedded the issue of trade policy within the wider context of the EU's macroeconomic strategy. It specifically included a sub-heading on 'deploying external policy instruments' where it was argued that these 'need to be deployed to foster European growth through our participation in open and fair markets world wide' (European Commission 2010c: 22). This may lead some to suggest that unlike 'Global Europe', where DG Trade independently seized upon the

Lisbon discourse for strategic purposes, the 'Trade, Growth and World Affairs' strategy was a product of wider forces within the EU political economy. DG Trade did not begin work on this new trade strategy until March 2010, when it was mandated to do so by higher forces within the Commission as part of the 'Europe 2020' agenda. But as I shall argue in the following sub-section, DG Trade still managed to establish ownership of this strategy, shaping it in order to fulfil similar discursive objectives as Lisbon did for 'Global Europe'.

Keeping 'protectionism' at bay in 'Trade, Growth and World Affairs'[6]

Although work on the 'Trade, Growth and World Affairs' strategy was initiated as part of the broader 'Europe 2020' agenda, DG Trade ensured that, from the beginning, it established discursive 'ownership' of this initiative. In its eyes there were very good reasons to do so, as it was Member States which were partly behind the drive for an 'external dimension' to the 'Europe 2020' competitiveness agenda. Whereas this drive was, in part, a reflection of the success of the 'Global Europe' agenda's discursive linking of the EU's internal and external competitiveness – which I have shown in earlier chapters to have been internalised strongly by most Member States – there was also a strong drive from certain Member States to include an emphasis on 'reciprocity' in EU trade policy – ostensibly in the more mercantilist-inspired protectionist vein long associated with certain members of the Council. Thus when drafting the 'Europe 2020' document, which included a page setting out the basic parameters of the future 'Trade, Growth and World Affairs' strategy, DG Trade worked hard (and ultimately successfully) to excise the term 'reciprocity' from the document given its potentially protectionist ramifications. Moreover, it also seems that DG Trade successfully sought the greatest degree of flexibility possible in drafting the 'Trade, Growth and World Affairs' strategy by ensuring that the 'Europe 2020' communication remained as non-committal as possible in this domain. The end result was that 'Europe 2020' was more vague on trade policy than on most other areas in terms of the specific policy prescriptions it put forward (European Commission 2010c: 24).

The next step of DG Trade's strategy consisted of seizing upon the discourse of external constraint at the heart of 'Europe 2020', much as it had with the Lisbon Agenda six years previously, in order to render its agenda of trade liberalisation discursively *necessary*, especially in response to the crisis (for a similar argument, see De Ville and Orbie 2013). This began with the consultation process and especially the 2010

'Issues Paper' used to frame it. Although the consultation itself was far less important in shaping the ensuing trade strategy than the equivalent process was for 'Global Europe', ironically DG Trade sought to institutionalise it to a far greater extent. This was a product of a desire to ensure a more inclusive consultation process, as the feeling among certain (especially civil society) actors was that the process under 'Global Europe' had not been transparent enough. This underscores the ultimately communicative nature of the exercise, particularly when compared to the previous consultation kicked off by the 2005 'Issues Paper' which yielded 'Global Europe'. As David O'Sullivan, Director-General for Trade, put it explicitly, the purpose of this process was 'to continue to *project publicly the benefits of trade and globalisation*, because recent events have given rise to some criticism and some suggestions that perhaps trade or globalisation might even have contributed to the difficulties' (O'Sullivan 2010: 4, emphasis added).

The 2010 'Issues Paper' was thus the first key document in DG Trade's discursive arsenal. It began by arguing that production was increasingly embedded in 'global supply chains'. This led it to contend that '[w]hile people may be wary about the impact of [open trade] on their job security and income, *the crisis has clearly shown that protectionism is not an option*' (European Commission 2010f: 3, emphasis added). Invoking the spectre of 'beggar-thy-neighbour' protectionism this argument was transposed – in parts almost *verbatim* – to the 'Trade, Growth and World Affairs' strategy. Both documents also explicitly situated such arguments in the context of the indispensability of meeting the 'Europe 2020' competitiveness goals, with the final strategy explicitly stating that 'trade and investment policy *must contribute to this objective*' (European Commission 2010j: 4, emphasis added).

Crucially, the '2020 Trade Strategy' also addressed the threat of protectionist 'reciprocity' by noting that while 'others [...] must match our [liberalisation] efforts, in a spirit of *reciprocity* and mutual benefit [...] [t]he EU *will remain an open economy*' (European Commission 2010j: 4, emphasis added). This was an act of discursively neutering the term 'reciprocity' of protectionist connotations; although DG Trade continued by stressing that the EU 'w[ould] remain vigilant in defence of European interests and European jobs', the implication, given the constraint posed by globalised markets, was that the EU would *have to* remain open in order not to jeopardise those interests. As the preceding paragraph had made clear, '[o]pen economies tend to grow faster than closed economies [...] [and as a result] Europe *must seize* the triple benefit from more open trade and investment: more growth and jobs and lower consumer prices' (European Commission 2010j: 4, emphasis added). This also underscored the importance attached to imports, as Europeans stood to lose out from protectionism not only as workers but also as consumers as neoclassical trade theory highlights. The necessitarian character attached to trade liberalisation as a result of the so-called 'triple benefits from trade' – which had featured in a more contingent form in DG Trade coordinative discourse – also featured in another key document, the 'Staff Working Paper on Trade as a Driver of Prosperity'. This came out in accompaniment to the strategy – to elaborate on areas the length and format-restricted '2020 Trade Strategy' could not address – and sought to '[make] the case again for open trade as an important driver for economic growth and job creation in the EU as well as worldwide, and as a *necessary condition* to strengthen the competitiveness of the EU in global markets' (European Commission 2010l: 3, emphasis added). Moreover it intended, as had the '2020 Trade Strategy', to underscore that 'reciprocity' *could not* imply a closure of the EU market, given the importance of imports within the EU political economy by noting that '[c]reating more growth and jobs in the EU will require a stronger export orientation *but without falling into mercantilism:* competitive exports *require* competitive imports' (European Commission 2010l: 4, emphasis added).

As in other chapters, one needs to ask whether this discourse of external constraint was invoked strategically, as it was under Mandelson. To do so, I deploy the analytical technique I developed earlier (see Chapter 2) to contrast DG Trade's coordinative and communicative discourses over this period. The findings are summarised in Table 6.1. As before, I find some contrast between the contingency arguments raised by policymakers in a coordinative setting and the rhetoric characterising the 'Trade, Growth and World Affairs' strategy. Where in the former case trade liberalisation was seen as desirable yet contingent on political pressure (Cernat's column in the Vox debate, for example, was tellingly sub-titled 'How to Maximise the Gains from Trade in a Globalised World'), the Commission's 2010 strategy sought to embed trade liberalisation in the context of 'Europe 2020' and was thus discursively rendering it indispensable. Although this may seem like a matter of differing emphasis, which I would not wish to overstate, the discrepancy between both discourses is more evident when turning to the issue of 'reciprocity'. Whereas in a coordinative setting Commission officials stressed that a lack thereof 'may lead to protectionist tendencies' (Cernat and Madsen 2011), in public they stressed that although 'for an open trade policy in Europe to succeed politically, others [...] must match our efforts [...] [t]he EU *will remain an open economy*' (European Commission 2010j: 4,

Table 6.1   DG Trade's diverging discourses on globalisation and trade liberalisation in the wake of the crisis

Vox publications by DG officials (January 2010–March 2011)	Globalisation (economic openness) as a **contingent** and **desirable** process.	'[R]ecent events have given rise to some criticism and some suggestions that perhaps trade or globalisation might even have contributed to the difficulties, whereas we would strongly maintain that *trade and globalisation are very much part of the solution* and not part of the problem.' (O'Sullivan 2010: 4–5, emphasis added)
Coordinative Discursive Setting	Trade liberalisation as a **contingent** and **desirable** process given the onset of the crisis (particularly if there is no reciprocity).	'[Most] Europeans believe that the EU has benefited greatly from international trade. However, they are less confident about the future, as [again most] think that trade will benefit more the emerging economies like Brazil, China, India, and Russia in the coming years. These views *may lead to protectionist tendencies,* if Europe's openness is perceived as being matched by EU's strategic trading partners with 'behind-the-border' policies acting as de facto discriminatory trade barriers.' (Cernat and Madsen 2011, emphasis added)
2010 'Issues Paper' (June 2010); 'Trade, Growth and World Affairs' and accompanying staff working document 'Trade as a Driver of Prosperity' (November 2010)	The '2020' competitiveness objectives as a **necessary** outcome … (given) Globalisation (in the form of competitive pressures in emerging markets) as an **external economic constraint.**	'This Communication is a crucial element of the external dimension of the *Europe 2020 strategy* and sets out how trade and investment policy *must contribute to this objective,* and to our external policies as a whole [...] By 2015, 90% of world growth will be generated outside Europe [...] So in the years to come, we need to seize the opportunity of higher levels of growth abroad, especially in East and South Asia. [...] The world economy and world trade have undergone profound changes in the recent past. The supply chain of many goods and services now encompasses factories and offices in various parts of the globe.' (European Commission 2010): 4, emphasis added)

| Communicative Discursive Setting | Trade liberalisation as a necessary process, especially in light of the crisis (even given concerns about 'reciprocity'). | 'The [staff working paper] starts by making the case again for *open trade* as an important driver for economic growth and job creation in the EU as well as worldwide, and as *a necessary condition to strengthen the competitiveness of the EU in global markets.*' (European Commission 2010l: 3, emphasis added)

'Open economies tend to grow faster than closed economies [...] Europe *must seize the triple benefit from more open trade and investment*: more growth and jobs and lower consumer prices. But for an open trade policy in Europe to succeed politically, others – including both our developed and emerging partners – must match our efforts, in a spirit of *reciprocity* and mutual benefit. Trade policy will not gain public support in Europe if we do not have fair access to raw materials, or if access to public procurement abroad is blocked, for example. The EU *will remain an open economy* but we will not be naïve. In particular, the Commission will remain vigilant in defence of European interests and European jobs.' (European Commission 2010j: 4, emphasis added) |

Sources: Author's interpretation, Cernat and Madsen (2011), O'Sullivan (2010) and European Commission (2010j,l).

emphasis added). The message, as I noted above, was that it had no choice to do so, given that in globalised markets '[o]pen economies tend to grow faster than closed economies' (European Commission 2010j: 4). As a result, I conclude that officials in DG Trade did not truly believe these to be binding material constraints and were thus invoking them, as before, in order to legitimate their neoliberal agenda of market opening.

Subsequent Commission documents and speeches by Commissioner De Gucht (see De Gucht 2012, 2013) have been broadly consistent with this rhetoric. Three new themes, however, have also emerged since the publication of 'Trade, Growth and World Affairs', although they draw on a very similar discursive armoury. In the context of the unfolding Eurozone Crisis the ongoing stagnation of demand in the EU, the politics of austerity (which has been imposed by the EU on debtor countries in the Eurozone) and competitiveness imbalances between Member States (seen as a keen contributor to the crisis, leading to current account deficits amongst debtor states in the Eurozone being financed through excessive borrowing) have all become increasingly relevant concerns (on these issues, see, amongst others, Hall 2012; Blyth 2013). As a result, in a July 2012 Staff Working Document on the 'External Sources of Growth' the Commission has underscored how, given weak EU demand 'economic recovery will [...] need to be consolidated by stronger links with the new global growth centres [in emerging economies]'. Secondly, it noted how '[b]oosting trade is one of the few means to bolster economic growth without drawing on severely constrained public finances' (European Commission 2012d: 4). As a result of these two (reinforcing) factors – reduced demand and public austerity – the Commission argued (in a February 2013 contribution to a debate in the European Council on 'Trade, Growth and Jobs') that '**[t]rade has never been more important for the European Union's economy**' (European Commission 2013a: 1, emphasis in the original). In other words, the EU's economic crisis ultimately heightens the need to bow to the imperatives of global market integration – one of the old leitmotifs of the Commission's communicative trade policy discourse.

The Commission has also begun to acknowledge in these two documents that 'differences in competitiveness' between Member States exist (European Commission 2013a: 2; see also European Commission 2012d: 8). This may seem like an important concession; referring to such pronouncements, De Ville and Orbie (2013: 13) note that 'usually, official documents and speeches [...] present the EU as a single "trading *bloc*"', while an important feature of the Commission's discourse since the

Single Market has been to present the EU as a single 'economic space' (Rosamond 2002). Ultimately, however, the Commission has only reinforced the necessitarian logic of achieving (global) competitiveness objectives: divergences in competitiveness are strenuously argued not to be 'a problem of trade policy', whose 'core objective […] must be to maintain, and where necessary, re-invent Europe's place in global supply chains' (European Commission 2013a: 3). There is no concession to the idea that exposure to global markets may have resulted in 'asymmetric shocks' amongst Member States (see Chen *et al.* 2012). Rather, not only do 'Member States' performances impl[y] a competitiveness problem' largely in terms of their trade with fellow Eurozone partners – rather than external third parties – but, more importantly, this lagging performance also requires structural reforms – in the context of the broader 'Europe 2020' strategy – so that they can 'step up their capacity to compete' (European Commission 2013a: 3). Promoting the EU's upmarket exports is ultimately presented as the only viable option for EU trade policy in the future.

Potential future limitations to the EU's trade and discursive strategy[7]

As the European demand crisis and public austerity continue to bite, the pressure on the Commission to deliver the 'promised' fruits of liberalisation – the 'growth and jobs' of the 'Europe 2020' Agenda rhetoric – will increase. Indeed, DG Trade is perfectly aware of the political limits of its neoliberal trade strategy – especially where others fail to reciprocate. This has led it to embrace 'reciprocity' to improve the EU's waning *leverage* with emerging economies. The hope is that this will yield the liberalisation gains that have remained elusive in so many cases and which will allow it to 'sell' liberalisation to the public and other political actors (given the more mercantilist reading of trade policy in general circulation). Aside from the obvious difficulties to realising this objective that such a strategy betrays, there are also a few reasons as to why banking unconditionally on free trade to deliver 'growth and jobs' may be problematic. My argument in this section is that this may put the EU's trade strategy and rhetoric under increased pressure in the future, even if so far neoliberalism and the discourses that underpin it have remained surprisingly 'resilient' during the current crisis (Schmidt and Thatcher 2013; see also Crouch 2011).

Firstly, there is the 'one-size-fits-all' approach to trade policy – which involves DG Trade dismissing the differential impact this has had on countries in the Eurozone. As is even argued in an article from a recent

ECB monthly bulletin, it is clear that '[t]he large and persistent current account imbalances recorded in some euro area countries in the years leading up to the global financial crisis generally reflected deficits vis-à-vis *both* intra-euro area *and extra-euro area partners*' (ECB 2013: 74, emphasis added; see also an International Monetary Fund [IMF] study on the issue, Chen *et al.* 2012: 4). Exposing the Eurozone's worst performers to the vicissitudes of the global, rather than just the European (Single) Market, is unlikely to be particularly helpful to their recovery and may become a source of political opposition to free trade in the future (De Ville and Orbie 2013: 13–14). This is especially relevant if we consider that it is precisely the economies of 'emerging Asia' which the EU is targeting for market-opening – either via its 'Global Europe' FTAs or other initiatives – that appear to be responsible for 'displacing exports' from Eurozone debtor countries (Chen *et al.* 2012: 12–18).

Secondly, even if we overlook the differential impacts of trade policy between Member States and focus on 'EU-wide' performance, the question remains as to how far the Commission can continue to legitimate its free trade policies given the potential for significant adjustment costs. There is as of yet only limited recognition of a potential problem among policymakers; the Issues Paper goes as far as to suggest that it is *desirable* for developing countries to catch up as it will allow for greater vertical *and* horizontal intra-industry specialisation (that is, differentiation in terms of, respectively, quality and variety) with reduced adjustment costs for EU industry in line with the expectations of neoclassical trade theory (European Commission 2005a: 36).

Although it is the Commission's long-term aspiration for this sort of model to develop in its trade with emerging economies, the fact remains that it still relies mostly on promoting vertical intra-industry specialisation. Even according to its own logic, this faith in vertical intra-industry specialisation is problematic. The 2005 'Issues Paper' acknowledged the long-term limitations of vertical intra-industry specialisation, arguing that this was likely to lead the EU to specialise in a very narrow subset of products if the living standards of emerging economies did not catch up and lead to horizontal specialisation (European Commission 2005a: 35–7). So far, furthermore, this problem has beset the EU's trade agreements with even relatively developed trading partners, where the pattern of specialisation has not been horizontal. The EU's proposed and agreed trade-offs in the context of its 'Global Europe' FTAs have so far been largely inter-sectoral in nature (in that DG Trade has consciously traded away protection in one sector for market access in another), with the clear potential for significant economic adjustment away from production in lower-end EU industries/services. This is particularly significant if one considers the case of the EU's FTA with South Korea. Despite being touted as an example of vertical intra-sectoral specialisation between both parties, given the relative maturity of the Korean economy, it is still likely to lead to inter-sectoral adjustment in the EU (in that the car sector is likely to contract as a whole and services likely to expand). One should not forget that this is what caused the already considerable political fallout from the FTA in the first place. The fact that the political trade-offs pursued in the context of an FTA with one of the most advanced economies targeted by 'Global Europe' are still likely to lead to inter-sectoral adjustment runs counter to the neoclassical economic optimism espoused by policymakers (and some political scientists) about the prospects for (supposedly less painful and politically less costly) intra-industry specialisation via FTAs (European Commission 2005a; Manger 2012).

Although the EU's discursive strategy has so far been successful at legitimating these painful trade-offs in terms of the important economic gains made for upmarket sectors, it is uncertain as to how it would fare in future. Although trade between the EU and emerging economies is still largely inter-sectoral in nature, as DG Trade itself admitted in the 2005 'Issues Paper', these economies are likely to move up the value chain and engage in more intra-industry trade with the EU; indeed, there is already evidence that such economies are gaining on the EU in terms of their competitiveness in such products (European Commission 2005a: 36; see also Rodrik 2006). Although, as I noted above, this is seen as a positive trend by officials in DG Trade, there are grounds for doubting this optimistic assessment. The EU's current upmarket export model is premised on the EU facing very little competition here given the inter-sectoral nature of political trade-offs that have been pursued and that are still being contemplated (for example in the case of the EU–India FTA, see García and Khorana 2013; Siles-Brügge 2013a). Its current FTA strategy may lead it to specialise in a narrower set of upmarket products to the detriment of a more diversified economy. The Commission's current trade strategy thus risks undermining the EU's manufacturing base while compensating gains at the higher end of the scale are increasingly likely to be put under pressure; trade liberalisation on its own is unlikely to lead to an improvement in competitiveness for upmarket exports as these typically do not perform on the basis of their price (Hay 2012). Whether the Commission would be able to legitimate continued openness by appealing to the external forces of globalisation if EU exporters were doing badly remains an open question.

Speaking more broadly, both of these issues have the potential to undermine the position of DG Trade's discursive strategy within the 'Europe 2020' macroeconomic consensus, as the gulf between the 'competitiveness' and 'social Europe' (the 'first' and 'second') pillars grows.[8] As I noted in Chapter 3, Pascal Lamy's pronouncements strongly suggested that he felt both could be reconciled, while Brittan's, Mandelson's and now De Gucht's discourse of external constraint does not explicitly speak to this issue. This is potentially problematic in light of the fact that some of the opposition to the EU's '2020 Trade Strategy' has already been registered in the EP under the banner of a social argument. For instance, a fear expressed by an EP resolution is that the Commission's new competence for investment negotiations might lead the EU to negotiate agreements that impinge on the national 'right to regulate' (European Parliament 2011b). By not explicitly resolving the inherent tension that might emerge within the Lisbon/'Europe 2020' discourse in light of the aforementioned developments in the world economy – beyond expressing a vague hope that trade will increasingly allow for intra-industry specialisation and the maintenance of a manufacturing base, when its policies have been moving the EU in the opposite direction – DG Trade's current and ongoing discursive strategy has the potential to undermine itself. While the Polanyian 'countermovement' – that is, the social re-embedding of neoliberal markets – has not yet occurred despite the crisis (*pace* predictions to this effect; see Caporaso and Tarrow 2009: 615–16), it remains to be seen how this struggle over a successor to 'embedded liberalism' will end.

Finally, and as I showed in Chapter 5, the rhetoric behind the EU's trade discourse has already been challenged successfully in the domain of development policy by anti-EPA campaigners. While future research is needed to understand how this discourse was successfully deconstructed, this raises all sorts of issues for the EU's trade agenda going forward. Indeed, although the EPA agenda has stagnated, the EU's 'commercial' and 'developmental' trade agendas remain heavily intertwined. The GSP reforms discussed in this chapter are the flagship policy of the Commission's 2012 communication on 'Trade, Growth and Development'. This has brought to the fore the theme of 'differentiating' between developing countries (especially between emerging economies and the rest) that has featured – albeit less prominently – in previous EU pronouncements on trade in the Doha Round (see Mandelson 2005b: 13). The aim (to quote the communication's subtitle) is to 'tailor[] trade and investment policy for those countries most in need', so that such states may also 'reap the benefits of open and increasingly integrated world markets' (European Commission 2012a: 2). However, these development-based arguments in favour of, among other things, reforming the GSP scheme – to help LDCs and 'vulnerable' economies – jar with the Commission's clear preference for placing trade relations with such countries on a contractually enshrined free trading basis via FTAs. In the past, at least the argument could be made that in seeking regulatory liberalisation as part of the EPAs, DG Trade was genuinely *convinced* of their value as developmental tools (as this was consistent with their behaviour in pushing for the inclusion of such provisions in the EPAs). Given that even this agenda was successfully challenged by anti-EPA actors, the increasingly visible subordination of 'developmental' to 'commercial' imperatives has the potential to further weaken DG Trade's neoliberal rhetoric in the area of development, even spilling over to its negotiations with emerging economies. In the case of the EU–India FTA, for example, the EU faces considerable opposition from civil society campaigners and certain MEPs over the agreement's IPR chapter and the issue of access to medicines (García and Khorana 2013: 692–3). This is viewed with some trepidation by some within the exporter and policy-making community, who fear that the EP may become a roadblock to the ratification of the EU–India FTA.

Conclusion

In this chapter I have focused on the evolution of the 'Global Europe' offensive trade agenda in the aftermath of the Financial and Eurozone Crises. I argued that, despite the potential for increased protectionist pressure from societal actors and the EP, EU trade policy has still been driven by a concern with servicing upmarket exporters at the expense of protected sectors in the EU economy. I have shown how the move towards emphasising reciprocity in the EU's trade relations with third parties has to be seen as serving this wider objective, specifically through the creation of a new offensive instrument in government procurement and by changing the shape of the GSP regime. Both initiatives are aimed at increasing EU leverage in negotiations with emerging country trade partners. I find that such developments are underpinned by continuity in the beliefs held by officials in DG Trade and the current Commissioner Karel De Gucht vis-à-vis their predecessors responsible for drafting 'Global Europe'. In the communicative sphere, this continuity is also reflected in the use of similar rhetorics of external constraint to legitimate free trade.

It is on the future success of this discursive strategy, however, that some open questions remain. Although it remains successful so far at legitimating DG Trade's neoliberal trade agenda, underscoring the argument of those within the field of IPE that have written about the 'resilience' of neoliberalism during the present crisis (for example, Schmidt and Thatcher 2013), the jury is still out on whether it will be able to do so in the future, especially if openness does not deliver 'growth and jobs' as promised by the Commission. More specifically, it remains to be seen to what extent DG Trade's emphasis on the external constraint posed by globalisation will be sustainable as the Eurozone crisis continues biting and as emerging economies' exports move up the value chain, directly threatening the EU's current export model. Similarly, it is unclear as to how successful such a discursive imperative will be at neutralising opposition from civil society as the competitiveness objectives of the EU increasingly impinge on its trade relationship with developing countries. Thus, and regardless of whether the discursive strategy continues being successful in future, ideas are likely to remain an important determinant of trade policy outcomes in the EU in years to come.

The June 2013 G8 summit in Lough Erne saw the EU and US formally announce they were launching talks on an EU–US FTA, the so-called Transatlantic Trade and Investment Partnership (TTIP). Interestingly, such a commercially significant FTA did not meet the criteria previously set down in 'Global Europe' in terms of 'market potential' (the US is a 'mature' market) and 'the level of protection against EU export interests' (its market is already largely open to the EU) (European Commission 2006g: 11).[9] The origin of these negotiations was a decision taken at the November 2011 EU–US summit to establish a High Level Working Group (HLWG) on Jobs and Growth composed of EU and US officials and led by De Gucht and USTR's Ron Kirk. Its task was 'to identify policies and measures to increase U.S.–EU trade and investment' (European Commission 2011e: 1). Its final report from February 2013 recommended the opening of FTA negotiations between both parties (HLWG 2013), with the EU's mandate for negotiations being authorised in a Council vote in June (Council of the EU 2013). Aside from sending a signal about the continuing stagnation of the Doha Round, the timing of this decision suggests that (on the EU side) it may also be partly driven by the Commission's frustration with emerging economy interlocutors and the perceived need to continue producing liberalisation results.[10] Indeed, in its impact assessment of the TTIP, the Commission argued that an ambitious FTA would not only deliver increases in national income for both partners of around 151 billion euro (author's calculation, using data from European Commission 2013b: 37), but also 'more jobs supported by trade, increases in wages for both unskilled and skilled employees, together with increases in competitiveness and an improved standing for both the EU and the US in respect of other global competitors' (European Commission 2013b: 56). While it is of course too early to say whether the agreement will deliver all that is promised, it suggests that DG Trade remains committed to putting its eggs in the bilateral liberalisation basket, with all the difficulties that this might entail.

7
Conclusion

The main argument in this book has been that trade is what actors make of it; 'a global idea of Europe' has been reproduced by actors and has led to an increasingly neoliberal orientation in EU trade policy. The more specific aim I set up in the introduction was to address three separate, albeit interrelated, research puzzles raised by conventional understandings of (EU) trade policy. Firstly, I was interested in why the EU adopted a preferential trade strategy at the time that it did. Secondly, I wanted to explore *why* this strategy was premised on trading away protection for market access and *how* the EU's trade negotiators in DG Trade were able to achieve this, particularly at a time of economic crisis and against the opposition of powerful sectoral interests. Finally, I sought to explore the reasons behind the increasing entwinement of the EU's 'commercial' and 'developmental' trade agendas. Deliberately eschewing institutionalist and purely rationalist IPE approaches, I arrived at a constructivist IPE explanation.

In the first section of this chapter I consider how I have contributed to scholarly understanding of 'Global Europe' and EU trade politics in light of these research puzzles. I also provide an overview of the arguments raised by each chapter in the book. In the second section I then turn to consider the broader theoretical insights that my constructivist framework offers the study of not only (EU) trade politics but also the international political economy more generally. In the process, I conclude the book by highlighting how these insights would inform a future research agenda in EU Studies and IPE.

'Global Europe' and EU trade politics: The role of interest groups and ideas

The first puzzle addressed in this book was prompted by the rational institutionalist EU Studies literature, which has been focused on the institutional constraints facing trade policymakers from either a 'multi-level' game or a PA approach. At the heart of such approaches has been a historical narrative about the depoliticisation of EU trade policymaking in the wake of increasing supranational integration in Europe. The argument is that this has meant that the Commission – insulated from societal and systemic pressures – has increasingly been able to act autonomously. The SMP, in particular, has been seen as a crucial turning point in this respect, shifting the balance of power between the Council and Commission in favour of the latter. This, so the argument goes, allowed the EU to ditch a generally defensive attitude vis-à-vis the multilateral trading system and adopt a more proactive stance premised on seeking commercial gains via multilateral trade liberalisation efforts. Institutionalist approaches, however, struggle to explain the turn to bilateralism in 'Global Europe' in the absence of institutional changes to the EU's trade policy machinery in the intervening period. Both the Treaties of Amsterdam (1997) and Nice (2001) – which introduced changes to the operation of the CCP – predated the new strategy (and even its gestation period) by several years. In the same way, the Treaty of Lisbon – which granted the EP a greater role in trade policymaking – only came into force in December 2009, over three years after 'Global Europe' was announced. Moreover, even if we focus on the gradual and informal ascendancy of the European Commission in EU trade policymaking – which explains the focus taken in this book on the Commission's role – this has long preceded the shift in policy and cannot account for its nature or sudden emergence: after all, Lamy (who rejected bilateralism) was working under very similar conditions to Mandelson (who embraced it). In sum, the timing of 'Global Europe' does not fit within an approach that emphasises the pre-eminence of institutional factors in shaping EU foreign economic policymaking.

The second puzzle for conventional understanding of (EU) trade policy that I raised in Chapter 1 concerned the content of 'Global Europe'. Crucially, the strategy was premised on exchanging the EU's remaining 'pockets of protection' for market access gains for the EU's upmarket exporters. This saw the EU trading away protection in the automobile sector for regulatory liberalisation in services and investment in the case of the EU–Korea FTA and at the time of the Financial Crisis. Although this galvanised the opposition to the FTA, especially from the powerful automobile industry which had access to policymakers at all levels of the EU machinery, DG Trade was still able to get the agreement signed, ratified and implemented. This was puzzling in the sense that it defied domestic IPE explanations of trade policy emphasising collective action dynamics – whereby protectionists remain influential even where exporters mobilise in support of trade liberalisation. Similarly, the rational institutionalist approach to emphasising the supranational insulation of EU trade policymaking is an insufficient explanation of *why* and *how* trade policymakers pursued this course of action in light of the fact that import-competing sectors were very active and had access to policymakers at different levels of EU trade governance.

The third puzzle was to explain the increasing entwinement of the EU's 'commercial' and 'developmental' trade agendas in the wake of 'Global Europe' when both are said to be driven by distinct imperatives. The EU's trade relations with the ACP – seen as a flagship of its international development policy – have usually been described as separate from the EU's economic interests further afield in the discourse of policymakers. This distinction has also found its way into the conventional (rational institutionalist) literature on EU–ACP trade relations, which has emphasised the functional differentiation between different Commission DGs (Trade and Development). Even where the entwinement of 'commercial' and 'developmental' imperatives has been acknowledged by such authors, these have tended to emphasise the shifting of functional responsibility for trade with the ACP from DG Development to DG Trade in the late 1990s. This, however, does fit the timing and content of the EU's EPAs with the ACP which, after Mandelson's arrival as Trade Commissioner, became part and parcel of the EU's bilateral trade strategy. Not only was there a renewed interest in these latter agreements, but DG Trade pushed very strongly for the inclusion of WTO-plus, regulatory provisions which bore a striking similarity to those it was seeking in 'Global Europe' FTAs (particularly in the area of services and investment).

In Chapter 2, I arrived at a constructivist IPE approach to explain these three developments. I began by arguing that mainstream IPE accounts marked an improvement on the EU Studies approach by focusing on the role of systemic pressures, domestic political competition between various economic interest groups, or a combination of both types of factors. This latter, 'combined' IPE literature was, in my eyes, particularly useful at highlighting important features of the current wave of regionalism of which the EU was a participant. These included its North–South focus, its competitive and discriminatory logic and the emphasis on regulatory liberalisation in services and investment (Manger 2009). However, it still neglected the important role played by ideas in constructing social reality. I built on an existing constructivist literature in IPE that has emphasised agential uncertainty (most notably, Blyth 2002) to argue that ideas matter in IPE because they are treated *as though they are material constraints*. This is particularly relevant if one considers the purchase of neoliberal economic discourse in policymaking (and academic) circles, derived specifically from neoclassical economic trade theory in this case. As a result, I developed a constructivist IPE approach that stressed the role of agents in constructing social reality, drawing on insights from a literature on so-called 'discourses of globalisation' (Hay and Rosamond 2002; Schmidt 2002b). I focused on two dimensions of discourse here. On the one hand, the strategic pathway to discourse focuses on the use actors made of particular rhetorics of economic constraint to legitimate politically contentious policy decisions. The reflexive pathway, in turn, is concerned with studying how particular ideas become internalised by actors and how these in turn also shape discourse strategies. I subsequently developed a novel analytical technique to determine the strategic invocation of discourse. My appeal to ideational logics of explanation, however, did not seek to detract from the insights of rationalist IPE when it came to explaining the preferences of interest groups and their influence with policymakers. I accommodated these insights within my ontologically consistent constructivism by recasting these groups' attempts at influence in terms of strategic discourse. This was premised on appeals to the external *threat* of commercial rivals.

The empirical story then began in Chapter 3. I started by charting the broad historical evolution of EU trade policy from the days of 'embedded liberalism' to the neoliberal shift implied by the SMP of the late 1980s and early 1990s. Crucially, this coincided with EU trade policymakers actively embracing the multilateral trading system following decades of EU defensiveness over agriculture and other issues (including NTBs). However, rather than seeing this as evidence of the increasing depoliticisation of trade policymaking – supposedly resulting from increased European integration and the supranational insulation of policymakers in the Commission – my focus was on the role played by interest groups and ideas in setting the EU trade policymaking agenda. Thus, the EU's new emphasis on commercial 'multilateralism' translated, in addition to a moratorium on new FTAs to emphasise the EU's priorities, into a constructive working relationship between interest groups and policymakers. Following the collapse of the Cancún summit, however, expectations for the Round receded amongst this constituency (especially as the Doha Round appeared to be increasingly stalled by 2005–06). In response, a discourse of external threat was constructed by these business actors, and in particular the services lobby, which sought to paint preferential liberalisation as a *must*, given the systemic pressures being exerted by the EU's competitors (especially the US). This ended up having its intended effects under Commissioner Peter Mandelson, who abandoned the 'multilateralism-first' approach of his predecessor to join the fray of preferential trade liberalisation. 'Global Europe' thus saw the EU initiate FTA talks with a group of emerging Asian economies (namely India, the ASEAN bloc and South Korea). This was in large part a result of the pressure of interest groups, which found in Mandelson and his DG a willing set of interlocutors. Moreover, the services lobby was not only particularly forceful – in part because it perceived itself to have a more urgent interest in preferential liberalisation given 'first mover' effects – but also successful at pushing its agenda. It managed to ensure that services and investment liberalisation was at the heart of the new strategy in the form of a new template for FTA talks (the 'Minimum Platform'). Focus on the reflexive dimension to discourse also explained why interest groups only invoked a competitive *threat* argument vis-à-vis policymakers after the failure of Cancún (even when EU rivals were pursuing PTAs earlier than that). Prior to that ill-fated summit, the discourse of trade multilateralism espoused by policymakers was still seen as viable.

In Chapter 3, I also explained why DG Trade not only chose to listen to interest groups but also why and how it explicitly sought to pursue politically costly trade-offs through its preferential trade strategy. I did so by focusing on the role of ideas. Specifically, I argued that policymakers had internalised neoliberal beliefs deriving from neoclassical trade theory that saw in economic restructuring – along the lines of international comparative advantage – a desirable (yet politically contingent) outcome. This would boost the EU's global competitiveness, which had to be pursued through further liberalisation of third party markets. These beliefs were used to explain why policymakers heeded the arguments of exporters over those of defensive interests. They also accounted for the moves taken by policymakers to encourage exporters to mobilise in favour of their neoliberal agenda of market opening. In addition, this meant that policymakers were susceptible to the arguments of such interests when they were clamouring for more market access abroad through FTAs at a time where the Doha Round appeared moribund (the so-called reflexive dimension to discourse). In order to legitimate this potentially controversial agenda, DG Trade strategically constructed a discursive imperative by linking 'Global Europe' to the Lisbon Agenda of macroeconomic reform. The argument they invoked was that the external constraint that Lisbon had identified – the notion that the EU had to face up to the challenges posed by globalising markets – necessitated an increasing emphasis on ensuring EU competitiveness. In this way, DG Trade was also able to seize discursive terrain within EU economic policymaking by linking internal rulemaking to external trade policymaking (the so-called 'external dimension of competitiveness').

In Chapter 4, I focused on explaining the content, negotiation and ratification of the EU–Korea FTA. This represents the most tangible embodiment of the 'Global Europe' project so far. In this respect, I built on some of the issues first explored in Chapter 3. I focused on the related issues of *why* DG Trade chose to pursue politically contentious liberalisation in the context of its agreement with Korea – where market access for European service providers was obtained in exchange for a liberalisation of trade in automobiles and other manufactured goods – and *how* it was then able to achieve this outcome despite the opposition of a major industry with powerful backers inside the EU policymaking machinery. I began in the chapter by providing some background to the agreement in terms of its likely distributive consequences and systemic context (competition with the KORUS FTA). I then showed how the FTA also highlighted the influence of services lobbyists during the negotiations, which were able to ensure that their preferences were heeded by invoking a competitive threat at the same time that import-competing interests were marginalised. DG Trade successfully made use of a similar ideational imperative for liberalisation created in 'Global Europe' to neutralise opposition to the FTA with South Korea. Indeed, the Commission was also able to draw on interest groups' *competitive threat* rhetoric – which was directed at the KORUS agreement – as a discursive resource in this task.

In Chapter 5, I sought to address the third puzzle I raised in the introduction, the issue of why the EU's 'developmental' and 'commercial' trade agendas have become increasingly entwined. I began by offering some historical background to the EU–ACP trade relationship, arguing that it originally developed separately from the GATT-oriented CCP, being premised on the principle of non-reciprocity (although it was of course not immune from commercial considerations). Following the shift to multilateralism in the EU's trade strategy, however, both regimes became increasingly linked, as the Commission sought to recast the

EU–ACP relationship in terms of WTO-compatible agreements. Following the arrival of Mandelson, moreover, the EPAs became an integral part of the EU's bilateral trade agenda, as the Commission more actively pursued these negotiations after a period of neglect under Lamy. Underscoring this point, I showed how the EU's 'Global Europe' FTAs and the EPAs bore a striking resemblance to one another in terms of their mutual emphasis on WTO-plus provisions, with services and investment provisions, in particular, being extremely similar in both types of agreement. I then began to explain this trend by situating the study of EU–ACP relations within my wider constructivist IPE of EU trade policy. As such, I saw the drivers of this change to be both interest group activism – again, from the services lobby which pushed hard for WTO-plus liberalisation in the EPAs – and policymakers' neoliberal beliefs that such liberalisation was not only good for the ACP but also for the EU. Their positive-sum view of free trade led them to see this as an opportunity for both sides to benefit from the forces of comparative advantage. This also explains why policymakers were susceptible to the arguments of (services) lobbyists on the issue, who made similar arguments to justify their advocacy of deregulating and liberalising ACP markets. Although DG Trade attempted, in the face of considerable opposition from NGOs and some Member States, to legitimate this agenda in terms of a 'Global Europe'-esque discourse of external constraint, they were ultimately unsuccessful in doing so.

In the final substantive chapter (Chapter 6) I focused on the ongoing evolution of the 'Global Europe' agenda in the context of the Financial and Eurozone Crises. DG Trade remains committed to pursuing the same objectives (as before) in the 'Trade, Growth and World Affairs' strategy, which has become the most recent overarching Commission statement on trade policy. I began in the chapter by highlighting that this is surprising given the context of the economic crisis, which might lead one to expect greater pressure from protectionist quarters (especially as the EP has gained a more prominent position in trade policy-making since the Treaty of Lisbon). Although I also highlighted that there was a new emphasis on 'reciprocity' in 'Trade, Growth and World Affairs', this is in fact aimed at improving the EU's leverage in ongoing trade negotiations with emerging economies (which are proceeding less well than it would like) rather than representing a turn towards protectionism or mercantilism. The reciprocity agenda has resulted in two specific initiatives: a reform of the EU's GSP scheme to reduce eligibility for preferences amongst emerging economies (including those the EU is currently negotiating an FTA with) and a proposed instrument to open third party government procurement markets through carefully managed closures (insulated from protectionist pressures) of the EU market. I also argued that the emphasis on 'reciprocity' betrayed an even more urgent realisation among policymakers that trade liberalisation was politically contingent in the aftermath of the Financial Crisis. This, in turn, made it even more important in their eyes to *communicate* the benefits of free trade. This was accomplished via a renewed strategic invocation of a discourse of external constraint, in this case furnished by 'Europe 2020' – the successor to the Lisbon competitiveness agenda. While this discourse, and the neoliberal orientation of EU trade policy more generally, remain resilient in the context of the current crisis, I considered a number of reasons why this may not hold in the future. These included the continued political pressure induced by the crisis, the possible erosion of the EU's performance in upmarket products in a world where the emerging economies are catching up and the challenge (predominantly from development NGOs) to the EU's trade-development discourse.

Broader contributions and future research agenda

My first theoretical aim in this book has been to add to the works on EU trade policy that situate it within the discipline of IPE (for instance, Dür 2007; Sbragia 2010), rather than treat it as *sui generis* (as in the rational institutionalist literature). For now, the 'political economy' turn in EU Studies (see Bache *et al.* 2011: 45–51) has mostly taken place from within a neo-Gramscian perspective (see, for example, van Apeldoorn 2002; Cafruny and Ryner 2003; Bieler 2006). What such works have been particularly useful at is highlighting the increasingly neoliberal nature of the EU political economy, especially in specific policy domains (Buch-Hansen and Wigger 2011; Horn 2011). The present study contributes to this latter field in particular – illustrating how the EU's trade policy has increasingly been linked to the marketisation of (aspects of) the European political economy by becoming the 'external dimension of competitiveness'. However, I would argue that there still remains much more room to incorporate studies of the EU into IPE and to move beyond the narrower problématique of this specific literature. This would be useful for two main reasons. Firstly, scholars could draw on a broader theoretical armoury to more fully explore the power relations at the heart of the EU. Secondly, it would be easier to interrogate the EU's place within the world. This is particularly important if one considers the status of the EU as a major economic power (and, in fact, the world's foremost trading entity).

Although the EU is not quite a state and does not always act cohesively, the fact remains that links between different actors within the EU are sufficiently established for it to be studied meaningfully from an IPE perspective. The sort of critically minded IPE that I advocate (see Chapter 2) explicitly acknowledges the importance of moving beyond a view of the international political economy as being composed of unitary and distinct state entities. The aim is breaking down artificial barriers between so-called 'levels of analysis' (that is, the so-called 'domestic' and 'systemic' spheres often found in IPE). In this respect the EU, with its multiple levels of policymaking, is not necessarily so different from the wider international political economy and the notion common in IPE circles that actors are engaged in a complex web of interactions (see, for instance, the theory of 'complex interdependence', see Keohane and Nye 1977; a more modern incarnation, 'transnational neopluralism', is found in Cerny 2011). There are thus many domains where the study of the EU's foreign and domestic economic policymaking could benefit from the theoretical insights of a being studied from within a broader IPE perspective. For instance, the EU has been playing a leading role in international negotiations to limit climate change. This has very important implications for the wider international political economy but, so far, studies of the EU in this domain have focused more on the domestic/institutional determinants of policymaking and less on the wider global context in which the EU is embedded (for example, Knill and Tosun 2009; Woolcock 2012: Ch. 5). Recognising that the EU is not that exceptional an entity in the international political economy is thus the first step towards better understanding its behaviour and place within global environmental governance, allowing researchers to draw on a wider literature on this issue existing in IPE (for instance, Clapp and Dauvergne 2011).

More specifically, I concur with Ryner's (2012) assessment that scholarship within EU Studies has been overly focused on explaining the drivers of European integration and has missed the underlying causes of the Eurozone Crisis; as he notes, the 'disciplinary politics' of the field (see Rosamond 2007) has ultimately prevented scholars from asking some of the broader questions about the nature of capitalism in Europe. The crisis thus represents a distinct opportunity to bring the EU into the study of IPE. I would also argue that the constructivist framework developed here offers important insights into the role of ideas in causing and sustaining the crisis. For one, the problems of the Eurozone have been underpinned by neoclassical economic doctrine; policymakers showed remarkable faith in monetary union as a source of financial stability when they created EMU (McNamara 1999) and continue to plump for austerity despite its, at best mixed, at worst counterproductive, macro-economic record (Blyth 2013). Moreover, during the Eurozone Crisis ideas have remained key to legitimating ongoing neoliberal agendas.

In this vein, and taking forward some of the more specific themes I began to explore in Chapters 4 and 6, it would be interesting to see how EU trade policy continues developing in the wake of this crisis as the discourse of external constraint invoked by Commission trade poli-cymakers has *so far* continued to allow them to legitimate trade liberali-sation policies. This seems to fit the findings of others, who have remarked on the 'resilience' of neoliberalism in the European political economy and have similarly pointed to the (successful) strategic use of ideas to legitimate unpopular policies (Schmidt and Thatcher 2013; see also Crouch 2011). But there is also the potential for such logics to be undone; DG Trade's discursive strategy may indeed face problems if the crisis continues biting. This raises important questions going forward as to what role such discourses can and will play in future EU trade policy (and within the European political economy more broadly) and whether they can continue to allow the Commission and other actors to neutralise opposition to neoliberalism.

The constraining role of agriculture within EU trade policy (where it has long tempered otherwise liberal policymaking impulses) also raises issues that a constructivist approach may be able to address. The prefer-ential approach to liberalisation pursued since 'Global Europe' has afforded DG Trade the opportunity to be more selective when picking off 'pockets of protection', avoiding a confrontation with the entrenched forces of agricultural protectionism as in the multilateral setting (con-strained by the parameters of the Single Undertaking); agriculture was never intended to be one of the 'pockets of protection' to be traded away for market access (unlike the automobile sector). Admittedly this is probably not only because the issue is not considered a stumbling block in most other 'Global Europe' FTA negotiations (with South Korea or India, for instance; see Chapter 4, García and Khorana 2013: 692) but rather also due to the special position of agriculture within EU trade policy. Although exploring this issue in detail has been beyond the scope of this study (given the low salience of the issue in the 'Global Europe' offensive trade agenda), it does raise questions about other EU trade negotiations where the *bête noire* of agriculture remains relevant – even as the Doha Round continues to stagnate and preferential agree-ments are seen as the only option for trade liberalisation. The role of EU agricultural protectionism has been a significant stumbling block in the still incomplete talks with MERCOSUR – which predated 'Global Europe' – and may even come to play a role in the FTA talks with the US (Egan 2013). The constructivist IPE approach developed in this book may thus contribute to a literature that suggests that EU 'agricultural exceptionalism' is not just a product of the constellation of interests but of institutionally embedded ideas in the international trading system (see Skogstad 1998; Daugbjerg and Swinbank 2009). Future work could move beyond the current focus on the politics of agricultural trade at the WTO to consider the role of agriculture as a potential constraint on preferential trade negotiations (including MERCOSUR and potentially the US).

My second major theoretical aim in this book was to bring ideas into the study of (EU) trade politics, as others have begun to do in the field, both adopting a constructivist IPE position (for example, Woll 2008; Bukovansky 2010) and/or focusing on the role of ideas, language and expertise in trade politics more broadly (Wilkinson 2009; De Ville and Orbie 2013; Trommer 2013). There is still very much a rationalist bias in this domain, not only within EU Studies but also within IPE. Indeed, other areas of empirical focus in IPE (such as production and finance) are already well-endowed with approaches that take ideational dynamics seriously (for example, Cox 1987; Seabrooke 2006). This does not mean, however, that there is nothing 'rationalist' scholars might wish to draw upon in my work. After all, I suggested that trade – and more specifically trade *liberalisation* – remains a very important issue within the international political economy despite the stagnation of the Doha Round in light of the continued proliferation of FTAs with a strong WTO-plus component. My findings in this book (drawing on Manger 2009) that services and investment liberalisation have been key drivers of this development are likely to interest future scholars, who may wish to further interrogate to what extent other developed countries are driven by a similar concern with regulatory liberalisation. Indeed, most of the literature on trade has focused on goods despite what Young and Peterson (2006: 795, emphasis added) call the 'deep trade agenda', that is, the increasing drive towards 'seeking […] [trade] agreements on the making of *domestic* rules'.

What is perhaps most interesting from my own constructivist perspective is that free trade itself (wrought by both FTAs and multilateral trade liberalisation efforts) has been remarkably resilient in the face of the crisis, not just in the EU but also further afield. Despite some concern over the measures taken by some members, the WTO's 2011 Annual Report stated that '[g]overnments appear to have learned the lessons from the past, with a clear rejection of the "beggar-thy-neighbour" protectionism that had such a disastrous effect in the Great Depression' (WTO 2011b: 10). This raises a puzzle for what could be called rational institutionalist explanations of the world trading system (what in the 'systemic' IPE/IR literature is often called 'neoliberal institutionalism') similar to that explored in this book. While many would stress the importance of the WTO in resisting protectionist pressures – and more specifically, its strong, judicialised system for the enforcement of international trade regulation and liberalisation commitments (for instance, Goldstein *et al.* 2007) – the fact remains that countries have continued to apply tariffs at lower rates than they are (legally) 'bound' to in the context of multilateral trade liberalisation talks (see Hoekman *et al.* 2007: 508). This specific puzzle suggests that my constructivist framework may be a useful approach. It would allow one to interrogate both the motivations of policymakers, but, more importantly why these policymakers have been able to legitimate the maintenance of free trade, despite the existence of political pressure for trade protection, by invoking an external constraint. Indeed, the excerpt cited from the 2011 WTO Annual Report suggests that policymakers are already invoking the spectre of the Great Depression in order to legitimate trade liberalisation (for the beginnings of such an argument, see Siles-Brügge 2013b).

Finally, in this book I have made a number of contributions to a wider constructivist research agenda. Firstly, I was able to illustrate that the study of discourses of external constraint can move beyond a focus on the hyperglobalisation thesis to study other forms of economic discourses. Secondly, I devised an analytical strategy to more parsimoniously determine whether such ideas were being invoked instrumentally by contrasting policymakers' 'coordinative' (private) and 'communicative' (public) discourses (the terms are taken from Schmidt 2002b). Combined, these two insights are likely to be interesting to political economists interrogating the dominant neoliberal economic policymaking paradigm in a variety of fields, from changes in the labour market (often justified in terms of needing to meet external competitive pressures, see Menz 2009) to reform of welfare provision or higher education along more free market lines (see Haskel 2008). In the context of the crisis and (often externally mandated) austerity packages, the insights I offer are likely to remain relevant to those wishing to understand how such projects are being legitimated (Blyth 2013; Schmidt and Thatcher 2013). Moreover, by broadening the way discourses of external constraint are conceptualised I have hopefully shown how my insights could be applied beyond the context of economic policymaking. Taking the arena of international security, for instance, it is clear that the discourse surrounding the 'global war on terror' has often been premised on constructing an external constraint. This takes the form of an amorphous threat from 'terrorists' that has been used to justify controversial domestic security and foreign policy agendas (on this, see Record 2004). Similarly, what some scholars have called the 'legal turn' in IR (Abbott *et al.* 2000) – the increasing judicialisation and constitutionalisation of international law – suggests that legal discourses are also, much like economic discourses, increasingly treated as external constraints. The specific approach to these issues taken in this book would allow scholars to determine *why* particular ideas have mattered rather than simply relying on uncertainty as an enabler for ideational explanation as in previous constructivist IPE accounts (see Blyth 2002; Woll 2008). This can help to overcome the criticism of some neo-Marxist scholars that constructivist approaches provide insufficient theoretical insight into why certain ideas trump others. Moreover, it avoids the overly deterministic and holistic approach of neo-Gramscianism, which pays insufficient attention to the role of particular agents in propagating specific ideas (such as neoliberalism).

In this vein, my third theoretical contribution to studies of constructivism was to add to the analytical purchase of the so-called 'reflexive dimension' of discourse by highlighting how ideas matter because they are internalised by actors and treated *as though they were material factors*. My specific application of this idea was to claim that this allowed one to rely on rationalist models to determine interest group perceptions of interest. At the same time, however, I was able to draw on constructivism to show why particular interests were more influential with policymakers than others and how interest groups' perceptions were potentially subject to change over time. This promises a whole host of insights into the role that interest groups play within trade policy and within economic policymaking more broadly for two reasons. Firstly, while interest groups' preferences are seen as grounded in some understanding of the material world, they are not fixed but changeable and context-dependent. This insight could allow scholars to study how the preferences of interest groups change over time in response to different external stimuli and why certain factors have a greater bearing on the preferences of economic interest groups. For instance, although scholars have studied the emergence of the services lobby in international trade negotiations as the product of the internalisation of particular ideas at times of uncertainty (for example, Drake and Nicolaïdis 1992; Woll 2008), the fact remains that this tells one little about why these specific ideas were influential in the first place or about the relationship between such ideas and the wider economic (and what could be called 'material') context. In other words, such an approach would offer additional explanatory power in assessing how interest groups respond to changes in their economic setting. This may be particularly useful to understand how business groups evaluate their interests in a world that is not only experiencing profound economic change following the Financial Crisis, but is also likely to see significant global environmental change over the coming years. Secondly, understanding the 'reflexive dimension' to discourse, and specifically interest group pronouncements, might help future researchers to understand why certain groups trump others (or indeed fail to persuade altogether) in permeable political systems. The key lies in drawing attention to the affinity between their arguments and the belief systems of policymakers. There is evidence to suggest that well-resourced and cohesive business groups may not always be as influential as rationalist theories might expect and that the 'stories' they 'tell' are key to the success of their lobbying efforts (Nilsson 2010). The approach developed in this book would provide some insight into the discursive strategies of business groups and why or why not they may be successful.

More broadly, the emphasis on actors internalising 'as if' material rationalities does not just provide an insight into the study of interest groups but also represents a step towards bridging the perceived gap between constructivism and rationalism. So far this has largely been done in the literature from an ontologically inconsistent position by claiming that actors behave according to two different logics of explanation at different times (see, for example, Schimmelfennig 2003; Jabko 2006). In contrast, the idea of 'as if' rationality that I have contributed to in this book suggests that rational behaviour itself can be treated as a construction. This can help researchers to understand why particular rationalities are internalised by all manner of actors and under what circumstances these are liable to change. In light of the increasing emphasis placed in IPE scholarship on 'everyday IPE' – that is, the behaviour of 'small-scale actors' – and the role of culture within such frameworks (see Hobson and Seabrooke 2007), it may be useful to future researchers to consider how particular cultural frameworks predisposition certain individuals to adopt certain courses of action which are deemed to be 'rational'. For instance, Langley (2007) discusses that although savings can take many forms, a particular form of 'mass investment culture' has taken hold in Anglo-American society (and further afield), with now well-known implications for the wider international political economy. The agent-focused constructivist approach developed in this book – and its emphasis on internalisation effects – may therefore be quite useful to such scholars interrogating the 'microfoundations' of IPE.

Finally, and to conclude, in this book I have highlighted that discourses of external constraint, while often successful, have the potential to fail; indeed, in Chapter 6 I provided some preliminary evidence to suggest that the Commission's own discursive strategy is likely to be increasingly put under pressure given the economic crisis and the entwinement of the EU's commercial and developmental trade agendas. This has so far not been considered very frequently in the literature and it raises important questions for future researchers. Why are necessitarian (economic, but also broader political) logics internalised (or otherwise successful) in certain contexts but not others? At what point do previously successful discourses of constraint become unviable? I have begun to suggest that discourses premised on an external material constraint have the potential to unravel themselves if that external (to an extent material) economic context (over which the Commission does not have total control) does not develop favourably (for example if the EU's high-end exporters face increased competition from emerging economies, invoking globalisation as an external constraint may be increasingly difficult). Similarly, in Chapter 5 I showed that in the domain of 'development' the Commission's necessitarian arguments in favour of the EPAs had very little truck with actors that were critical of its agenda. In contrast, in the area of 'commercial' trade policy even import-competing interests acknowledged the economic logic advanced by the Commission in defence of the EU–Korea FTA. This hints at the fact that the success of such discourses may be, to an extent, context-dependent. It remains, however, an area that requires further study, especially if scholars are to better understand the eminently complex relationship between the material world and societal actors' interpretation of it, which shapes much political life.

Appendix: Coding and Selecting Texts for Discursive Analysis

In the preceding chapters, I relied on selecting particular texts (and especially policymaking documents) to determine policymakers' coordinative discourse (which corresponds to their beliefs), which I then contrasted to their communicative discourse to identify strategic uses of discourses of external constraint (the distinction between both types of discourse is from Schmidt 2002b; for more theoretically-informed definitions of the terms 'coordinative' and 'communicative' discourse, see Chapter 2). The purpose of this appendix is to provide a methodological justification for the coding and selection of these texts.

Coding texts

While communicative discourse may be relatively easy to infer from examining public texts, one of the most significant problems facing researchers in this domain is how to distinguish this from coordinative discourse. This is particularly relevant in light of Hay and Smith's (2010: 904) argument that studies predicated on studying public pronouncements through texts 'are simply incapable of providing the detailed picture of policymakers' assumptions and understandings of globalisation [...] that we increasingly seem to acknowledge that we need'. Their reasoning is two-fold. Firstly, they highlight that one cannot simply infer 'cognitions' from public pronouncements given the potential for a strategic invocation of particular ideas. Secondly, they argue that policymakers often make only a passing reference to the term globalisation in their pronouncements, precluding an in-depth study of their understanding of the term from such data. As a result, they argue that there is 'no substitute for raw attitudinal data' (Hay and Smith 2010: 904) collected via surveys. A survey-based approach to gauging policymakers' beliefs has also been popular in other constructivist work in IPE, such as Chwieroth's (2010) study of the IMF. Data collected in this manner is then analysed in terms of either the descriptive statistics it yields or by using a more sophisticated quantitative technique such as factor analysis (for example in Hay and Smith 2010).

In contrast, the nature of my analytical strategy to determine the strategic invocation of discourses of external constraint (see Chapter 2) informs the methodological approach I take in this book to infer policymakers' beliefs from the texts (and especially documents) used in policy formulation. In my view it is not just the fact that discourse is private that allows one to conclude that it is coordinative. Although coordinative discourse may at times only be found in purely internal documentation, there will be occasions when one can arrive at it by studying publicly available texts, provided one understands the context in which they originate.

This claim requires some more detail and substantiation. I do this with specific reference to the argument that Schmidt (2002b: 230–9) develops regarding the nature of coordinative and communicative discourses. To recap the definitions of both of these terms, coordinative discourse 'serves to provide policy actors with a common language and ideational framework through which they can together construct a policy programme' while communicative discourse 'serves political actors as the means for persuading the public' (or, if we generalise the concept, those outside 'the common language and ideational framework' in which policy is constructed). Moreover, not only does the coordinative phase of policy construction precede the communicative phase of political legitimation, but, crucially, these two discourses are 'analytically and empirically separable' (Schmidt 2002b: 230). Schmidt (2002b: 231) identifies how, among other things, they feature different intended audiences (fellow policy actors in the case of the former and the public in the case of the latter); 'purposes' ('construct[ing] a policy programme' vs. 'communicat[ing] to the public') and 'forms' ('provid[ing] language and framework for policy [...] deliberation' vs. 'translat[ing] programme[s] into accessible language for public [...] deliberation'). Aside from the content of particular discourses we have to be aware of the broader context in which they arise; in other words, 'the interactive process involved in articulating a discourse' becomes as important as the discourse itself (Schmidt 2002b: 230). This is why I speak of coordinative and communicative *settings* to denote the importance of *locating* a particular set of ideas. In this vein, Schmidt (2002b: 232) also distinguishes between the nature of actors involved in articulating discourses (with 'policy actors' being associated with a coordinative discourse and 'political actors' being associated with communicative discourse). That being said, her recognition that the same actors are often involved across discursive settings suggests that this is a more fluid (and hence less reliable) indicator of where to situate ideas. Indeed, in the case of this book, the Commission was the prime articulator of discourses in both coordinative and communicative settings. As a result, I would argue that what her distinction between 'policy' and 'political' actors fundamentally points to is the logic of behaviour existing in different discursive arenas, rather than the exact actors involved.

This leaves me with the methodological claim that we can distinguish between coordinative (or non-strategic) and communicative (strategic) discourses by exploring their intended audience, purpose and form. For one, what need do policymakers have to invoke ideas instrumentally *when they are speaking to* stakeholders with which they share – referring to part of Schmidt's (2002b: 230) key definition of coordinative discourse – a 'common language and ideational framework'? The fact that the *purpose* of such discussions is to draft policy only adds grist to the mill, especially as we can distinguish this phase of discourse articulation from a 'communicative' one. Indeed, as Schmidt (2002b: 233, 237–8) points out, she is not alone in seeing evidence of ideas taking on very different logics depending on their purpose: she shows how the literatures on 'epistemic communities' (such as Haas 1992) or 'advocacy coalitions' (for example, Sabatier 1998) operate within a coordinative discursive frame; in contrast, 'political entrepreneurs' deploying communicative ideas have been discussed within the literature on external economic constraints considered at length above. Finally, discourses intended for policy discussions are likely to take on very different *forms* to those for public (or more broadly *political*) consumption; coordinative texts are likely to feature the language of *insiders* to policy construction and are thus likely to be more technical, while discourse that is intended to communicate to *outsiders* is likely to take on a more accessible form.

The obvious limitation of relying on these criteria to select particular texts for analysis is that coordinative documents may well be hard to come by (especially in a specific field like trade policy). Any judgment in this respect is thus likely to be empirical and circumscribed, placing a considerable premium on text selection. It is a 'small-n', qualitative method – as opposed to methods involving the collection of a large amount of texts, and perhaps analysing them using quantitative methods, or those drawing on attitudinal data (for example, Chwieroth 2010; Hay and Smith 2010). Similarly, my approach is likely to offer a less detailed insight into the ideas of policymakers than attitudinal or 'large-n' studies.

That being said, there are a number of reasons why such an approach is preferred, especially given the limited availability of 'coordinative' documents. For one, I argue that determining the 'setting' of a document is crucial, especially as the analytical technique I have developed in Chapter 2 relies on contrasting texts originating in different discursive contexts. 'Large-n' approaches to studying policymakers' ideas and beliefs, such as comparative cognitive mapping, are ultimately reliant on the public statements made by political actors (Axelrod 1976; Verbeeck 2003), with the presumption often being that what is said in private is very similar to what is said in public – otherwise such approaches might lack the data necessary to infer the beliefs of policymakers. Of course, this is not a criticism that I can level at Hay and Smith's (2010) or Chwieroth's (2010) approach to collecting 'raw attitudinal data' – which, like 'large-n' studies of texts, offers more detailed insight into the nature of policymaker beliefs – but I have two additional reasons for plumping for my method. Firstly, mine is a more parsimonious method to reliably arrive at the general outline of policymakers' beliefs, as I am not interested in a genealogy or 'anthropology' – to use Hay's (2004b) term – of the emergence of neoliberal ideas in EU trade policy (similar in its aims to, for example, Polanyi 1957). The 'snapshots' I garner through textual analysis, in turn, are sufficient for the purposes of identifying the main content of such beliefs, to both tell these apart from other types of ideas (for example, distinguishing neoliberalism from other variants of liberalism) and to deploy my analytical strategy to unmask the strategic nature of appeals to an external economic constraint. Secondly, I am interested in the ideas of policymakers at a particular moment in time; collecting attitudinal data is constrained in this regard by the potential for such problems as memory failure that plague retrospective surveys (Oppenheim 1992: 130) and interviews (Seldon 1996: 355–6).[1]

Selecting texts[2]

As noted above, my method for coding texts is reliant on making appropriate document selection. In this section I provide an overview of the most important documents used to arrive at coordinative and communicative discourse throughout the book. These were selected on the basis of the three criteria I set forth in the preceding section: *intended audience*, *purpose* and *form*.

The easier task (as noted above) was determining communicative discourse. For this, I relied primarily on the two major and authoritative Commission communications on trade policy issued over the period the 2006 'Global Europe' and 2010 'Trade, Growth and World Affairs' strategies. Both of these were intended for a broad audience of not just trade policymakers but for wider political consumption. Both feature(d) prominently on DG Trade's website, were attractively formatted as brochures and were announced with much fanfare. In terms of their purpose, they were the distinct product of a preceding period of policy deliberation and sought to *communicate* its outcome (indeed, both were termed 'communications'). Moreover, they were written in a generally quite accessible form, seeking to translate technical trade discussions into accessible language.[3] For the communicative discourse surrounding the EPA negotiations, I relied on a series of speeches and articles by Commissioners Peter Mandelson and Louis Michel as well as a 'factsheet' about the EPAs (European Commission 2008a). These were clearly intended to sell the Commission's policy to a broad audience of critical actors and were formulated in a non-technical language.

The judgments involved in selecting documents that reflected coordinative discourse were altogether trickier, and therefore I dedicate a bit more space to discuss the main documents selected for each of the three chapters (3, 5 and 6) making use of documents in this way. Before turning to these more detailed discussions, a few words on the general criteria used for selecting documents are in order. As opposed to the main texts used to arrive at communicative discourse – which were Commission 'communications' – I generally selected documents which I judged to be for a largely internal audience, whose purpose was to feed into policy discussions and which were written in a technical (rather than more accessible) form. These included 'Staff Working Papers' and 'Issues Papers', often (albeit not always) more broadly known as 'SEC' documents – which are of a more specialised nature and more limited circulation than 'COM'-labelled documents, such as Commission communications (Peterson 1995: 479–80). Where possible, I also relied on documents that were mentioned to me by Commission officials as being important in the discussion of policy. Where this was not possible – especially given the limited availability of internal documents on trade policy, which are often exempt from data access requests given their sensitive nature – I drew on documents that generally fit the criteria for coordinative documents enumerated above. While this may lead some to consider that there may have been bias in the selection of documents, I drew on numerous personal interviews with Commission policymakers (especially in DG Trade) to triangulate the findings of my textual analysis. Crucially, such officials consistently espoused views that mirrored the coordinative discourse found in the documents discussed below.

In Chapter 3, where I discussed the drafting of 'Global Europe', the two main documents used to arrive at coordinative discourse were the 1996 'Market Access Strategy' (authored under Brittan) and the 2005 'Issues Paper on Trade and Competitiveness' (authored under Mandelson) (European Commission 1996a, 2005a). Despite being available publicly (the former being circulated as a COM document), the primary audience was one of actors sympathetic to the general goal of trade liberalisation, namely exporters. In this sense, neither had the flavour of an 'advocacy' document directed at an external audience that may have been neutral or indeed hostile with regards to the basic principles they espoused. The 1996 'Market Access Strategy' was the product of a desire to more actively involve business interests in the setting of trade policy, which spawned (among other things) the Market Access Database and the Market Access Symposium (European Commission 2007c) – a regular meeting organised by DG Trade to which it invited policymakers from other EU institutions but predominantly like-minded business organisations (van der Stichele *et al.* 2006: 13). Indeed, the strategy itself was presented at the first of these symposia in February 1996 (Shaffer 2003: 68). Similarly, although the 'Issues Paper' was formally presented at the equally public 2005 'Market Access Symposium' its main purpose was to stimulate policy discussions that would feed into the formulation of a new trade strategy (what ultimately became 'Global Europe') rather than to 'convince' its readers of the desirability of trade liberalisation.[4] Although the process involved consultations with potentially hostile Member States and DGs (such as Enterprise and Industry) – potentially lending the document a more communicative purpose – participants in these discussions noted how DG Trade failed to engage in a very meaningful or extensive dialogue with such actors. Rather, the main intended external audience for the 'Issues Paper' (as for the 1996 'Market Access Strategy') were exporters which, although not formally part of the Commission machinery, were sympathetic to the aims of achieving further access to third party markets. In fact, DG Trade was extremely keen that they be actively involved in the internal drafting of its policy positions. Moreover, in terms of form, neither document made an effort to translate its findings to a broader audience; one of the charges often levied against the 'Issues Paper' was that it was overly 'dry' and 'academic', hardly the stuff of persuasive rhetoric.

In Chapter 5, where I discussed the EU's trade agreements with the ACP (the so-called EPAs), I relied on a number of (mostly) internal Commission texts to arrive at coordinative discourse over different periods of time. The first such document is the 1996 'Green Paper on Relations between the EU and ACP countries' (European Commission 1996b), whose role and importance as a document in policymaking discussions has been widely documented elsewhere (see, for example, Holland and Doidge 2012: 66–7). For my purposes, it is important to note that it presented several policy options in a very technical form, rather than seeking to communicate policy decisions. The chapter also draws on the (unfortunately abridged) version of the confidential EPA mandate of 2002 (which, given its continued restricted nature, was clearly intended for internal discussion; European Commission 2002). To arrive at the views of policymakers on the issues under Mandelson, I rely on a number of 'Commission staff working paper(s)' (which are SEC documents) authored on the subject under his tenure (European Commission 2005c, 2006i) as well as an information note from both Mandelson and Louis Michel (the Development Commissioner) to their fellow Commissioners (European Commission 2007e). I also compare these views to those espoused in a similarly internal 'Staff Working Paper' from DG Development from 2007 (European Commission 2007d).

In Chapter 6, given the lack of available internal documents for De Gucht's period in office – which may be a reflection of the fact that the Commission is more sensitive about the disclosure of more recent documents – I focus on the contributions made (in a private capacity) by figures in DG Trade's Chief Economist's unit to a debate organised by the online 'policy portal' VoxEU.org over 2010–11. Vox is a collaborative online portal set up by the Centre for Economic Policy Research – an economics think tank based in London – which also involves a series of other European economics research organisations and websites (see Vox 2013). The purpose of this debate was to feed into the EU's policymaking discussions on the '2020 Trade Strategy'. This was in tune with Vox's wider aim of 'promot[ing] *research-based policy analysis and commentary* by leading scholars [whose] [...] *intended audience is economists in governments, international organisations, academia and the private sector as well as journalists specialising in economics, finance and business*' (Vox 2013, emphasis added). With only around a couple thousand visits to the online debate, and a mere thirteen contributions largely from neoclassical economists (see Vox 2010), one can see that this forum, albeit publicly accessible on the web, was not so much aimed at policy *communication* as policy discussion among a group of actors sympathetic to the aims of EU policymakers. Moreover, the self-professed *form* such deliberations took was one of 'research-based policy analysis and commentary'. Although, given the online format, this was more accessible than some of the Commission documents consulted for other chapters, entries on the website were still written using broadly technical language.

Notes

1 Introduction

1   I use the term 'EU' to refer to the supranational European entity throughout its history. This is done for the sake of consistency and simplicity. When EU policy documents are cited, however, the designation has not been altered. These sources (which all date from after the 1967 Merger Treaty) may thus still refer to the European Community (EC) or, more simply, to the Community. This is because, even post-Maastricht, the entity officially concluding trade agreements was the EC. This arrangement has only recently changed, with the 2009 Treaty of Lisbon giving the EU a 'legal personality' to enter into international agreements.

2   Until 1999, the entity in the Commission that handled trade negotiations was known as DG I (Directorate General for External Economic Relations). It was renamed DG Trade with the reorganisation of the Commission under the leadership of Romano Prodi (Nugent 2000). As these changes were largely cosmetic, I refer throughout this book to 'DG Trade' for the sake of consistency, irrespective of the historical period concerned.

3   Although 'Global Europe' also mentioned the emerging economies of Latin America (specifically the Common Market of the Southern Cone, also known by its Spanish acronym MERCOSUR) as desirable targets for bilateral activism, the focus was largely on the specific Asian economies it mentioned. Negotiations with MERCOSUR had already been initiated earlier and were stuck in the doldrums due to disagreements over agriculture (see Doctor 2007; Jank et al. 2004).

4   It should be said that some of these authors have either identified themselves as 'historical institutionalists' (see Young 2002; in part Elsig 2002) or implicitly drawn on the insights of this approach (for example, Hanson 1998), writing about the effects of informal and/or unintended institutional processes over time and emphasising the role of path dependence (for more on historical institutionalism in the study of the EU see, for example, Pierson 1996). However, the fact remains that they still have largely taken a rationalist view of institutions and actor preferences and have often deployed similar analytical and methodological tools to rational choice scholars.

5   These include an increased diversity of Member State interests as a result of enlargement (Elsig 2010: 793) to a decision by Member States to 'reallocate resources away from trade policy, given that it is the Commission which has the responsibility to negotiate on their behalf' (Baldwin 2006: 930).

6   More specifically, I conducted 40 interviews in DG Trade; 4 interviews in DG Development; 2 interviews in DG Agriculture and 3 interviews with members of what were then still Commission delegations.

2 Trade Is What You Make of It: The Social Construction of EU Commercial Policy

1 On the use of this terminology, see Mansfield (1998: 524).

2 In other words, it has tended to take for granted a certain set of 'rational choice' assumptions, which depict political actors as rational (and selfish) utility maximisers with *a priori* well-defined preferences (see Dunleavy 1991: 3–4).

3 While some, more nuanced accounts place emphasis on the mediating role of political institutions and the independent interests of policymakers (for example, Goldstein 1988), these have not been nearly as influential as those scholars working on the basis of rational choice theories.

4 I am of course not suggesting that all constructivists in IPE have explicitly drawn on this particular author and his work on uncertainty. Rather, what I am underscoring is that in addition to developing this particular framework, Blyth has had a considerable impact in terms of (re)stating the case for ideas in the field of IPE.

5 While not all constructivists in the field of IPE have emphasised causality (or indeed have done so in an explicitly Humean sense) it has been a self-conscious feature of much of the literature considered here (see, for example, Abdelal *et al.* 2010b: 17–19) and an analytical move that this book replicates.

6 This can be said of the highly influential Schimmelfennig's (2003) research, whose aim is to combine a constructivist streak that stresses the strategic use of ideas with a rationalist reading of actor interests (see also van den Hoven 2004; Jabko 2006). The problem with these approaches is thus their ontological inconsistency; although they may point to the use that actors make of particular ideas, they are no better than Blyth (2002) in that they cannot accommodate ideas within their frameworks without appealing to non-ideational 'enabling' factors. For his part, although Parsons (2003: 19–22) avoids the trap of metatheoretical inconsistency, his approach to explaining 'which ideas win' cannot explain why certain ideas *themselves* may trump others, relying instead on a framework that focuses on wider processes of ideational institutionalisation.

7 Although there appear to be some parallels here with the 'critical realist' ontology and epistemology of Bhaskar (1979), what distinguishes my approach is that it sees underlying material structures as *real* (or significant) in a social and political context only in the sense that their materiality is often internalised and/or acted upon by actors. I also distinguish myself from Hay (2005), who refers to his metatheoretical position as one of 'as-if-realism' and is thus avowedly closer to critical realism (see also Gofas and Hay 2010).

8 While focusing on specific policy domains (rather than European integration as a whole) has mitigated this in some neo-Gramscian works, to an extent, these still inherit the broader tendency to overstate the prevalence of neoliberalism within the European integration project. As van Apeldoorn and Horn (2007: 222) note, for example, of the 'marketisation of corporate control', '[t]his project is [...] part and parcel of a broader neoliberal project of European integration'.

9 In contrast, Actor A from Figure 1 might just be repeating an internalised discourse, rather than disingenuously trying to bring about the outcome associated with such a belief.

3 Charting the Rise of 'Global Europe'

1 In this sub-section I draw on an interview with interest group representatives, Brussels, 14 September and 8 October 2009.

2 While there are other pro-liberalisation interest groups other than exporters, including import-consuming industries such as retailers (see Heron 2007; De Bièvre and Eckhardt 2011), these have arguably played a much smaller role in shaping policymaking on EU trade policy than exporters. Moreover, my focus in this book is largely on the pursuit of external market access, where such groups have a less obvious interest.

3 The lobby was 'cross-sectoral' in the sense that it represented the interests of all tradable service suppliers.

4 Although the Transatlantic Business Dialogue was also borne of similar efforts, its focus was on bringing together business interests from both sides of the Atlantic (Cowles 2001: 168–70). It would thus become less relevant in driving policy in the era of 'competitive liberalisation', although EU–US FTA talks have more recently taken off (see Chapter 6). The European Roundtable of Industrialists (ERT), for its part, has traditionally concerned itself with strategic policy direction and less with the perceived 'day-to-day' of Commission consultations on trade policy (see also Greenwood 2011: 75).

5 In this sub-section I draw on interviews with interest group representatives, Brussels, 14 September 2009 and on a telephone interview with a European Commission official, 5 May 2010.

6 Even though negotiations subsequently resumed, these came to very little and the Doha Round was officially suspended in July 2008 (Wilkinson 2014: Ch. 1). Despite attempts since to revive the talks, at the time of writing it appears unlikely that the Round will yield significant liberalisation gains anytime soon.

7 In this sub-section I draw on interviews with European Commission officials and interest group representatives, Brussels, September–October 2009; on a telephone interview with a European Commission official, 5 May 2010 and on an interview with a Member State official, Brussels, 20 May 2010.

8 In this sub-section I draw on interviews with interest group representatives, Brussels, 14 September 2009 and on a telephone interview with a European Commission official, Brussels, 11 March 2010.

9 While multilateral dysfunction did play a role in shaping the preferences of interest groups (and to an extent policymakers, see the sub-section on the 'reflexive dimension' to discourse at the end of this chapter) it should be apparent that I am treating it in a constructivist fashion as a factor influencing actors' (contingent) perceptions of their interests. This stands in contrast to the rationalist systemic IPE perspectives on the issue (for example, Mansfield and Reinhardt 2008), which treat multilateral institutions as structural constraints on actor behaviour.

10 This does not require the use of the analytical technique described in Figure 2.2 as interest group pronouncements can be taken to be *intrinsically* strategic.

11 In this section I draw on interviews with European Commission officials, Brussels, September–October 2009 and May 2011.

12 The text of the 'Minimum Platform' cited in this book is that of a leaked, and now freely available, draft presented to the Council's Article 133 Committee in July 2006. The final text is still of 'restricted' circulation. However, it should be noted that the final text is unlikely to have changed very much

from this draft in the case of the negotiations considered in this volume. The EU's subsequent FTA with South Korea and EPA with the Caribbean region seem to mirror it quite closely (see Chapters 4 and 5). Included with this draft was an explanatory memorandum, which is cited separately.

13 Since then, of course, the Treaty of Lisbon has come into force, which in Article 207 does give the Commission sole authority to negotiate agreements on investment (see Woolcock 2010a).

14 It reflected a compromise between the Commission's desire for additional competences and Member States' concern for sovereignty in two ways. For one, it provided an arrangement to overcome competing claims for competence by providing the Commission with the 'minimum' tools necessary to effectively negotiate ambitious trade agreements. For another, it led both parties to settle on a particular formula for EU services and investment FTAs. This was the GATS-style model with a 'positive list' for liberalisation (only sectors explicitly committed would be liberalised) – as Member States wanted to preserve some regulatory 'wiggle room' – and an MFN clause (to capture future liberalisation undertaken by the partner in an FTA) rather than the more ambitious North American Free Trade Agreement (NAFTA) style agreement that DG Trade (and the ESF) had wanted. This would have entailed a 'negative list' (binding all liberalisation not explicitly excluded) and a ratchet clause which would have bound any future autonomous liberalisation undertaken by the partner.

15 In an interview conducted in March 2006 with an EU official on EU bilateral trade agreements, the official in question promptly produced a copy of the EU–Chile FTA and noted that it represented a 'model' agreement.

16 The 'Issues Paper' referred to these as 'pockets of distortion' as these were the few remaining sectors in the EU still enjoying significant trade 'protection' potentially at the expense, it argued, of both broader economic efficiency and/or the competitiveness of upmarket producers (European Commission 2005a: 11–17).

17 In this sub-section I draw on interviews with European Commission officials, Brussels, September–October 2009 and May 2011; on a telephone interview with a European Commission official, 5 May 2010; on interviews with interest group representatives, Brussels, September–October 2009 and 21 May 2010 and on an interview with an EU official, Brussels 6 May 2010.

18 Author's translation: 'that exports are also a tool for the continual improvement of our firms' competitiveness'.

19 The 'Issues Paper' had a whole section dedicated to 'Drawing upon EU Comparative Advantages', but only mentioned economies of scale in passing (European Commission 2005a: 3, 29–33). This underscores how policymakers placed a lot more emphasis on promoting vertical intra-industry specialisation (where neo-classical economics sees the forces of comparative advantage being relevant) than horizontal specialisation (where economies of scale are important).

20 The implicit suggestion was, of course, that this turn to openness following the 'new protectionism' had helped stop the decline of European business.

21 That being said, no major conflict with protectionist interests emerged over the drafting of the 'Global Europe' strategy itself.

22 In the following sub-section I draw on interviews with European Commission officials, Brussels, September–October and 16 December 2009; on an interview with an interest group representatives, Brussels, 21 September 2009 and on an interview with an EU official, Brussels, 6 May 2010.

23 To an extent, this was a product of perceived animosity and rivalry between Verheugen and Mandelson. However, it also suggested a strategic appeal to the idea of Lisbon, as argued below.

24 In this sub-section I draw on interviews with interest group representatives, Brussels, 14 September 2009.

4 Resisting 'Protectionism': The EU–Korea Free Trade Agreement

1 In this section I draw on an interview with an interest group representative, Brussels, 21 May 2010 and with an official in the office of United States Trade Representative (USTR), Geneva, 15 March 2010.

2 The study foresaw two partial FTA scenarios and one full FTA scenario. For more details, see Copenhagen Economics and Francois (2006: 24).

3 The baseline against which both of the scenarios were being compared included completion of the Doha Round (including a liberalisation of tariffs for several sensitive products) as well as various Korean FTAs with third parties (for details, see Copenhagen Economics and Francois 2006: 56). Although a number of these FTAs have since been concluded, the same cannot be said of the Doha Round. This means that the losses for the automobile sector (which still benefits from relatively high MFN rates of protection) could actually be greater than predicted by this model.

4 Although the output gain and sectoral trade expansion figures are derived from a full FTA and partial FTA scenario, respectively, it makes sense to consider them alongside one another because the difference between them relates to the degree of services (rather than tariff) liberalisation undertaken (and the presence, or not, of some trade facilitation measures, whose impact is likely to be negligible).

5 In this sub-section I draw on interviews with European Commission officials, Brussels, September and December 2009.

6 As duty drawback was largely used by emerging economies as a tool to facilitate industrial production for export, the fact that it was permitted in the context of preferential trade relations with some developing countries – for instance under the EU's Generalised System of Preferences (GSP) or under its EPAs with the ACP – can, to a great extent, be explained in terms of the relatively modest industrial capacity of these economies.

7 That being said, the fact that South Korea pushed the issue so strongly and ended up accepting the EU proposal for 'limited' duty drawback suggests that the concession had some significance.

8 In this sub-section (including Table 4.2) I draw on interviews with European Commission officials, Brussels, 23 and 29 September 2009 and 11 May 2010, and on interviews with interest group representatives, Brussels, 14 September 2009.

9 In this sub-section I draw on interviews with an interest group representatives, Brussels, 14 September 2009; on interviews with European Commission officials, Brussels, September–October and 17 December 2009; on an interview with Mr. Erik Bergelin, Director of the Trade and Economics Section at ACEA, Brussels, 24 September 2009; on an interview with a Member state official, Brussels, 20 May 2011 and on an interview with an official in the office of the USTR, Geneva, 15 March 2010.

10   Seeking ratification from national parliaments (mandated by the Treaties in the case of mixed agreements) was not mentioned by pro-FTA interviewees as an area that was particularly problematic, nor did it feature prominently as an issue during the debates surrounding ratification (another recent study of the EU–Korea FTA does not even mention it, see Elsig and Dupont 2012). Indeed, the agreement has been in force since July 2011 despite the lack of 'formal' ratification from national parliaments, following the established practice of 'provisionally applying' agreements upon their conclusion. Highlighting the relative weight attached to the EP – as opposed to national parliaments – the Commission chose not to 'provisionally apply' the EU–Korea FTA until after EP had ratified it despite having the authority to do so (see De Gucht 2010: 3–4).

11   In this sub-section I draw on an interview with an interest group representative, 14 September 2009 and on an interview with an EU official, Brussels, 6 May 2010.

12   Under full liberalisation, the contraction in output was estimated at 1.78 per cent, while under two partial liberalisation scenarios it was estimated at only 1.08 per cent and 0.9 per cent (Copenhagen Economics and Francois 2006: 29).

13   In late November 2010 the Korean government, anticipating the imminent entry into force of the agreement, offered its livestock farmers 2 trillion won in aid (approximately 1.7 billion US dollars at November 2010 exchange rates) to mitigate the effects of trade liberalisation with the EU (Cheong Wa Dae 2010).

5   'Global Europe' and the Economic Partnership Agreements

1   'Asymmetry' refers to the fact that, in view of their development status, ACP countries are expected to undertake less liberalisation than the EU.

2   In this sub-section I draw on an interview with a European Commission official, Brussels, 23 September 2009.

3   As if to underscore the fragmentation of the ACP, in November 2007 the five member states of the East African Community (EAC) – Burundi, Kenya, Rwanda, Tanzania and Uganda – would break away from the East and Southern Africa 'region' and sign a separate interim EPA with the EU.

4   Although an EPA would offer such countries more relaxed 'rules of origin' – which are often seen to be one of the principal trade barriers for LDCs (Brenton 2003) – most LDCs have since still been deterred by the prospect of having to offer reciprocity.

5   In this sub-section I draw on interviews with European Commission officials, Brussels, 16 and 23 September 2009 and on an interview with an NGO representative, Brussels, 2 October 2009.

6   Many ACP delegations were allegedly pressured into agreeing to these provisions by being presented with draft IEPAs for initialling that included imminent expiry dates.

7   In this section I draw on interviews with European Commission officials, Brussels, September–October, 15 December 2009 and 26 May 2011.

8   In this sub-section I draw on interviews with European Commission officials, Brussels, September–October 2009.

9 In this sub-section I draw on interviews with European Commission officials, September–October and December 2009.

10 DG Trade was still committed to some form of 'special and differential' treatment but, as I highlighted for the EU–CARIFORUM agreement, this does not detract from the argument that it was strongly pushing for a significant measure of WTO-plus liberalisation in the ACP.

11 In this sub-section I draw on interviews with European Commission officials, Brussels, September–October 2009 and 22 January 2013.

12 Although my argument in this chapter also suggests that one needs to also consider how these material incentives are *mediated* by ideas.

13 These interim agreements have become institutionalised, with EU policymakers acutely aware that they cannot withdraw any market access commitments for ACP countries – say as a negotiating tactic in order to encourage such countries to move towards signing a full EPA – without serious political repercussions.

6 'Global Europe' during the Crisis: Reciprocity and the Political Limits to Liberalisation

1 In this sub-section I draw on interviews with European Commission officials, Brussels, September–October, 2009, May 2011 and January 2013.

2 The new investment policy communication of the Commission was to spell this out by stressing that one 'objective' of the Commission's new investment policy was 'the integration of investment into the common commercial policy' as part of its unfolding FTA agenda (European Commission 2010g: 7); as a result, DG Trade managed to incorporate an investment protection mandate into FTA negotiations with India, Canada and Singapore (Council of the EU 2011). The Commission has also adopted a 'negative list' approach for services liberalisation in FTA talks with Canada – which is seen by many, including the ESF (2006), to enhance the ability of the EU to pursue wide-ranging liberalisation when compared to the MFN clause/positive list model – although it remains to be seen whether this approach will be adopted in other FTAs.

3 In this sub-section I draw on interviews with European Commission officials, Brussels, September–October, 2009, 25 and 27 May 2011 and 21 January 2013 and on an interview with an interest group representative, Brussels, 20 May 2011.

4 In this sub-section, I draw on interviews with European Commission officials, Brussels, May 2011 and January 2013.

5 In one contribution to Vox, Cernat and Pajot (2012) would highlight how the EU's export performance is boosted by 'inward processing trade', where intermediate products for use in exports are imported duty-free, making a very similar argument to the 2005 'Issues Paper' about the role of cheap inputs in shaping EU competitiveness.

6 In this sub-section I draw on an interview with a European Commission official, Brussels, 17 May 2011.

7 In this sub-section, I draw on interviews with European Commission officials, Brussels, May 2011 and January 2013, and on an interview with an interest group representative, Brussels, 20 May 2011.

8   Some authors within the neo-Gramscian tradition have also suggested that the EU's 'embedded neoliberal' compromise is internally contradictory (for example, van Apeldoorn 2010).

9   Similarly, an FTA between the EU and the US had been broadly seen as unthinkable only a few years prior due to the perceived difficulties in negotiating and ratifying such a large-scale agreement (Peterson *et al.* 2004: 76–7).

10   The EU also launched FTA talks in March 2013 with Japan, concluding the first round of talks in April of that year. While Commission officials have noted how Japan was the *demandeur* of these talks, fearing the competition resulting from the EU–Korea FTA (see Elsig and Dupont 2012: 505–6), the fact remains that such negotiations with a major trading partner were not being contemplated in 'Global Europe' and may thus also signal growing frustration with emerging economies and the slow pace of liberalisation.

Appendix: Coding and Selecting Texts for Discursive Analysis

1   As a result, I only use interviews as a means of 'triangulating' information already garnered via document analysis.

2   In this section I draw on interviews with European Commission officials, Brussels, September–October 2009, May 2011 and January 2013, interviews with interest group representatives, Brussels, 14 September 2009 and an interview with an EU official, Brussels, 6 May 2010.

3   The 'Issues Paper' and 'Commission Staff Working Papers' accompanying 'Trade, Growth and World Affairs' (European Commission 2010k,l) were also treated as communicative (even if these types of documents were usually coded as coordinative). This is based on the judgment that they had an intended audiences beyond trade policymakers and their constituents; a purpose of communicating (rather than arriving at) trade policy decisions and were presented as glossy brochures and/or in a fairly accessible language. Both were part of a broader communicative exercise aimed at selling the benefits of free trade in the context of the crisis (see Chapter 6). A similar judgment also informed the decision to treat a subsequent 'Staff Working Paper' – suggestively entitled 'External Sources of Growth' (European Commission 2012d) – and the Commission's 'contribution' to a Council meeting (European Commission 2013a) as communicative.

4   The purpose of the 'Issues Paper' is also discussed in European Commission (2006h: 4).

References

Abbott, R.W., Keohane, R.O., Moravcsik, A., Slaughter, A.-M. and Snidal, D. (2000), 'The Concept of Legalization', *International Organization*, 54 (3), pp. 401–19.

Abdelal, R. and Meunier, S. (2010), 'Managed Globalisation: Doctrine, Practice and Promise', *Journal of European Public Policy*, 17 (3), pp. 350–67.

Abdelal, R., Blyth, M. and Parsons, C. (eds) (2010a), *Constructing the International Economy* (Ithaca, NY: Cornell University Press).

Abdelal, R., Blyth, M. and Parsons, C. (2010b), 'Introduction: Constructing the International Economy', in R. Abdelal, M. Blyth and C. Parsons (eds), *Constructing the International Economy* (Ithaca, NY: Cornell University Press), pp. 1–19.

Ablordeppey, S.D. (2007), 'ECOWAS Looks for Good Partnership', 15 March, *Daily Graphic*. Online edition. Available from: http://www.modernghana.com/news/125551/1/ecowas-looks-for-good-partnership.html [accessed 8 May 2011].

ACEA (2009), 'Trade Deal with Korea Goes against the Interest of Major European Industries and Their Workforce', Brussels: ACEA. Available from: http://www.acea.be/index.php/news/news_detail/trade_deal_with_korea_goes_against_the_interest_of_major_european_industrie [accessed 2 November 2010].

ACEA (2010), 'Free Trade Agreement with South Korea', Brussels: ACEA. Available from: http://www.acea.be/index.php/news/news_detail/free_trade_agreement_with_south_korea/ [accessed 2 November 2010].

Action Aid (2005), 'The Trade Escape: WTO Rules and Alternatives to Free Trade Economic Partnership Agreements', Johannesburg: Action Aid.

Adler, E. (1997), 'Seizing the Middle Ground: Constructivism in World Politics', *European Journal of International Relations*, 3 (3), pp. 319–63.

AFX News (2005), 'Pacific Countries Confident of Making Deadline for EU Trade Agreement', 25 October, *AFX News*. Available from: http://www.bilaterals.org/spip.php?article2980 [accessed 8 May 2011].

Alter, K.J. and Meunier, S. (2006), 'Nested and Overlapping Regimes in the Transatlantic Banana Trade Dispute', *Journal of European Public Policy*, 13 (3), pp. 362–82.

Amin, A. and Thrift, N. (1994), 'Holding down the Global', in A. Amin and N. Thrift (eds), *Globalization, Institutions and Regional Development in Europe* (Oxford: Oxford University Press), pp. 257–60.

Anderson, R.D. and Arrowsmith, S. (2011), 'The WTO Regime on Government Procurement: Past, Present and Future', in S. Arrowsmith and R.D. Anderson (eds), *The WTO Regime on Government Procurement: Challenge and Reform* (Cambridge: Cambridge University Press), pp. 3–58.

Axelrod, R. (ed.) (1976), *The Structure of Decision: The Cognitive Maps of Political Elites* (Princeton, NJ: Princeton University Press).

Babarinde, O. and Faber, G. (eds) (2005), *The European Union and the Developing Countries: The Cotonou Agreement* (Leiden: Martinus Nijhoff Publishers).

Bache, I., George, S. and Bulmer, S. (2011), *Politics in the European Union*, 3rd edn (Oxford: Oxford University Press).

Bailey, M.A., Goldstein, J. and Weingast, B.R. (1997), 'The Institutional Roots of American Trade Policy', *World Politics*, 49 (3), pp. 309–38.

Balassa, B. (1978), 'The "New Protectionism" and the International Economic Order', *Journal of World Trade Law*, 12, pp. 409–36.

Baldwin, M. (2006), 'EU Trade Politics – Heaven or Hell?', *Journal of European Public Policy*, 13 (6), pp. 926–42.

Baldwin, R.E. (1985), *The Political Economy of US Import Policy* (Cambridge, MA: MIT Press).

Baldwin, R.E. (1992), 'Measurable Dynamic Gains from Trade', *Journal of Political Economy*, 100 (1), pp. 162–74.

Baldwin, R.E. (1993), 'A Domino Theory of Regionalism', Working Paper No. 4465, Cambridge, MA: National Bureau of Economic Research (NBER).

Beattie, A. (2006), 'UK Urges Brussels to Relent over New Trade Rules for Poor Nations', *The Financial Times*, 16 October. Online edition. Available from: http://www.ft.com/cms/s/0/224da378-5cb3-11db-9e7e -0000779e2340.html#ax zz1LlGYAXnw [accessed 8 May 2011].

Beckert, J. (1996), 'What is Sociological about Economic Sociology? Uncertainty and the Embeddedness of Economic Action', *Theory and Society*, 25 (6), pp. 803–40.

Bell, S.D. (2011), 'Do We Really Need a New "Constructivist Institutionalism"?', *British Journal of Politics and International Relations*, 41 (4), pp. 883–906.

Bell, S.D. (2012), 'The Power of Ideas: The Ideational Shaping of the Structural Power of Business', *International Studies Quarterly*, 56 (4), pp. 661–73.

Benoit, B. (2008), 'Berlin Set to Give Opel €1bn Guarantee', *The Financial Times*, 18 November. Online edition. Available from: http://www.ft.com/cms/6d816998-b511-11dd-b780-0000779fd18c.html [accessed 22 November 2010].

Berghahn, V. and Young, B. (2013), 'Reflections on Werner Bonefeld's "Freedom and the Strong State: On German Ordoliberalism" and the Continuing Importance of the Ideas of Ordoliberalism to Understand Germany's (Contested) Role in Resolving the Eurozone Crisis', *New Political Economy*, 18 (5), pp. 768–78.

Bergsten, C.F. (1997), 'Open Regionalism', Working Paper No. 97-3, Washington, DC: Peterson Institute for International Economics.

Bernard, A. and Jensen, J.B. (2004), 'Exporting and Productivity in the USA', *Oxford Review of Economic Policy*, 20 (3), pp. 343–57.

Best, J. (2008), *The Limits of Transparency: Ambiguity and the History of International Finance* (Ithaca, NY: Cornell University Press).

Best, J. and Widmaier, W.W. (2006), 'Micro- or Macro-Moralities? Economic Discourses and Policy Possibilities', *Review of International Political Economy*, 13 (4), pp. 609–31.

Bhaskar, R. (1979), *The Limits of Naturalism* (Brighton: Harvester Wheatsheaf).

Bieler, A. (2006), *The Struggle for a Social Europe: Trade Unions and EMU in Times of Global Restructuring* (Manchester: Manchester University Press).

Bieler, A. (2013), 'The EU, Global Europe and the Process of Uneven and Combined Development: The Problem of Transnational Labour Solidarity', *Review of International Studies*, 39 (1), pp. 161–83.

Bieler, A. and Morton, A.D. (2008), 'The Deficits of Discourse in IPE: Turning Base Metal into Gold?', *International Studies Quarterly*, 52 (1), pp. 103–28.

Billiet, S. (2006), 'From GATT to the WTO: The Internal Struggle for External Competences in the EU', *Journal of Common Market Studies*, 44 (5), pp. 899–919.

Bishop, M.L., Heron, T. and Payne, A. (2013), 'Caribbean Development Alternatives and the European Union–CARIFORUM Economic Partnership Agreement', *Journal of International Relations and Development*, 16 (1), pp. 82–110.

Blyth, M. (2002), *Great Transformations: Economic Ideas and Political Change in the Twentieth Century* (Cambridge: Cambridge University Press).

Blyth, M. (2006), 'Great Punctuations: Prediction, Randomness, and the Evolution of Comparative Political Science', *American Political Science Review*, 100 (4), pp. 493–8.

Blyth, M. (2010), 'Ideas, Uncertainty and Evolution', in D. Béland and R.H. Cox (eds), *Ideas and Politics in Social Science Research* (Oxford: Oxford University Press), pp. 83–100.

Blyth, M. (2013), *Austerity: The History of a Dangerous Idea* (Oxford: Oxford University Press).

Bounds, A. and Fifield, A. (2007), 'EU Told to Exclude N Korea Enclave from Pact', *The Financial Times*, 16 October. Online edition. Available from: http://www.ft.com/cms/s/0/d7bd5ffe-7b80-11dc-8c53-0000779fd2ac.html [accessed 1 September 2010].

Brand, C. and Vogel, T. (2010), 'Parliament Delays Vote on Free-Trade Safeguards', *European Voice*. Online edition. Available from: http://www.europeanvoice.com/article/imported/parliament-delays-vote-on-free-trade-safeguards/69201.aspx [accessed 1 November 2010].

Brenton, P. (2003), 'Integrating Least Developed Countries into the World Trading System: The Current Impact of EU Preferences under Everything But Arms', World Bank Policy Research Paper No. 3018, Washington, DC: World Bank.

Brittan, L. (1999), 'European Service Leaders' Group', speech delivered to the European Service Leaders' Group, Brussels, 26 January. Available from: http://www.esf.be/pdfs/documents/speeches/splb0199.pdf [accessed 10 June 2010].

Buch-Hansen, H. and Wigger, A. (2011), *The Politics of European Competition Regulation: A Critical Political Economy Perspective* (Abingdon: Routledge).

Bukovansky, M. (2010), 'Institutionalised Hypocrisy and the Politics of Agricultural Trade', in R. Abdelal, M. Blyth and C. Parsons (eds), *Constructing the International Economy* (Ithaca, NY: Cornell University Press), pp. 68–89.

Bungenberg, M. (2011), 'The Division of Competences between the EU and Its Member States in the Area of Investment Politics', in M. Bungenberg, J. Griebel and S. Hindelang (eds), *International Investment Law and EU Law* (Heidelberg: Springer), pp. 29–42.

Cafruny, A.W. and Ryner, M. (eds) (2003), *A Ruined Fortress? Neoliberal Hegemony and Transformation in Europe* (Lanham, MD: Rowman & Littlefield).

Caporaso, J. and Tarrow, S. (2009), 'Polanyi in Brussels: Supranational Institutions and the Transnational Embedding of Markets', *International Organization*, 63 (4), pp. 593–620.

Casella, A. (1996), 'Large Countries, Small Countries and the Enlargement of Trade Blocs', *European Economic Review*, 40 (2), pp. 389–415.

Cernat, L. (2010), 'Shaping the Future of EU Trade Policy: How to Maximise the Gains from Trade in a Globalised World?', *Vox*, 7 September. Available from: http://trade.ec.europa.eu/doclib/docs/2010/november/tradoc_146932.pdf [accessed 19 July 2011].

Cernat, L. and Madsen, M.R. (2011), 'Murky Protectionism and Behind-the-Border Barriers: How Big an Issue? The 100€ Billion Question', *Vox*, 23 March. Available from: http://www.voxeu.org/index.php?q=node/6274 [accessed 19 July 2011].

Cernat, L. and Pajot, M. (2012), 'Assembled in Europe: The Role of Processing Trade in EU Export Performance', *Vox*, 17 September. Available from: http://www.voxeu. org/article/assembled-europe-role-processing-trade-eu-export-performance [accessed 14 July 2013].

Cernat, L. and Susa, N. (2010), 'The Impact of Crisis-Driven Protectionism on EU Exports: The "Russian Doll" Effect', *Vox*, 9 January. Available from: http://www. voxeu.org/index.php?q=node/4464 [accessed 19 July 2011].

Cerny, P.G. (1995), 'Globalization and Other Stories: The Search for a New Paradigm in International Relations', *International Journal*, 51 (4), pp. 617–37.

Cerny, P.G. (2011), *Rethinking World Politics: A Theory of Transnational Pluralism* (Oxford: Oxford University Press).

Chang, H.J. (2002), *Kicking Away the Ladder: Development Strategy in Historical Perspective* (London: Anthem Press).

Chase, K.A. (2005), *Trading Blocs: States, Firms, and Regions in the World Economy* (Ann Arbor: The University of Michigan Press).

Checkel, J. (2005), 'International Institutions and Socialization in Europe: Introduction and Framework', *International Organization*, 59 (4), pp. 801–26.

Chen, R., Milesi-Ferreti, G.M. and Tressel, T. (2012), 'External Imbalances in the Euro Area', IMF Working Paper No. WP/12/236, Washington, DC: IMF.

Cheong Wa Dae (2010), 'Seoul to Support Livestock Industry', Seoul, Cheong Wa Dae. Available from: http://english.president.go.kr/koreain/issue/issue_view. php?uno=4372&board_no=E07 [accessed 29 November 2010].

Chorev, N. and Babb, S. (2009), 'The Crisis of Neoliberalism and the Future of International Institutions: A Comparison of the IMF and the WTO', *Theory and Society*, 38 (5), pp. 459–84.

Chosun Ilbo (2010), 'EU–Korea Business Club Unhappy with Revised FTA with US', 7 December. Available from: http://english.chosun.com/site/data/html_ dir/2010/12/07/2010120701056.html [accessed 8 December 2010].

Christian Aid, Catholic Overseas Development Agency, Action Aid, Both Ends, Africa Trade Network, Agir Ici, Eurostep, Environment and Development Action in the Third World, EcoNews Africa, Mwengo, Third World Network-Africa, Southern and Eastern African Trade Information and Negotiations Institute, Oxfam, Traidcraft and 11.11.11 (2004), 'Six Reasons to Oppose EPAs in Their Current Form'. Available from: http://www.stopepa.de/img/ six-questions-on-epas.pdf [accessed 8 May 2011].

Chwieroth, J.M. (2010), *Capital Ideas: The IMF and the Rise of Financial Liberalization* (Princeton, NJ: Princeton University Press).

Clapp, J. and Dauvergne, P. (2011), *Paths to a Green World: The Political Economy of the Global Environment*, 2nd edn (Cambridge, MA: MIT Press).

Cockfield, F. (1988), *Europe without Frontiers – Completing the Internal Market*, 2nd edn, Periodical 3/1988 (Luxembourg: Office for Official Publications of the European Communities).

Collinson, S. (1999), 'Issue-Systems, Multi-Level Games, and the Analysis of the EU's External Commercial and Associated Policies: A Research Agenda', *Journal of European Public Policy*, 6 (2), pp. 206–24.

Commission for Africa (2005), 'Our Common Interest: Report of the Commission for Africa', London: Commission for Africa.

Copenhagen Economics and Francois, J.F. (2006), *Economic Impact of a Potential Free Trade Agreement (FTA) between the European Union and South Korea* (Copenhagen: Copenhagen Economics).

Corporate Europe Observatory (2008), 'Global Europe: An Open Door for Big Business Lobbyists at DG Trade', Brussels: Corporate Europe Observatory.

Corporate Europe Observatory (2009), 'Pulling the Strings of African Business: How the EU Commission Orchestrated Support from African Business for EPAs', Brussels: Corporate Europe Observatory.

Council of the EU (2006), 'Draft Conclusions on "Global Europe: Competing in the World": Amendments Proposed by the French Delegation', Council document no. 15018/06, 9 November, Brussels: General Secretariat of the Council of the EU. Available from: http://register.consilium.europa.eu/pdf/en/06/st15/st15018.en06.pdf [accessed 16 October 2009].

Council of the EU (2009), 'Council (Competitiveness): Council Conclusions on the Automotive Industry', Council document no. 7367/1/09 REV 1, 5–6 March, Brussels: General Secretariat of the Council of the EU. Available from: http://register.consilium.europa.eu/pdf/en/09/st07/st07367-re01.en09.pdf [accessed 5 January 2011].

Council of the EU (2011), 'EU Negotiating Mandates on Investment'. Available from: http://www.bilaterals.org/spip.php?article20272 [accessed 14 June 2013].

Council of the EU (2013), 'Council Gives the Green Light to Launch Free-Trade Talks with the United States', 14 June. Available from: http://www.consilium.europa.eu/homepage/highlights/council-gives-the-green-light-to-launch-free-trade-talks-with-the-united-states?lang=en [accessed 14 July 2013].

Cowles, M.G. (2001), 'The TABD and Domestic Business-Government Relations', in M.G. Cowles, J. Caporaso and T. Risse (eds), *Transforming Europe: Europeanization and Domestic Change* (Ithaca, NY: Cornell University Press), pp. 159–79.

Cox, R.W. (1981), 'Social Forces, States and World Orders: Beyond International Relations Theory', *Millennium: Journal of International Studies*, 10 (2), pp. 126–55.

Cox, R.W. (1987), *Production, Power, and World Order: Social Forces in the Making of History* (New York: Columbia University Press).

Cox, R.W. (1996), 'Influences and Commitments', in R.W. Cox with T.J. Sinclair (eds), *Approaches to World Order* (Cambridge: Cambridge University Press), pp. 19–38.

Crawford, G. (1996), 'Whither Lomé? The Mid-Term Review and the Decline of Partnership', *Journal of Modern African Studies*, 34 (3), pp. 503–18.

CRNM (2007), 'Getting to Know the EPA', 5 December, Christ Church, Barbados: CRNM. Available from: http://www.crnm.org/index.php?option=com_docman&task=doc_download&gid=293&Itemid=95 [accessed 12 September 2011].

Crouch, C. (2011), *The Strange Non-Death of Neo-Liberalism* (Cambridge: Polity Press).

Daugbjerg, C. and Swinbank, A. (2009), *Ideas, Institutions, and Trade: The WTO and the Curious Case of EU Farm Policy in Trade Liberalization* (Oxford: Oxford University Press).

De Bièvre, D. and Eckhardt, J. (2011), 'Interest Groups and the Failure of EU Anti-Dumping Reform', *Journal of European Public Policy*, 18 (3), pp. 338–59.

De Gucht, K. (2010), 'The Implications of the Lisbon Treaty for EU Trade Policy', speech at the S&D Seminar on EU Trade Policy, Porto, 8 October. Available from: http://trade.ec.europa.eu/doclib/docs/2010/october/tradoc_146719.pdf [accessed 16 January 2013].

De Gucht, K. (2012), 'EU Trade Policy in Times of Protectionism', speech at the Roundtable with the Centre for European Political Practical Excellence,

Brussels, 28 March. Available from: http://trade.ec.europa.eu/doclib/docs/2012/march/tradoc_149256.pdf [accessed 10 July 2013].

De Gucht, K. (2013), 'Open Markets: Making the Case', speech at the World Federation of Advertisers Annual Conference, Brussels, 6 March. Available from: http://trade.ec.europa.eu/doclib/docs/2013/march/tradoc_150732.pdf [accessed 10 July 2013].

De Ville, F. and Orbie, J. (2013), 'The European Commission's Neoliberal Trade Discourse since the Crisis: Legitimising Continuity Through Subtle Discursive Change', *British Journal of Politics and International Relations*, DOI: 10.1111/1467-856X.12022.

Del Felice, C. (2012), 'Power in Discursive Practices: The Case of the STOP EPAs Campaign', *European Journal of International Relations*, DOI: 10.1177/1354066112437769.

Denzin, N. (2006), *Sociological Methods: A Sourcebook*, 5th edn (Chicago, IL: Aldine).

Deraniyagala, S. and Fine, B. (2001), 'New Trade Theory versus Old Trade Policy: A Continuing Enigma', *Cambridge Journal of Economics*, 25 (6), pp. 809–25.

Destler, I.M. (2005), *American Trade Politics*, 4th edn (Washington, DC: Institute for International Economics).

Deutsche Presse Agentur (2010), 'Italy to Hold out Until Thursday on EU–South Korea Veto', *Deutsche Presse Agentur*, 13 September. Available from: http://www.bilaterals.org/spip.php?article18091 [accessed 1 October 2010].

Devuyst, Y. (1995), 'The European Community and the Conclusion of the Uruguay Round', in C. Rhodes and S. Mazey (eds), *The State of the European Union*, Vol. III (Boulder, CO: Lynne Rienner), pp. 449–67.

Doctor, M. (2007), 'Why Bother with Interregionalism? Negotiations for a European Union–Mercosur Agreement', *Journal of Common Market Studies*, 45 (2), pp. 281–314.

Drake, W.J. and Nicolaïdis, K. (1992), 'Ideas, Interests and Institutionalization: "Trade in Services" and the Uruguay Round', *International Organization*, 46 (1), pp. 37–100.

Duddy, J.-M. (2012), 'EU Backs Down on EPA Deadline', *The Namibian*, 18 September. Online edition. Available from: http://www.namibian.com.na/indexx.php?archive_id=100045&page_type=archive_story_detail&page=678 [accessed 3 September 2013].

Dunleavy, P. (1991), *Democracy, Bureaucracy and Public Choice: Economic Explanations in Political Science* (Hemel Hempstead: Wheatsheaf).

Dür, A. (2007), 'EU Trade Policy as Protection for Exporters: The Agreements with Chile and Mexico', *Journal of Common Market Studies*, 45 (4), pp. 833–55.

Dür, A. (2008), 'Bringing Economic Interests Back into the Study of EU Trade Policy-Making', *British Journal of Politics and International Relations*, 10 (1), pp. 27–45.

Dür, A. (2010), *Protection for Exporters: Power and Discrimination in Transatlantic Trade Relations, 1930–2010* (Ithaca, NY: Cornell University Press).

Dür, A. and De Bièvre, D. (2007), 'Inclusion without Influence: NGOs in European Trade Policy', *Journal of Public Policy*, 27 (1), pp. 79–101.

ECB (2013), 'Intra-Euro Area Trade Linkages and External Adjustment', *European Central Bank Monthly Bulletin*, January, pp. 59–74.

ECLAC (2008), 'Review of CARIFORUM–EU EPA in Development Cooperation and WTO Compatibility', Santiago: ECLAC. Available from: http://www.eclac.org/publicaciones/xml/5/34435/L.177.pdf [accessed 8 May 2011].

EC–Mexico Joint Council (2001), 'Decision No. 2/2001 of the EU–Mexico Joint Council of 27 February 2001', Brussels: General Secretariat of the Council of the EU. Available from: http://eur-lex.europa.eu/LexUriServ/LexUriServ.do?uri=OJ: L:2001:070:0007:0050:EN:PDF [accessed 3 March 2010].

EcoNews Africa and Traidcraft (2005), 'EPAs: Through the Lens of Kenya', Nairobi and London: EcoNews Africa and Traidcraft.

Egan, M. (2013), 'From EU–US FTA to TTIP: Promises and Pitfalls', Transworld Op-Ed. Available from: http://www.transworld-fp7.eu/?p=1060 [accessed 15 July 2013].

Egeberg, M. (2002), 'The European Commission – The Evolving Executive', Working Paper No. 02/30, Oslo: ARENA Centre for European Studies.

Egger, H., Egger, P. and Greenaway, P. (2007), 'Intra-Industry Trade with Multinational Firms', *European Economic Review*, 51 (8), pp. 1959–84.

Elgström, O. and Pilegaard, J. (2008), 'Imposed Incoherence: Negotiating Economic Partnership Agreements', *Journal of European Integration*, 30 (3), pp. 363–80.

Elsig, M. (2002), *The EU's Common Commercial Policy: Institutions, Interests and Ideas* (London: Ashgate).

Elsig, M. (2007), 'The EU's Choice of Regulatory Venues for Trade Negotiations: A Tale of Agency Power?', *Journal of Common Market Studies*, 45 (4), pp. 927–48.

Elsig, M. (2010), 'European Union Trade Policy after Enlargement: Larger Crowds, Shifting Priorities and Informal Decision-Making', *Journal of European Public Policy*, 17 (6), pp. 781–98.

Elsig, M. and Dupont, C. (2012), 'European Union Meets South Korea: Bureaucratic Interests, Exporter Discrimination and the Negotiations of Trade Agreements', *Journal of Common Market Studies*, 50 (3), pp. 492–507.

EPA Watch (2013), 'EPA Watch: About Us'. Available from: http://epawatch.eu/about/ [accessed 14 July 2013].

ESF (2003a), 'ESF Calls for Progress towards a Multilateral Agreement on Trade and Competition', Brussels: ESF. Available from: http://www.esf.be/new/wp-content/uploads/2009/06/esf-position-paper-on-trade-competition-final.pdf [accessed 8 January 2010].

ESF (2003b), 'New ESF Priorities for the DDA', Brussels: ESF. Available from: http://www.esf.be/new/wp-content/uploads/2009/01/esf-new-priorities-for-the-dda.pdf [accessed 8 April 2010].

ESF (2006), 'The Negative List Approach in Bilateral Services Negotiations', Brussels: ESF. Available from: http://www.esf.be/new/wp-content/uploads/2009/01/esf2006-40-mandelson-negative-approach.pdf [accessed 8 January 2010].

ESF (2007a), 'ESF Position Paper on EU Free Trade Agreements', Brussels: ESF. Available from: http://www.esf.be/new/wp-content/uploads/2009/01/esf-position-paper-on-eu-free-trade-agreements-final.pdf [accessed 8 January 2010].

ESF (2007b), 'Call for Ambitious Services Result in the DDA', 17 April, Brussels: ESF.

ESF (2007c), 'ESF Response to DG Trade Questionnaire on FTAs', Brussels: ESF. Available from: http://www.esf.be/new/wp-content/uploads/2009/01/esf2007-17-ftas-questionnaire-aguiar-machado-final-consolidated-version.pdf [accessed 8 January 2010].

ESF (2007d), 'Negotiations of Services Commitments in the European Partnership Agreements', 1 November, Brussels: ESF. Available from: http://www.esf.be/pdfs/documents/position_papers/ESF2007-27%20Peter%20Mandelson%20-%20Services%20in%20EPAs.pdf [accessed 8 May 2011].

ESF (2008a), 'What Ambitions for the EPA on Services & Investment: The European Private Sector's Views', presentation to the SADC Workshop on Trade in Services & Investment in the EPA Negotiations in Cape Town, 20–22 February. Available from: www.tralac.org/unique/tralac/pdf/20070229_Kerneis. ppt [accessed 8 May 2011].

ESF (2008b), 'Business Perspective/Ambitions: The EU Views', presentation to the ESA-EAC Workshop on Trade in Services & Investment in the EPA Negotiations in Kampala, 28–30 May. Available from: http://trade.ec.europa.eu/doclib/docs/2008/june/tradoc_139115.pdf [accessed 8 May 2011].

ESF (2009), 'Services Industry Calls for a Swift Conclusion of the EU–Korea FTA', Brussels: ESF. Available from: http://www.esf.be/new/wp-content/uploads/2009/01/esf-korea-letter-to-barroso-july-6-2009.pdf [accessed 8 January 2010].

ESF (2010), 'The Benefits of the FTA for the European Services Sectors', presentation to the INTA public hearing on the FTA between the EU and Its Member States and the Republic of Korea, Brussels, 23 June. Available from: http://www.esf.be/new/wp-content/uploads/2010/06/EU-Korea-FTA-INTA-Hearing-23-06-2010-ESF-Presentation.pdf [accessed 1 November 2010].

ESF (2013), 'Our Members from A–Z' [online], Brussels: ESF. Available from: http://www.esf.be/new/?page_id=87 [accessed 17 July 2013].

ESF, Panafrican Federation of Employers, Australian Services Roundtable, Australian Chamber of Commerce and Industry, Confederação Nacional da Indústria, Confederación de la Producción y del Comercio, Federation of Egyptian Industries, UNICE, Hong Kong Coalition of Service Industries, Hong Kong General Chamber of Commerce, Japan Business Federation, Mexican Confederation of Employers and Confédération Générale des Entreprises du Maroc (2003), 'Joint Business Charter for Cancún: Business Is United in Support of the WTO Multilateral Trading System'. Available from: http://www.hkcsi.org.hk/reports/cancun/08Joint_Business_Charter_final_110903.pdf [accessed 7 March 2010].

Estevadeordal, A. and Suominen, K. (2006), 'Mapping and Measuring Rules of Origin around the World', in O. Cadot, A. Estevadeordal, A. Suwa-Eisenmann and T. Verdier (eds), *The Origin of Goods: Rules of Origin in Regional Trade Agreements* (Oxford: Oxford University Press), pp. 69–113.

Ethier, W.J. (2009), 'The Greater the Differences, the Greater the Gains?', *Trade and Development Review*, 2 (2), pp. 70–8.

EU–Africa Chamber of Commerce (2013), 'MEPs Extend Deadline for Ending Free EU Market Access for ACP Countries'. Available from: http://www.eu-africa-cc.org/index.php/en/component/k2/item/688-meps-extend-deadline-for-ending-free-eu-market-access-for-acp-countries [accessed 14 July 2013].

Eun-Joo, J. (2012), 'After KORUS FTA, New Pressures on the Horizon', *The Hankyoreh*, 15 March. Online edition. Available from: http://english.hani.co.kr/arti/english_edition/e_business/523643.html [accessed 15 November 2012].

EurActiv (2010), 'EU–Korea Trade Deal Ups Pressure on Taiwan, Japan', 14 December. Online edition. Available from: http://www.euractiv.com/en/global-europe/eu-korea-trade-deal-ups-pressure-taiwan-japan-news-500555 [accessed 9 February 2011].

European Centre for Development Policy Management (ECDPM) (2006), 'Update on Regional EPA Negotiations', *In Brief*, No. 15E, November, Maastricht: ECDPM.

European Commission (1987), 'Second Report on the Implementation of the Commission's White Paper on Completing the Internal Market', COM(87) 203 final, Brussels: European Commission.

European Commission (1995), 'Free Trade Areas: An Appraisal', SEC(95) 322 final, Brussels: European Commission.

European Commission (1996a), 'The Global Challenge of International Trade: A Market Access Strategy for the European Union', COM(96) 53 final, Brussels: European Commission.

European Commission (1996b), 'Green Paper on Relations between the European Union and the ACP Countries on the Eve of the 21st Century: Challenges and Options for a New Partnership', COM(96) 570 final, Brussels: European Commission.

European Commission (1999), 'The EU Approach to the Millennium Round', Brussels: European Commission. Available from: http://trade.ec.europa.eu/doclib/docs/2006/december/tradoc_111111.pdf [accessed 1 February 2011].

European Commission (2002), 'Recommendation for a Council Decision Authorising the Commission to Negotiate Economic Partnership Agreements with the ACP Countries and Regions: Explanatory Memorandum', SEC(2002) 351 final, Brussels: European Commission.

European Commission (2005a), 'Trade and Competitiveness: Issues Paper', Brussels: European Commission. Available from: http://trade.ec.europa.eu/doclib/docs/2005/november/tradoc_125859.pdf [accessed 16 October 2009].

European Commission (2005b), 'Workshop 3: External Aspects of Competitiveness', summary of proceedings at the Market Access Symposium, 19 September, Brussels: European Commission. Available from: http://trade.ec.europa.eu/doclib/docs/2005/october/tradoc_125018.pdf [accessed 16 October 2009].

European Commission (2005c), 'Commission Staff Working Document: The Trade and Development Aspects of EPA Negotiations', SEC(2005) 1459, Brussels: European Commission.

European Commission (2005d), 'Economic Partnership Agreements: EU and West Africa Agree on Next Phase of Negotiations', press release, 28 October. Available from: http://www.europa-eu-un.org/articles/en/article_5214_en.htm [accessed 8 May 2011].

European Commission (2006a), 'CARS 21: A Competitive Automotive Regulatory Framework for the 21st Century, Final Report', Brussels: European Commission. Available from: http://ec.europa.eu/enterprise/sectors/automotive/files/pages-background/competitiveness/cars21finalreport_en.pdf [accessed 8 January 2010].

European Commission (2006b), 'Report – "External Aspects of Competitiveness": Consultation of EU Business Federations – 18 January 2006', Brussels: European Commission.

European Commission (2006c), 'Trade and Competitiveness: Record of Civil Society Dialogue Meeting Held 8 March 2006', Brussels: European Commission. Available from: http://trade.ec.europa.eu/doclib/docs/2006/march/tradoc_127897.pdf [accessed 16 October 2009].

European Commission (2006d), 'Draft Communication on External Aspects of Competitiveness', reference 318/06, 28 June, Brussels: European Commission. Available from: http://www.s2bnetwork.org/download/globaleurope_draft [accessed 25 September 2009].

European Commission (2006e), 'Note for the Attention of the 133 Committee: Minimum Platform on Investment for EU FTAs – Provisions on Establishment in Template for a Title on "Establishment, Trade in Services and E-commerce"', D(2006) 9219, Brussels: European Commission. Available from: http://www.iisd.org/pdf/2006/itn_ecom.pdf [accessed 25 September 2009].

European Commission (2006f), 'Note for the Attention of the 133 Committee: Minimum Platform on Investment for EU FTAs – Provisions on Establishment in Template for a Title on "Establishment, Trade in Services and E-commerce" – Explanatory Memorandum', D(2006) 9219, Brussels: European Commission. Available from: http://www.iisd.org/pdf/2006/itn_ecom.pdf [accessed 25 September 2009].

European Commission (2006g), 'Global Europe: Competing in the World', COM(2006) 567 final, Brussels: European Commission.

European Commission (2006h), 'Global Europe: Competing in the World – Impact Assessment Report', SEC(2006) 1228, Brussels: European Commission.

European Commission (2006i), 'Commission Staff Working Document: Accompanying Document to the Communication to Modify the Directives for the Negotiations of Economic Partnership Agreements with ACP Countries and Regions', SEC(2006) 1427, Brussels: European Commission.

European Commission (2007a), 'EU Draft Mandate for ASEAN'. Available from: http://www.bilaterals.org/spip.php?article8211 [accessed 8 May 2011].

European Commission (2007b), 'EU Draft Mandate for India'. Available from: http://www.bilaterals.org/IMG/doc_India_draft_mandate_061206.doc [accessed 8 May 2011].

European Commission (2007c), 'Global Europe: A Stronger Partnership to Deliver Market Access for European Exporters', COM(2007) 183 final, Brussels: European Commission.

European Commission (2007d), 'Commission Staff Working Paper Accompanying the Commission Working Paper: EU Report on Policy Coherence for Development', SEC(2007) 1202, Brussels: European Commission.

European Commission (2007e), 'Economic Partnership Agreements: Information Note from Commissioners Mandelson and Michel', SEC(2007) 1743, Brussels: European Commission.

European Commission (2008a), 'Six Common Misconceptions about Economic Partnership Agreements (EPAs)'. Available from: http://trade.ec.europa.eu/doclib/docs/2008/january/tradoc_137484.pdf [accessed 8 May 2011].

European Commission (2008b), 'CARS 21: Mid-Term Review High Level Conference, Conclusions and Report', Brussels: European Commission. Available from: http://ec.europa.eu/enterprise/sectors/automotive/files/pagesbackground/competitiveness/cars21_mtr_report_en.pdf [accessed 8 January 2010].

European Commission (2009a), 'Commission Reacts to ACEA Press Release on Korea Free Trade Deal', Brussels: European Commission. Available from: http://trade.ec.europa.eu/doclib/press/index.cfm?id=155&serie=139&langId=en [accessed 20 October 2010].

European Commission (2009b), 'Introduction to the CARIFORUM–EC EPA'. Available from: http://trade.ec.europa.eu/doclib/docs/2010/march/tradoc_145879.pdf [accessed 8 May 2011].

European Commission (2010a), 'Proposal for a Regulation of the European Parliament and of the Council Implementing the Bilateral Safeguard Clause of the EU–Korea Free Trade Agreement', COM(2010) 49 final, Brussels: European Commission.

European Commission (2010b), 'The Feature of "Duty Drawback" in the Rules of Origin of EU Free Trade Agreements', COM(2010) 77 final, Brussels: European Commission.

European Commission (2010c), 'Europe 2020: A Strategy for Smart, Sustainable and Inclusive Growth', COM(2010) 2020 final, Brussels: European Commission.

European Commission (2010d), 'South Korea: EU Bilateral Trade and Trade with the World', Brussels: European Commission. Available from: http://trade.ec.europa.eu/doclib/docs/2006/september/tradoc_113448.pdf [accessed 18 November 2010].

European Commission (2010e), 'Services and Investment in EPAs & Scheduling Specific Services Commitments: The EPA Approach Proposed by the EU', presentation to the West Africa Technical Workshop in Praia, 18 March. Available from: http://trade.ec.europa.eu/doclib/docs/2010/may/tradoc_146188.pdf [accessed 8 May 2011].

European Commission (2010f), 'Public Consultation on a Future Trade Policy: Issues Paper', Brussels: European Commission. Available from: http://trade.ec.europa.eu/doclib/docs/2010/june/tradoc_146220.pdf [accessed 18 July 2011].

European Commission (2010g), 'Towards a Comprehensive European International Investment Policy', COM(2010) 343 final, Brussels: European Commission.

European Commission (2010h), 'Public Consultation on the EU Generalised System of Preferences (GSP): Listing of Answers Received', Brussels: European Commission. Available from: http://trade.ec.europa.eu/doclib/docs/2010/september/tradoc_146463.edited.pdf [accessed 18 July 2011].

European Commission (2010i), 'EU–South Korea Free Trade Agreement: A Quick Reading Guide', October 2010, Brussels: European Commission. Available from: http://trade.ec.europa.eu/doclib/docs/2009/october/tradoc_145203.pdf [accessed 11 January 2012].

European Commission (2010j), 'Trade, Growth and World Affairs: Trade as a Core Component of the EU's 2020 Strategy', COM(2010) 612, Brussels: European Commission.

European Commission (2010k), 'Report on Progress Achieved on the Global Europe Strategy, 2006–2010: Commission Staff Working Document Accompanying the Commission's Communication on "Trade, Growth and World Affairs"', SEC(2010) 1268/2, Brussels: European Commission.

European Commission (2010l), 'Trade as a Driver of Prosperity: Commission Staff Working Document Accompanying the Commission's Communication on "Trade, Growth and World Affairs"', SEC(2010) 1269, Brussels: European Commission.

European Commission (2011a), 'Trade and Investment Barriers Report 2011', COM(2011) 114, Brussels: European Commission.

European Commission (2011b), 'Proposal for a Regulation of the European Parliament and of the Council Applying a Scheme of Generalised Tariff Preferences', COM(2011) 241 final, Brussels: European Commission.

European Commission (2011c), 'Vol. I: Commission Staff Working Paper: Impact Assessment, Accompanying the Document for a Proposal for a Regulation of the European Parliament and of the Council Applying a Scheme of Generalised Tariff Preferences', SEC(2011) 536 final, Brussels: European Commission.

European Commission (2011d), 'Access to EU Markets for Exporters from African, Caribbean and Pacific Countries', Brussels: European Commission. Available from: http://trade.ec.europa.eu/doclib/docs/2011/september/tradoc_148215. pdf [accessed 30 September 2011].

European Commission (2011e), 'EU–US Summit: Factsheet on High-Level Working Group on Jobs and Growth'. Available from: http://trade.ec.europa. eu/doclib/docs/2011/november/tradoc_148387.pdf [accessed 14 July 2013].

European Commission (2012a), 'Trade, Growth and Development: Tailoring Trade and Investment Policy for those Countries Most in Need', COM(2012) 22 final, Brussels: European Commission.

European Commission (2012b), 'Les Services Culturelles dans le cadre de l'APE CARIFORUM–UE: Quelles Opportunités pour Haïti?', presentation to the seminar 'L'Union Européenne au Service du Secteur Privé Haitien', 20 March. Available from: http://trade.ec.europa.eu/doclib/docs/2012/june/tradoc_149555.pdf [accessed 25 November 2012].

European Commission (2012c), 'Proposal for a Regulation of the European Parliament and of the Council on the Access of Third-Country Goods and Services to the Union's Internal Market in Public Procurement and Procedures Supporting Negotiations on Access of Union Goods and Services to the Public Procurement Markets of Third Countries', COM(2012) 124 final, Brussels: European Commission.

European Commission (2012d), 'External Sources of Growth: Progress Report on EU Trade and Investment Relationship with Key Economic Partners', Brussels: European Commission.

European Commission (2013a), 'Trade: A Key Source of Growth and Jobs for the EU – Commission Contribution to the European Council of 7–8 February', Brussels: European Commission. Available from: http://ec.europa.eu/commission_ 2010-2014/president/news/archives/2013/02/pdf/20130205_2_en.pdf [accessed 14 July 2013].

European Commission (2013b), 'Impact Assessment Report on the Future of EU–US Trade Relations', SWD(2013) 68 final, Strasbourg: European Commission.

European Commission (2013c), 'EU–Korea FTA Sees Strong Rise in EU Exports', IP/13/626, Brussels: European Commission. Available from: http://europa.eu/ rapid/press-release_IP-13-626_en.htm [accessed 14 July 2013].

European Commission (2013d), 'Overview of FTA and Other Trade Negotiations: Updated 1 August', Brussels: European Commission. Available from: http:// trade.ec.europa.eu/doclib/docs/2006/december/tradoc_118238.pdf [accessed 9 September 2013].

European Commission (2013e), 'Overview of EPA: Updated 7 August', Brussels: European Commission. Available from: http://trade.ec.europa.eu/doclib/ docs/2009/september/tradoc_144912.pdf [accessed 9 September 2013].

European Council (2000), 'Lisbon European Council Conclusions: 23 and 24 March 2000', Brussels: General Secretariat of the Council of the EU. Available from: http://www.europarl.europa.eu/summits/lis1_en.htm [1 September 2010].

European Council (2005), 'Brussels European Council Conclusions: 22 and 23 March 2005', Brussels: General Secretariat of the Council of the EU. Available from: http://www.consilium.europa.eu/uedocs/cms_data/docs/pressdata/en/ ec/84335.pdf [accessed 1 September 2010].

European Council (2010a), 'Brussels European Council Conclusions: 17 June 2010', Brussels: General Secretariat of the Council of the EU. Available from: http://ec.europa.eu/eu2020/pdf/council_conclusion_17_june_en.pdf [accessed 19 July 2011].

European Council (2010b), 'Brussels European Council Conclusions: 28–29 October 2010', Brussels: General Secretariat of the Council of the EU. Available from: http://www.consilium.europa.eu/uedocs/cms_data/docs/pressdata/en/ec/117496.pdf [accessed 20 December 2010].

European Parliament (2009), 'Debates – Monday, 14 September 2009: 22. Free Trade Agreement with South Korea: Impact on European Industry', Brussels: European Parliament. Available from: http://www.europarl.europa.eu/sides/getDoc.do?type=CRE&reference=20090914&secondRef=ITEM-022&language=EN [accessed 12 November 2010].

European Parliament (2010a), 'Report on the Proposal for a Regulation of the European Parliament and of the Council Implementing the Bilateral Safeguard Clause of the EU–Korea Free Trade Agreement', A7-0210/2010, Brussels: European Parliament.

European Parliament (2010b), 'Green Light from Trade Committee for Safeguard Clause in EU–South Korea Trade Accord', Brussels: European Parliament. Available from: http://www.europarl.europa.eu/en/pressroom/content/20100621IPR76426/ [accessed 28 October 2010].

European Parliament (2011a), 'EU–South Korea Free Trade Accord: MEPs Agree on the Safeguard Clause', Brussels: European Parliament. Available from: http://www.europarl.europa.eu/en/pressroom/content/20110124IPR12357/html/EU-South-Korea-free-trade-accord-MEPs-agree-on-the-safeguard-clause [accessed 9 February 2011].

European Parliament (2011b), 'European Parliament Resolution of 6 April 2011 on the Future European International Investment Policy', Brussels: European Parliament. Available from: http://www.europarl.europa.eu/sides/getDoc.do?type=TA&reference=P7-TA-2011-0141&language=EN [accessed 1 June 2011].

Eurostat (2008), *European Union Foreign Direct Investment Yearbook 2008: Data 2001–2006* [online] (Brussels: European Commission). Available from: http://epp.eurostat.ec.europa.eu/cache/ITY_OFFPUB/KS-BK-08-001/EN/KS-BK-08-001-EN.PDF [15 April 2010].

Eurostat (2013a), 'The EU in the World 2013: A Statistical Portrait', Brussels: European Commission. Available from: http://epp.eurostat.ec.europa.eu/cache/ITY_OFFPUB/KS-30-12-861/EN/KS-30-12-861-EN.PDF [accessed 15 July 2013].

Eurostat (2013b), *COMEXT Database* [online] (Brussels: European Commission). Available from: http://epp.eurostat.ec.europa.eu/portal/page/portal/external_trade/data/database [accessed 15 July 2013].

Faber, G. and Orbie, J. (eds) (2009), *Beyond Market Access for Economic Development: EU–Africa Relations in Transition* (Abingdon: Routledge).

Fairbrother, M. (2010), 'Trade Policymaking in the Real World: Elites' Conflicting Worldviews and North American Integration', *Review of International Political Economy*, 17 (2), pp. 319–47.

Fine, B. (2001), *Social Capital Versus Social Theory: Political Economy and Social Science at the Turn of the Millennium* (Abingdon: Routledge).

Fisher, E.O'N. (2011), 'Heckscher-Ohlin Theory When Countries Have Different Technologies', *International Review of Economics and Finance*, 20 (2), pp. 202–10.

Flam, H. and Helpman, E. (1987), 'Vertical Product Differentiation and North–South Trade', *American Economic Review*, 77 (5), pp. 810–22.

García, M. and Khorana, S. (2013), 'European Union–India Negotiations: One Step Forward, One Back?', *Journal of Common Market Studies*, 51 (4), pp. 684–700.

George, J. (1994), *Discourses of Global Politics: A Critical (Re)introduction to International Relations* (London: Lynne Rienner).

Gibb, R. (2000), 'Post-Lomé: The European Union and the South', *Third World Quarterly*, 21 (4), pp. 457–81.

Gill, S. (1998), 'European Governance and New Constitutionalism: Economic and Monetary Union and Alternatives to Disciplinary Neoliberalism in Europe', *New Political Economy*, 3 (1), pp. 5–26.

Gilligan, M. (1997), *Empowering Exporters: Reciprocity, Delegation and Collective Action in American Trade Policy* (Ann Arbour: University of Michigan Press).

Gofas, A. and Hay, C. (2010), 'Varieties of Ideational Explanation', in A. Gofas and C. Hay (eds), *The Role of Ideas in Political Analysis: A Portrait of Contemporary Debates* (Abingdon: Routledge), pp. 13–55.

Goldirova, R. (2009), 'Brussels Divided over Korean Trade Deal', *Bloomberg Business Week*, 22 July. Available from: http://www.businessweek.com/global-biz/content/jul2009/gb20090722_028291.htm [accessed 1 November 2010].

Goldstein, J. (1988), 'Ideas, Institutions, and American Trade Policy', *International Organization*, 42 (1), pp. 179–217.

Goldstein, J. and Keohane, R.O. (eds) (1993), *Ideas and Foreign Policy: Beliefs, Institutions, and Political Change* (Ithaca, NY: Cornell University Press).

Goldstein, J., Rivers, D. and Tomz, M. (2007), 'Institutions in International Relations: Understanding the Effects of the GATT and the WTO on World Trade', *International Organization*, 61 (1), pp. 37–67.

Greenwood, J. (2011), *Interest Representation in the European Union*, 3rd edn (Basingstoke: Palgrave Macmillan).

Grieco, J.M. (1988), 'Anarchy and the Limits of Cooperation: A Realist Critique of the Newest Liberal Institutionalism', *International Organization* 42 (3), pp. 485–507.

Grossman, G.M. and Helpman, E. (1994), 'Protection for Sale', *American Economic Review*, 84 (4), pp. 833–50.

Grubel, H.G. and Lloyd, P.J. (1975), *Intra-Industry Trade* (London: Macmillan).

Guerin, S.S., Edwards, T.H., Glania, G., Kim, H., Lee, H., Matthes, J. and Tekce, M. (2007), *A Qualitative Analysis of a Potential Free Trade Agreement between the European Union and South Korea* (Brussels and Seoul: Centre for European Policy Studies [CEPS] and Korean Institute for International and Economic Policy [KIEP] Study).

Haas, P. (1992), 'Introduction: Epistemic Communities and International Policy Coordination', *International Organization*, 46 (1), pp. 1–35.

Hacking, I. (1999), *The Social Construction of What?* (Cambridge, MA: Harvard University Press).

Hall, P.A. (2012), 'The Economics and Politics of the Euro Crisis', *German Politics*, 21 (4), pp. 355–71.

Hall, P.A. and Taylor, R.C.R. (1996), 'Political Science and the Three New Institutionalisms', *Political Studies*, 44 (4), pp. 936–57.

Hanson, B.T. (1998), 'What Happened to Fortress Europe? External Trade Policy Liberalization in the European Union', *International Organization*, 52 (1), pp. 55–85.

Haskel, B. (2008), 'When Can a Weak Process Generate Strong Results? Entrepreneurial Alliances in the Bologna Process to Create a European Higher Education Area', Working Paper No. 165, Cambridge, MA: Harvard Center for European Studies.

Hay, C. (2002), *Political Analysis: A Critical Introduction* (Basingstoke: Palgrave).

Hay, C. (2004a), 'Theory, Stylised Heuristic, or Self-Fulfilling Prophecy? The Status of Rational Choice Theory in Public Administration', *Public Administration*, 82 (1), pp. 39–62.

Hay, C. (2004b), 'Ideas, Interests and Institutions in the Comparative Political Economy of Great Transformations', *Review of International Political Economy*, 11 (1), pp. 204–26.

Hay, C. (2004c), 'The Normalizing Role of Rationalist Assumptions in the Institutional Embedding of Neoliberalism', *Economy and Society*, 33 (4), pp. 500–27.

Hay, C. (2005), 'Making Hay... or Clutching at Ontological Straws? Notes on Realism, "As-if-Realism" and Actualism', *Politics*, 25 (1), pp. 39–45.

Hay, C. (2007), 'What Doesn't Kill You Can Only Make You Stronger: The Doha Development Round, the Services Directive, and the EU's Conception of Competitiveness', *Journal of Common Market Studies*, 45, Annual Review, pp. 25–43.

Hay, C. (2012), 'The Dangerous Obsession with Cost Competitiveness... and the Not So Dangerous Obsession with Competitiveness', *Cambridge Journal of Economics*, 36 (2), pp. 463–79.

Hay, C. and Rosamond, B. (2002), 'Globalization, European Integration and the Discursive Construction of Economic Imperatives', *Journal of European Public Policy*, 9 (2), pp. 147–67.

Hay, C. and Smith, N. (2005), 'Horses for Courses? The Political Discourse of Globalization and European Integration in the UK and Ireland', *West European Politics*, 28 (1), pp. 124–58.

Hay, C. and Smith, N. (2010), 'How Policy-Makers (Really) Understand Globalization: The Internal Architecture of Anglophone Globalization Discourse in Europe', *Public Administration*, 88 (4), pp. 903–27.

Hayes, J.P. (1993), *Making Trade Policy in the European Community* (New York: St. Martin's Press).

Heckscher, E. and Ohlin, B. (1991), in H. Flam and M.J. Flanders (eds), with a foreword by P.A. Samuelson. *Heckscher-Ohlin Trade Theory* (Cambridge, MA: MIT Press).

Heron, T. (2007), 'European Trade Diplomacy and the Politics of Global Development: Reflections on the EU–China "Bra Wars" Dispute', *Government and Opposition*, 42 (2), pp. 190–214.

Heron, T. (2011), 'Asymmetric Bargaining and Development Tradeoffs in the CARIFORUM–European Union Economic Partnership Agreement', *Review of International Political Economy*, 18 (3), pp. 328–57.

Heron, T. (2013), *Pathways from Preferential Trade: The Politics of Trade Adjustment in Africa, the Caribbean and Pacific* (Basingstoke: Palgrave Macmillan).

Heron, T. and Siles-Brügge, G. (2012), 'Competitive Liberalisation and the "Global Europe" Services and Investment Agenda: Locating the Commercial Drivers of the EU–ACP Economic Partnership Agreements', *Journal of Common Market Studies*, 50 (2), pp. 250–66.

Hettne, B. (1993), 'Neo-Mercantilism: The Pursuit of Regionness', *Cooperation and Conflict* 28 (3), pp. 211–32.

Hindley, B. (2007), 'Antidumping Policy in the EU: A Comment on the Green Paper on Trade Defence Instruments', Policy Brief No. 03/2007, Brussels: European Centre for International Political Economy (ECIPE).

Hirst, P. and Thompson, G. (1999), *Globalization in Question: The International Economy and the Possibilities of Governance*, 2nd edn (Cambridge: Polity Press).

Hiscox, M. (2002), *International Trade and Political Conflict: Commerce, Coalitions and Mobility* (Princeton, NJ: Princeton University Press).

HLWG (2013), 'Final Report', 11 February. Available from: http://trade.ec.europa.eu/doclib/docs/2013/february/tradoc_150519.pdf [accessed 14 July 2013].

Hobson, J.M. and Seabrooke, L. (eds) (2007), *Everyday Politics of the World Economy* (Cambridge: Cambridge University Press).

Hoekman, B., Mattoo, A. and Sapir, A. (2007), 'The Political Economy of Services Trade Liberalisation: A Case for International Regulatory Cooperation?', *Oxford Review of Economic Policy*, 23 (3), pp. 367–91.

Holland, M. and Doidge, M. (2012), *Development Policy of the European Union* (Basingstoke: Palgrave Macmillan).

Horn, L. (2011), *Regulating Corporate Governance in the EU: Towards a Marketisation of Corporate Control* (Basingstoke: Palgrave Macmillan).

Howse, R. (2002), 'From Politics to Technocracy – And Back Again: The Fate of the Multilateral Trading Regime', *The American Journal of International Law*, 96 (1), pp. 94–117.

Hurt, S.R. (2003), 'Co-Operation and Coercion? The Cotonou Agreement between the European Union and ACP States and the End of the Lomé Convention', *Third World Quarterly*, 24 (1), pp. 161–76.

Hurt, S.R., Lee, D. and Lorenz, U. (2013), 'The Argumentative Dimension to the EPAs', *International Negotiation*, 18 (1), pp. 67–87.

ICTSD (2010), 'Obama Administration, South Korea Clinch Long-Awaited FTA', *Bridges Weekly Trade News Digest*, 9 December. Available from: http://ictsd.org/i/news/bridgesweekly/97746/ [accessed 9 December 2010].

International Development Committee (2005), *Fair Trade? The European Union's Trade Agreements with African, Caribbean and Pacific Countries* (London: The Stationery Office).

Jabko, N. (2006), *Playing the Market: A Political Strategy for Uniting Europe* (Ithaca, NY: Cornell University Press).

Jackson, P.T. (2010), *The Conduct of Inquiry in International Relations: Philosophy of Science and Its Implications for the Study of World Politics* (Abingdon: Routledge).

Jamaica Gleaner (2008), 'Guyana Gives In', *Jamaica Gleaner*, 22 October. Online edition. Available from: http://jamaica-gleaner.com/gleaner/20081022/business/business5.html [accessed 8 May 2011].

Jank, M.S., Carfantan, J., Kutas, G., Meirelles Netto, A.J., Nassar, A.M. and Cunha Filho, J.H. (2004), 'Scenarios for Untying the Agriculture Knot', in A. Valladão, F. Peña and P. Messerlin (eds), *Concluding the EU–Mercosur Agreement: Feasible Scenarios* (Paris: Chaire Mercosur de Sciences Po).

Kahler, M. (1985), 'European Protectionism in Theory and Practice', *World Politics*, 37 (4), pp. 475–502.

Katzenstein, P.J., Keohane, R.O. and Krasner, S.D. (1998), 'International Organization and the Study of World Politics', *International Organization*, 52 (4), pp. 645–85.

Keohane, R.O. (1984), *After Hegemony: Cooperation and Discord in the World Political Economy* (Princeton, NJ: Princeton University Press).

Keohane, R.O. and Nye, J. (eds) (1977), *Power and Interdependence: World Politics in Transition* (Boston: Little, Brown).

Keynes, J.M. (1931), 'Mitigation by Tariff', in J.M. Keynes (ed.), *Essays in Persuasion* (London: Macmillan), pp. 271–87.

Kim, H. (2005), *An Analysis of the Economic Effects of an EU–Korea FTA* (Seoul: KIEP).

Kitson, M. and Michie, J. (1995), 'Conflict, Cooperation and Change: The Political Economy of Trade and Trade Policy', *Review of International Political Economy*, 2 (4), pp. 632–57.

Knight, F.H. (1921), *Risk, Uncertainty and Profit* (New York: Houghton Mifflin Company).

Knill, C. and Tosun, J. (2009), 'Hierarchy, Networks, or Markets: How Does the EU Shape Environmental Policy Adoptions Within and Beyond Its Borders', *Journal of European Public Policy*, 16 (6), pp. 873–94.

Kohler-Koch, B. and Rittberger, B. (2006), 'Review Article: The "Governance Turn" in EU Studies', *Journal of Common Market Studies*, 44, Annual Review, pp. 27–49.

Korea JoongAng Daily (2010), 'EU–Korea FTA Hits Final Delay', *Korea JoongAng Daily*, 11 September. Online edition. Available from: http://joongangdaily. joins.com/article/view.asp?aid=2925867 [accessed 1 October 2010].

Krebs, R.R. and Jackson, P.T. (2007), 'Twisting Tongues and Twisting Arms: The Power of Political Rhetoric', *European Journal of International Relations*, 13 (1), pp. 35–66.

Krugman, P. (1981), 'Intraindustry Specialization and the Gains from Trade', *Journal of Political Economy*, 89 (5), pp. 959–73.

Krugman, P. (1986), *Strategic Trade Policy and the New International Economics* (Cambridge, MA: MIT Press).

Krugman, P. (1994), 'Competitiveness: A Dangerous Obsession', *Foreign Affairs*, 73 (2), pp. 28–44.

Kurki, M. (2006), 'Causes of a Divided Discipline: Rethinking the Concept of Cause in IR', *Review of International Studies*, 32 (2), pp. 189–216.

Lake, D.A. and McCubbins, M.D. (2006), 'The Logic of Delegation to International Organizations', in D.G Hawkins, D.A. Lake, D.L. Nielson and M.J. Tierney (eds), *Delegation and Agency in International Organizations* (Cambridge: Cambridge University Press), pp. 341–68.

Lamy, P. (1999), 'Globalisation: A Win–Win Process', speech delivered in Brussels, 15 September. Available from: http://trade.ec.europa.eu/doclib/docs/2005/january/tradoc_121059.pdf [accessed 20 June 2011].

Lamy, P. (2000), 'Faire Tomber les Barrières Ne Suffira Pas', speech delivered at the Market Access Symposium, 28 November. Available from: http://trade.ec.europa.eu/doclib/docs/2005/january/tradoc_121051.pdf [accessed 24 July 2011].

Lamy, P. (2002), 'Stepping Stones or Stumbling Blocks? The EU's Approach Towards the Problem of Multilateralism vs. Regionalism in Trade Policy', *The World Economy*, 25 (10), pp. 1399–413.

Lamy, P. (2003), '"Trade Crisis?"', speech delivered to the European Institute, Washington, DC, 4 November. Available from: http://www.europa-eu-un.org/articles/en/article_2970_en.htm [accessed 1 June 2008].

Lamy, P. (2004), 'The Future of the WTO', speech delivered to the European Parliament Kangaroo Group, Brussels, 27 January. Available from: http://trade.ec.europa.eu/doclib/docs/2004/june/tradoc_115726.pdf [accessed 1 June 2008].

Langan, M. (2011), 'Private Sector Development as Poverty and Strategic Discourse: PSD in the Political Economy of EU–Africa Relations', *Journal of Modern African Studies*, 49 (1), pp. 83–113.

Langley, P. (2007), 'Everyday Investor Subjects and Global Financial Change: The Rise of Anglo-American Mass Investment', in J.M. Hobson and L. Seabrookes (eds), *Everyday Politics of the World Economy* (Cambridge: Cambridge University Press), pp. 103–19.

Larsén, M.F. (2007), 'Trade Negotiations between the EU and South Africa: A Three-Level Game', *Journal of Common Market Studies*, 45 (4), pp. 857–81.

Lawrence, R. (1996), *Regionalism, Multilateralism and Deeper Integration* (Washington, DC: The Brookings Institution).

Lietaert, M. (2009), 'New Strategy, New Partnership: The EU Commission and the City of London in Trade in Services Policy', paper presented to the Political Studies Association Annual Conference, 7–9 April 2009.

List, F. (1904 [1841]), *The National System of Political Economy* (London: Longmans).

MacDonald, K. (2001), 'Using Documents', in N. Gilbert (ed.), *Researching Social Life*, 2nd edn (London: Sage), pp. 194–210.

Maier, C.S. (1988), *In Search of Stability: Explorations in Historical Political Economy* (Cambridge: Cambridge University Press).

Mandelson, P. (2005a), 'Economic Partnership Agreements: Putting a Rigorous Priority on Development', speech delivered by Peter Mandelson to the Civil Society Dialogue Group, 20 January. Available from: http://trade.ec.europa.eu/doclib/docs/2005/january/tradoc_121095.pdf [accessed 8 May 2011].

Mandelson, P. (2005b), 'Trade at the Service of Development', speech delivered at the London School of Economics, 4 February. Available from: http://www2.lse.ac.uk/publicEvents/pdf/20050204-Mandelson.pdf [accessed 19 March 2013].

Mandelson, P. (2005c), 'Europe's Global Trading Challenge and the Future of Free Trade Agreements', speech delivered by Peter Mandelson to the Foreign Policy Centre Debate, 26 September. Available from: http://trade.ec.europa.eu/doclib/docs/2005/september/tradoc_124783.pdf [accessed 20 August 2011].

Mandelson, P. (2006a), 'Address to the European Socialist Party Conference on Economic Partnership Agreements', speech delivered at the European Parliament, 19 October. Available from: http://www.delnga.ec.europa.eu/epas/Address%20to%20the%20European%20Socialist%20Party%20Conference%20on%20Economic%20Partnership%20Agreements.pdf [accessed 8 May 2011].

Mandelson, P. (2006b), 'The Challenges and Opportunities of the Economic Partnership Agreements', speech delivered to the EU–Africa Business Forum, 16 November. Available from: http://trade.ec.europa.eu/doclib/docs/2006/november/tradoc_131207.pdf [accessed 8 May 2011].

Mandelson, P. (2008), 'Commission Seminar on Economic Partnership Agreements: Remarks by Peter Mandelson', speech delivered at the European Parliament, 17 April. Available from: http://trade.ec.europa.eu/doclib/docs/2008/april/tradoc_138558.pdf [accessed 8 May 2011].

Mandelson, P. and Michel, L. (2007), 'This Is Not a Poker Game: Critics of the EU's Trade Agreements Are Gambling with Livelihoods in the Developing World', *The Guardian*, 31 October. Online edition. Available from: http://www.guardian.co.uk/commentisfree/2007/oct/31/comment.eu [accessed 8 May 2011].

Manger, M. (2005), 'Competition and Bilateralism in Trade Policy: The Case of Japan's Free Trade Agreements', *Review of International Political Economy*, 12 (5), pp. 804–28.

Manger, M. (2008), 'International Investment Agreements and Services Markets: Locking in Market Failure?', *World Development*, 36 (11), pp. 2456–69.

Manger, M. (2009), *Investing in Protection: The Politics of Preferential Trade Agreements between North and South* (Cambridge: Cambridge University Press).

Manger, M. (2012), 'Vertical Specialization and the Formation of North–South PTAs', *World Politics*, 64 (4), pp. 622–58.

Mansfield, E.D. (1998), 'The Proliferation of Preferential Trading Arrangements', *The Journal of Conflict Resolution*, 42 (5), pp. 523–43.

Mansfield, E.D. and Milner, H.V. (1999), 'The New Wave of Regionalism', *International Organization*, 53 (3), pp. 589–627.

Mansfield, E.D. and Reinhardt, E. (2008), 'International Institutions and the Volatility of International Trade', *International Organization*, 62 (4), pp. 621–52.

McGuire, S.M. and Lindeque, J.P. (2010), 'The Diminishing Returns to Trade Policy in the European Union', *Journal of Common Market Studies*, 48 (5), pp. 1329–49.

McNamara, K.R. (1999), *The Currency of Ideas: Monetary Politics in the European Union* (Ithaca, NY: Cornell University Press).

Menz, G. (2009), *The Political Economy of Managed Migration: Nonstate Actors, Europeanization, and the Politics of Designing Migration Policies* (Oxford: Oxford University Press).

Meunier, S. (2005), *Trading Voices: The European Union in International Commercial Negotiations* (Princeton, NJ: Princeton University Press).

Meunier, S. (2007), 'Managing Globalization? The EU in International Trade Negotiations', *Journal of Common Market Studies*, 45 (4), pp. 905–26.

Meunier, S. and Nicolaïdis, K. (1999), 'Who Speaks for Europe? The Delegation of Trade Authority in the EU', *Journal of Common Market Studies*, 37 (3), pp. 477–501.

Meunier, S. and Nicolaïdis, K. (2006), 'The European Union as a Conflicted Trade Power', *Journal of European Public Policy*, 13 (6), pp. 906–25.

Meyn, M. (2006), 'Regional Integration and EPA Configurations in Southern and Eastern Africa: What Are the Feasible Alternatives?', *SEATINI Bulletin*, 9 (7), pp. 1–9.

Milner, H.V. (1997), 'Industries, Governments, and the Creation of Regional Trade Blocs', in E.D. Mansfield and H.V. Milner (eds), *The Political Economy of Regionalism* (New York, NY: Columbia University Press), pp. 77–106.

Moravcsik, A. (1998), *The Choice for Europe: Social Purpose and State Power from Messina to Maastricht* (Ithaca, NY: Cornell University Press).

Murphy, P. (2007), 'West Africa to Miss EU Trade Partnership Deadline', *Reuters*, 5 October. Available from: http://www.reuters.com/article/2007/10/05/idUSL0511548 [accessed 8 May 2011].

Natarajan, P.T. (2011), 'EU–South Korea Free Trade Agreement: Synergistic or Lopsided?', Frost and Sullivan Market Insight. Available from: http://www.frost.com/sublib/display-market-insight-top.do?id=238793895 [accessed 16 November 2012].

Nilsson, A. (2010), *Telling Stories About...: Business Representation of Giant Corporations*, unpublished PhD thesis, University of Manchester.

North, D.C. (1990), *Institutions, Institutional Change, and Economic Performance* (Cambridge: Cambridge University Press).

Nugent, N. (2000), *The European Commission* (Basingstoke: Palgrave Macmillan).

Nunn, A. and Price, S. (2004), 'Managing Development: EU and African Relations Through the Evolution of the Lomé and Cotonou Agreements', *Historical Materialism*, 12 (4), pp. 203–30.

O'Boyle, M. (2005), 'Mexico, European Union Exchange Proposals to Deepen FTA in Services, Farm, Investment', *International Trade Reporter*, 14 March. Available from: http://bilaterals.org/spip.php?article1443 [accessed 1 March 2010].

O'Sullivan, D. (2010), Interview by Viv Davies in 'The Future of EU Trade Policy: A Vox EU Debate Moderated by Richard Baldwin'. Available from: http://trade.ec.europa.eu/doclib/docs/2010/november/tradoc_146932.pdf [accessed 19 July 2011].

ODI (2011), 'The Poverty Impact of the Proposed Graduation Threshold in the Generalised System of Preferences (GSP) Trade Scheme', October, London: ODI.

Ohmae, K. (1995), *The End of the Nation State: The Rise of Regional Economies* (London: Harper Collins).

Olson, M. (1965), *The Logic of Collective Action* (Cambridge, MA: Harvard University Press).

Oppenheim, A.N. (1992), *Questionnaire Design, Interviewing and Attitude Measurement*, new edn (London: Continuum).

Oxfam (2006a), 'Unequal Partners: How EU–ACP Economic Partnership Agreements (EPAs) Could Harm the Development Prospects of Many of the World's Poorest Countries', Oxford: Oxfam.

Oxfam (2006b), 'Slamming the Door on Development: Analysis of the EU's Response to the Pacific's EPA Negotiating Proposals', Oxford: Oxfam.

Pacific Islands Forum Secretariat (2007), 'EPA Must Offer Better Preferences', press release, 17 May. Available from: http://www.forumsec.org.fj/pages.cfm/news-room/press-statements/2007/epa-must-offer-better-preferences.html [accessed 8 May 2011].

Paemen, H. and Bensch, A. (1995), *From the GATT to the WTO: The European Community in the Uruguay Round* (Louvain: Leuven University Press).

Parker, O. (2008), 'Challenging "New Constitutionalism" in the EU: French Resistance, "Social Europe" and "Soft" Governance', *New Political Economy*, 13 (4), pp. 397–417.

Parsons, C. (2003), *A Certain Idea of Europe* (Ithaca, NY: Cornell University Press).

Parsons, C. (2007), *How to Map Arguments in Political Science* (Oxford: Oxford University Press).

Peck, J. (2010), *Constructions of Neoliberal Reason* (Oxford: Oxford University Press).

Peters, B.G. (1992), 'Bureaucratic Politics and the Institutions of the European Community', in A.M. Sbragia (ed.), *Euro-Politics: Institutions and Policy-Making in the 'New' European Community* (Washington, DC: The Brookings Institution), pp. 75–122.

Peterson, J. (1995), 'Playing the Transparency Game: Consultation and Policy-Making in the European Commission', *Public Administration*, 73 (3), pp. 473–92.

Peterson, J., Doherty, R., Van Cutsem, M., Wallace, H., Epstein, R., Burwell, F., Pollack, M.A., Quinlan, J.P. and Young, A.R. (2004), *Review of the Framework for*

Relations between the European Union and the United States: An Independent Study (Final Report) (Brussels: European Commission).

Pierson, P. (1996), 'The Path to European Integration: A Historical Institutionalist Account', *Comparative Political Studies*, 29 (2), pp. 123–63.

Polanyi, K. (1944), *The Great Transformation: The Political and Economic Origins of Our Time* (New York, NY: Rinehart).

Polanyi, K. (1957), 'The Economy as Instituted Process', in K. Polanyi, C.M. Ahrenberg and H. Pearson (eds), *Trade Market in the Early Empires* (New York: Free Press), pp. 243–70.

Poletti, A. and De Bièvre, D. (2013), 'The Political Science of European Trade Policy: A Literature Review with a Research Outlook', *Comparative European Politics*, DOI: 10.1057/cep.2012.35.

Pollack, M.A. (2003), *The Engines of European Integration: Delegation, Agency and Agenda Setting in the EU* (Oxford: Oxford University Press).

Pomfret, R.W.T. (1988), *Unequal Trade: The Economics of Discriminatory International Trade Policies* (Oxford: Basil Blackwell).

Preeg, E.H. (1970), *Traders and Diplomats: An Analysis of the Kennedy Round of Negotiations under the General Agreement on Tariffs and Trade* (Washington, DC: The Brookings Institution).

Putnam, R.D. (1988), 'Diplomacy and Domestic Politics: The Logic of Two-Level Games', *International Organization*, 42 (3), pp. 427–60.

Ravenhill, J. (1985), *Collective Clientelism: The Lomé Conventions and North–South Relations* (New York, NY: Columbia University Press).

Ravenhill, J. (2003), 'The New Bilateralism in the Asia Pacific', *Third World Quarterly*, 24 (2), pp. 299–317.

Ravenhill, J. (2004), 'Back to the Nest? Europe's Relations with the African, Caribbean and Pacific Group of Countries', in V.K. Aggarwal and E.A. Fogarty (eds), *EU Trade Strategies: Between Regionalism and Globalism* (London: Palgrave Macmillan), pp. 118–47.

Ravenhill, J. (2008), 'The Move to Preferential Trade on the Western Pacific Rim: Some Initial Conclusions', *Australian Journal of International Affairs*, 62 (2), pp. 129–50.

Raza, W. (2007), 'European Union Trade Politics: Pursuit of Neo-Mercantilism in Different Fora?', in W. Blaas and J. Becker (eds), *Strategic Arena Switching in International Trade Negotiations* (Farnham: Ashgate).

Record, J. (2004), *Bounding the Global War on Terrorism* (Honolulu, HI: University Press of the Pacific).

Reus-Smit, C. (1997), 'The Constitutional Structure of International Society and the Nature of Fundamental Institutions', *International Organization*, 51 (4), pp. 555–89.

Reuters (2010), 'EU Signs Free Trade Deal with South Korea, Its First with an Asian Nation', *Reuters*, 7 October. Available from: http://www.bilaterals.org/spip.php?article18252 [accessed 10 October 2010].

Ricardo, D. (2002 [1817]), *The Principles of Political Economy and Taxation* (London: Empiricus Books).

Richardson, B.J. (2009), 'Restructuring the EU–ACP Sugar Regime: Out of the Strong There Came Forth Sweetness', *Review of International Political Economy*, 16 (4), pp. 673–97.

Rieger, E. (2005), 'Agricultural Policy: Constrained Reforms', in H. Wallace, W. Wallace and M.A. Pollack (eds), *Policy-Making in the European Union*, 5th edn (Oxford: Oxford University Press), pp. 161–90.

Rodrik, D. (2006), 'What's So Special about China's Exports', *China & World Economy*, 14 (5), pp. 1–19.

Rosamond, B. (2000), 'Europeanization and Discourses of Globalization: Narratives of External Structural Context in the European Commission', Working Paper No. 51/00, Coventry: Centre for the Study of Globalization and Regionalization.

Rosamond, B. (2002), 'Imagining the European Economy: "Competitiveness" and the Social Construction of "Europe" as an Economic Space', *New Political Economy*, 7 (2), pp. 157–77.

Rosamond, B. (2007), 'European Integration and the Social Science of EU Studies: The Disciplinary Politics of a Subfield', *International Affairs*, 83 (2), pp. 231–52.

Rosamond, B. (2013), 'Three Ways of Speaking Europe to the World: Markets, Peace, Cosmopolitan Duty and the EU's Normative Power', *British Journal of Politics and International Relations*, DOI: 10.1111/1467-856X.12013.

Ruggie, J.G. (1982), 'International Regimes, Transactions and Change: Embedded Liberalism in the Post-War Order', *International Organization*, 36 (3), pp. 379–415.

Ryner, M. (2012), 'Financial Crisis, Orthodoxy and Heterodoxy in the Production of Knowledge about the EU', *Millennium: Journal of International Studies*, 40 (3), pp. 647–73.

Sabatier, P.A. (1998), 'The Advocacy Coalition Framework: Revisions and Relevance for Europe', *Journal of European Public Policy*, 5 (1), pp. 98–130.

Sandholtz, W. and Zysman, J. (1989), '1992: Recasting the European Bargain', *World Politics*, 42 (1), pp. 95–128.

Sang-Hun, C. (2011), 'South Korea Approves Free Trade Pact with US', *The New York Times*, 22 November. Online edition. Available from: http://www.nytimes.com/2011/11/23/business/global/seoul-votes-a-chaotic-yes-to-free-trade-with-us.html?pagewanted=all&_r=0 [accessed 15 November 2012].

Saurugger, S. (2013), 'Constructivism and Public Policy Approaches in the EU: From Ideas to Power Games', *Journal of European Public Policy*, 20 (6), pp. 888–906.

Sbragia, A. (2010), 'The EU, the US, and Trade Policy: Competitive Interdependence in the Management of Globalization', *Journal of European Public Policy*, 17 (3), pp. 368–82.

Scharpf, F. (2002), 'The European Social Model: Coping with the Challenges of Diversity', *Journal of Common Market Studies* 40 (4), pp. 645–70.

Schiek, D., Liebert, U. and Schneider, H. (eds) (2011), *European Economic and Social Constitutionalism after the Treaty of Lisbon* (Cambridge: Cambridge University Press).

Schimmelfennig, F. (2003), *The EU, NATO and the Integration of Europe: Rules and Rhetoric* (Cambridge: Cambridge University Press).

Schmidt, V. (2002a), 'Does Discourse Matter in the Politics of Welfare Adjustment?', *Comparative Political Studies*, 35 (2), pp. 168–93.

Schmidt, V. (2002b), *The Futures of European Capitalism* (Oxford: Oxford University Press).

Schmidt, V. (2008), 'Discursive Institutionalism: The Explanatory Power of Ideas and Discourse', *Annual Review of Political Science*, 11, pp. 303–26.

Schmidt, V. and Thatcher, M. (eds) (2013), *Resilient Liberalism in Europe's Political Economy* (Cambridge: Cambridge University Press).

Schott, J. (2004), *Free Trade Agreements: US Strategies and Priorities* (Washington, DC: Institute for International Economics).

Seabrooke, L. (2006), *The Social Sources of Financial Power: Domestic Legitimacy and International Financial Orders* (Ithaca, NY: Cornell University Press).

Seabrooke, L. (2010), 'Everyday Legitimacy and Institutional Change', in A. Gofas and C. Hay (eds), *The Role of Ideas in Political Analysis: A Portrait of Contemporary Debates* (Abingdon: Routledge), pp. 78–94.

Seldon, A. (1996), 'Elite Interviews', in B. Brivati, J. Buxton and A. Seldon (eds), *The Contemporary History Handbook* (Manchester: Manchester University Press), pp. 353–65.

Shaffer, G.C. (2003), *Defending Interests: Public–Private Partnerships in WTO Litigation* (Washington, DC: The Brookings Institution).

Siles-Brügge, G. (2011), 'Resisting Protectionism after the Crisis: Strategic Economic Discourse and the EU–Korea Free Trade Agreement', *New Political Economy*, 16 (5), pp. 627–53.

Siles-Brügge, G. (2013a), 'The Power of Economic Ideas: A Constructivist Political Economy of EU Trade Policy', *Journal of Contemporary European Research*, 9 (4), pp. 597–617.

Siles-Brügge, G. (2013b), 'Explaining the Resilience of Free Trade: The Smoot-Hawley Myth and the Crisis', *Review of International Political Economy*, DOI: 10.1080/09692290.2013.830979.

Skogstad, G. (1998), 'Ideas, Paradigms and Institutions: Agricultural Exceptionalism in the European Union and the United States', *Governance*, 11 (4), pp. 463–90.

Smith, S. (2000), 'Wendt's World', *Review of International Studies*, 26 (1), pp. 151–63.

Stearns, J. (2011), 'EU, South Korea Trade Agreement Overcomes Final European Hurdle', *Bloomberg*, 17 February. Available from: http://www.bloomberg.com/news/2011-02-17/eu-south-korea-trade-agreement-overcomes-final-european-hurdle.html [accessed 18 February 2011].

Stevens, C. (2000), 'Trade with Developing Countries: Banana Skins and Turf Wars', in H. Wallace and W. Wallace (eds), *Policy-Making in the European Union*, 3rd edn (Oxford: Oxford University Press), pp. 401–26.

Strange, S. (1970), 'International Economics and International Relations: A Case of Mutual Neglect', *International Affairs*, 46 (2), pp. 304–15.

Strange, S. (1979), 'The Management of Surplus Capacity: Or How Does Theory Stand Up to Protectionism 1970s Style?', *International Organization*, 33 (3), pp. 303–34.

Strange, S. (1994), 'Wake up, Krasner! The World *Has* Changed', *Review of International Political Economy*, 1 (2), pp. 209–19.

te Velde, D. (2004), 'Special and Differential Treatment in Post-Cotonou Services Negotiations', *Trade Negotiations Insights*, 3 (3), pp. 4–5.

ter Haar, B. and Copeland, P. (2010), 'What Are the Future Prospects for the European Social Model? An Analysis of EU Equal Opportunities and Employment Policy', *European Law Journal*, 16 (3), pp. 273–91.

The Dong-A Ilbo (2010), 'Chief EU Delegate Rules Out Renegotiation of FTA', 10 December. Online edition. Available from: http://english.donga.com/srv/service.php3?bicode=020000&biid=2010121092338 [accessed 8 February 2011].

The Economist (2013), 'Lexington: A Transatlantic Tipping Point', *The Economist*, 27 April. Online edition. Available from: http://www.economist.com/news/united-states/21576704-historic-trade-pact-between-america-and-europe-needs-saving-transatlantic [accessed 14 July 2013].

The Eleutheran (2008), 'Jamaica's Prime Minister Defends EPA Agreement', 16 September. Available from: http://www.eleutheranews.com/caribbean/117.html [accessed 8 May 2011].

Trade Negotiations Insights (2007), 'EPAs: There Is No Plan B – An Interview with Peter Mandelson', *Trade Negotiations Insights*, 6 (5), pp. 1–3.

Trommer, S. (2013), 'Legal Opportunity in Trade Negotiations: International Law, Opportunity Structures and the Political Economy of Trade Agreements', *New Political Economy*, DOI: 10.1080/13563467.2012.753520.

Tsoukalis, L. and da Silva Ferreira, A. (1980), 'Management of Industrial Surplus Capacity in the European Community', *International Organization*, 34 (3), pp. 355–76.

UNICE (2005), 'Competing for Growth and Jobs in a Global Market: UNICE Preliminary Views on the External Dimension of the Lisbon Strategy', Brussels: UNICE. Available from: http://trade.ec.europa.eu/doclib/docs/2005/october/tradoc_124909.pdf [accessed 16 October 2009].

UNICE (2006), 'Trade & Competitiveness: Initial Reaction to Commission Strategy Paper', 7 August, Brussels: UNICE.

van Apeldoorn, B. (2002), *Transnational Capitalism and the Struggle over European Integration* (London: Routledge).

van Apeldoorn, B. (2010), 'The Social Purpose of New Governance: Lisbon and the Limits to Legitimacy', *Journal of International Relations and Development*, 13 (3), pp. 209–38.

van Apeldoorn, B. and Horn, L. (2007), 'The Marketisation of Corporate Control: A Critical Political Economy Perspective', *New Political Economy*, 12 (2), pp. 211–35.

van Apeldoorn, B. and Overbeek, H. (2012), 'Introduction: The Life Course of the Neoliberal Project and the Global Crisis', in H. Overbeek and B. van Apeldoorn (eds), *Neoliberalism in Crisis* (Basingstoke: Palgrave Macmillan), pp. 1–20.

van den Hoven, A. (2004), 'Assuming Leadership in Multilateral Economic Institutions: The EU's "Development" Discourse and Strategy', *West European Politics*, 27 (2), pp. 256–83.

van der Stichele, M., Bizzarri, K. and Plank, L. (2006), 'Corporate Power over EU Trade Policy: Good for Business, Bad for the World', Brussels: Seattle to Brussels Network.

Verbeeck, B. (2003), *Decision-Making in Britain during the Suez Crisis: Small Groups and a Persistent Leader* (Aldershot: Ashgate).

Viner, J. (1948), 'Power versus Plenty as Objectives of Foreign Policy in the Seventeenth and Eighteenth Centuries', *World Politics*, 1 (1), pp. 1–29.

Viner, J. (1950), *The Customs Union Issue* (New York, NY: Carnegie Endowment for International Peace).

Vox (2010), 'The Future of EU Trade Policy: A Vox EU Debate Moderated by Richard Baldwin – Introduction'. Available from: http://trade.ec.europa.eu/doclib/docs/2010/november/tradoc_146932.pdf [accessed 19 July 2011].

Vox (2013), 'About: Vox'. Available from: http://www.voxeu.org/pages/about-vox [accessed 12 July 2013].

Wallace, A. (2004), 'Completing the Single Market: The Lisbon Strategy', in M.G. Cowles and D. Dinan (eds), *Developments in the European Union 2* (Basingstoke: Palgrave Macmillan), pp. 100–18.

Ward, T. and Loire, P. (2008), *Employment, Skills and Occupational Trends in the Automotive Industry: Annex Report* (Cambridge/Brussels and Paris: Alphametrics and Groupe Alpha).

Watkins, S. (2010), 'Shifting Sands', *New Left Review*, 61 (1), pp. 5–27.

Watson, M. and Hay, C. (2003), 'The Discourse of Globalization and the Logic of No Alternative: Rendering the Contingent Necessary in the Political Economy of New Labour', *Policy & Politics*, 31 (3), pp. 289–305.

Weaver, C. (2008), *Organised Hypocrisy: The World Bank and the Poverty of Reform* (Princeton, NJ: Princeton University Press).

Wendt, A. (1994), 'Collective Identity Formation and the International State', *American Political Science Review*, 88 (2), pp. 384–96.

Wendt, A. (1999), *Social Theory of International Politics* (Cambridge: Cambridge University Press).

Wiesman, G. (2010), 'German Warnings on "Aggressive" Chinese Rivals', *The Financial Times*, 14 October. Online edition. Available from: http://www.ft.com/cms/s/0/63f81280-d7c1-11df-b478-00144feabdc0.html#axzz1STaoQF8O [accessed 18 July 2011].

Wilkinson, R. (2009), 'Language, Power and Multilateral Trade Negotiations', *Review of International Political Economy*, 16 (4), pp. 597–619.

Wilkinson, R. (2014), *What's Wrong with the WTO and How to Fix It* (Cambridge, Polity).

Wilkinson, R. and Lee, D. (2007), 'The WTO after Hong Kong: Setting the Scene for Understanding the Round', in D. Lee and R. Wilkinson (eds), *The WTO after Hong Kong: Progress in, and Prospects for, the Doha Development Agenda* (Abingdon: Routledge), pp. 3–25.

Winham, G.R. (1986), *International Trade and the Tokyo Round Negotiation* (Princeton, NJ: Princeton University Press).

Wolfe, R. (2005), 'See You in Geneva? Legal (Mis)Representations of the Trading System', *European Journal of International Relations*, 11 (3), pp. 339–65.

Woll, C. (2008), *Firm Interests: How Governments Shape Business Lobbying on Global Trade* (Ithaca, NY: Cornell University Press).

Woll, C. (2009), 'Who Captures Whom? Trade Policy Lobbying in the European Union', in D. Coen and J. Richardson (eds), *Lobbying in the European Union: Institutions, Actors and Issues* (Oxford: Oxford University Press), pp. 268–88.

Woolcock, S. (2005), 'Trade Policy: From Uruguay to Doha and Beyond', in H. Wallace, W. Wallace and M. Pollack (eds), *Policy-Making in the European Union*, 5th edn (Oxford: Oxford University Press), pp. 377–99.

Woolcock, S. (2007), 'European Union Policy Towards Free Trade Agreements', ECIP Working Paper No. 03/2007, Brussels: ECIPE.

Woolcock, S. (2008), 'The Potential Impact of the Lisbon Treaty on European Union External Trade Policy', *European Policy Analysis*, 8, pp. 1–6.

Woolcock, S. (2010a), 'EU Trade and Investment Policymaking after the Lisbon Treaty', *Intereconomics*, 45 (1), pp. 22–5.

Woolcock, S. (2010b), 'Trade Policy: A Further Shift towards Brussels', in H. Wallace, M.A. Pollack and A.R. Young (eds), *Policy-Making in the European Union*, 6th edn (Oxford: Oxford University Press), pp. 381–98.

Woolcock, S. (2012), *European Union Economic Diplomacy: The Role of the EU in External Economic Relations* (Farnham: Ashgate).

Woolcock, S. and Hodges, M. (1996), 'EU Policy in the Uruguay Round', in H. Wallace and W. Wallace (eds), *Policy-Making in the European Union*, 3rd edn (Oxford: Oxford University Press), pp. 301–24.

WTO (2011a), 'Trade Policy Review: European Union', WT/TPR/S/248, Geneva: WTO. Available from: http://www.wto.org/english/tratop_e/tpr_e/s248_sum_e. pdf [accessed 19 July 2011].

WTO (2011b), 'World Trade Organisation: Annual Report 2011', Geneva: WTO. Available from: http://www.wto.org/english/res_e/booksp_e/anrep_e/anrep11_e. pdf [accessed 16 December 2011].

WTO (2013), 'Regional Trade Agreements Information System', Geneva: WTO. Available from: http://rtais.wto.org/UI/PublicAllRTAList.aspx [accessed 14 July 2013].

Yarbrough, B.V. and Yarbrough, R.M. (1992), *Cooperation and Governance in International Trade: The Strategic Organizational Approach* (Princeton, NJ: Princeton University Press).

Young, A.R. (2002), *Extending European Cooperation: The European Union and the "New" International Trade Agenda* (Manchester: Manchester University Press).

Young, A.R. (2006), 'Bringing Politics Back in: EU Trade Policy and the Doha Round', paper presented to the 47th Annual International Studies Association (ISA) Convention, San Diego, 22–25 March.

Young, A.R. (2007), 'Negotiating with Diminished Expectations: The EU and the Doha Development Round', in D. Lee and R. Wilkinson (eds), *The WTO after Hong Kong: Progress in, and Prospects for, the Doha Development Agenda* (Abingdon: Routledge), pp. 119–36.

Young, A.R. (2011), 'The Rise (and Fall?) of the EU's Performance in the Multilateral Trading System', *Journal of European Integration*, 33 (6), pp. 715–29.

Young, A.R. and Peterson, J. (2006), 'The EU and the New Trade Politics', *Journal of European Public Policy*, 13 (6), pp. 795–814.

Zoellick, R.B. (2002), 'Unleashing the Trade Winds', *The Economist*, 5 December. Online edition. Available from: http://www.economist.com/node/1477509 [accessed 14 July 2013].

Index

258   *Index*

Printed and bound by CPI Group (UK) Ltd, Croydon, CR0 4YY